The Seven Rays of Life

compiled by a student
from the writings of
Alice A. Bailey
and
The Tibetan Master,
Djwhal Khul

This compilation is extracted from
books by Alice A. Bailey for which
the Lucis Trust holds copyrights.

First printing 1995

ISBN 0 85330 142 5

Lucis Press Ltd.
Suite 54
3 Whitehall Court
London SW1A 2EF
U.K.

Lucis Publishing Company
120 Wall Street
New York, N.Y. 10005
U.S.A.

Manufactured in the United States of America by
FORT ORANGE PRESS, INC., ALBANY, N.Y.

Contents

Reference Index

**Books by the Tibetan (Djwhal Khul)
through Alice Bailey**

NOTE

At the end of every extract in this book is to be found a reference number, e.g. (DN–40/1). This means that the extract is taken from 'The Destiny of the Nations', pages 40 to 41.

Foreword

The books of Alice Bailey and the Tibetan are the result of a conscious co-operation earlier this century between a working disciple and a member of the Spiritual Hierarchy. Their shared desire was to precipitate a further phase of the ageless wisdom teachings that would enable humanity to better perceive and take advantage of the opportunities for progress that are now uniquely and powerfully available.

One of the most important features of their work is the detailed information on the seven rays. Recent years have seen a considerable growth of interest in this subject, and many people are now enthusiastically grappling with 'the science of the rays', recognising that the understanding it gives will enable them to work with greater skill and effectiveness in their chosen field of activity.

As the publishers of their books, we are delighted to issue this new compilation – "The Seven Rays of Life" – which is intended to serve as an introduction to the whole subject of the rays. The information in this book should not be regarded as complete or definitive, but rather as a signpost that can direct people to experiencing the reality of the seven rays for themselves. This requires more than an intellectual approach; it demands, and can foster, the unfoldment of the intuition. This inclusive quality of awareness goes beyond the thoughtforms that veil spiritual truth. It will enable those who persist in their quest for wisdom to have a direct experience of some inner reality, in this case the significance and the quality, as well as the outer effects, of the seven rays.

To explore the rays more fully we must, of course, point you in the direction of the originating books themselves, in particular the books on esoteric psychology, astrology, healing, and initiation which together comprise the 'Treatise on the Seven Rays'. A full list of titles is on page v.

Extract From a Statement by The Tibetan

Published August 1934.

Suffice it to say, that I am a Tibetan disciple of a certain degree, and this tells you but little, for all are disciples from the humblest aspirant up to, and beyond, the Christ Himself. I live in a physical body like other men, on the borders of Tibet, and at times (from the exoteric standpoint) preside over a large group of Tibetan lamas, when my other duties permit. It is this fact that has caused it to be reported that I am an abbot of this particular lamasery. Those associated with me in the work of the Hierarchy (and all true disciples are associated in this work) know me by still another name and office. A.A.B. knows who I am and recognises me by two of my names.

I am a brother of yours, who has travelled a little longer upon the Path than has the average student, and has therefore incurred greater responsibilities. I am one who has wrestled and fought his way into a greater measure of light than has the aspirant who will read this article, and I must therefore act as a transmitter of the light, no matter what the cost. I am not an old man, as age counts among the teachers, yet I am not young or inexperienced. My work is to teach and spread the knowledge of the Ageless Wisdom wherever I can find a response, and I have been doing this for many years. I seek also to help the Master M. and the Master K.H. whenever opportunity offers, for I have been long connected with Them and with Their work. In all the above, I have told you much; yet at the same time I have told you nothing which would lead you to offer me that blind obedience and the foolish devotion which the emotional aspirant offers to the Guru and Master Whom he is as yet unable to contact. Nor will he make that desired contact until he has transmuted emotional devotion into unselfish service to humanity, – not to the Master.

The books that I have written are sent out with no claim for their acceptance. They may, or may not, be correct, true and useful. It is for you to ascertain their truth by right practice and by the exercise of the intuition. Neither I nor A.A.B. is the least interested in having them acclaimed as inspired writings, or in having anyone speak of them (with bated breath) as being the work of one of the Masters. If they present truth in such a way that it follows sequentially upon that already offered in the world teachings, if the information given raises the aspiration and the will-to-serve from the plane of the emotions to that of the mind (the plane whereon the Masters *can* be found) then they will have served their purpose. If the teaching conveyed calls forth a response from the illumined mind of the worker in the world, and brings a flashing forth of his intuition, then let that teaching be accepted. But not otherwise. If the statements meet with eventual corroboration, or are deemed true under the test of the Law of Correspondences, then that is well and good. But should this not be so, let not the student accept what is said.

The Great Invocation

From the point of Light within the Mind of God
Let light stream forth into the minds of men.
Let Light descend on Earth.

From the point of Love within the Heart of God
Let love stream forth into the hearts of men.
May Christ return to Earth.

From the centre where the Will of God is known
Let purpose guide the little wills of men –
The purpose which the Masters know and serve.

From the centre which we call the race of men
Let the Plan of Love and Light work out
And may it seal the door where evil dwells.

Let Light and Love and Power restore the Plan on Earth.

"The above Invocation or Prayer does not belong to any person or group but to all humanity. The beauty and the strength of this Invocation lies in its simplicity, and in its expression of certain central truths which all men, innately and normally, accept – the truth of the existence of a basic Intelligence to Whom we vaguely give the name of God; the truth that behind all outer seeming, the motivating power of the universe is Love; the truth that a great Individuality came to earth, called by Christians, the Christ, and embodied that love so that we could understand; the truth that both love and intelligence are effects of what is called the Will of God; and finally the self-evident truth that only through *humanity* itself can the Divine Plan work out."

ALICE A. BAILEY

Introduction

Ten Basic Propositions

• ...Before starting on our real study of the rays, I seek to formulate for you the fundamental propositions upon which all this teaching is founded. They are for me, a humble worker in the Hierarchy, as they are for the Great White Lodge as a whole, a statement of fact and of truth. For students and seekers they must be accepted as an hypothesis:

One: There is one Life, which expresses Itself primarily through seven basic qualities or aspects, and secondarily through the myriad diversity of forms.

Two: These seven radiant qualities are the seven Rays, the seven Lives, Who give Their life to the forms, and give the form world its meaning, its laws, and its urge to evolution.

Three: Life, quality and appearance, or spirit, soul and body constitute all that exists. They are existence itself, with its capacity for growth, for activity, for manifestation of beauty, and for full conformity to the Plan. This Plan is rooted in the consciousness of the seven ray Lives.

Four: These seven Lives, Whose nature is consciousness and Whose expression is sentiency and specific quality, produce cyclically the manifested world; They work together in the closest union and harmony, and co-operate intelligently with the Plan of which They are the custodians. They are the seven Builders, Who produce the radiant temple of the Lord, under the guidance of the Mind of the Great

Architect of the Universe.

Five: Each ray Life is predominantly expressing Itself through one of the seven sacred planets, but the life of all the seven flows through every planet, including the Earth, and thus qualifies every form. On each planet is a small replica of the general scheme, and every planet conforms to the intent and purpose of the whole.

Six: Humanity, with which this treatise deals, is an expression of the life of God, and every human being has come forth along one line or other of the seven ray forces. The nature of his soul is qualified or determined by the ray Life which breathed him forth, and his form nature is coloured by the ray Life which – in its cyclic appearance on the physical plane at any particular time – sets the quality of the race life and of the forms in the kingdoms of nature. The soul nature or quality remains the same throughout a world period; its form life and nature change from life to life, according to its cyclic need and the environing group condition. This latter is determined by the ray or rays in incarnation at the time.

Seven: The Monad is the Life, lived in unison with the seven ray Lives. One Monad, seven rays and myriads of forms, – this is the structure behind the manifested worlds.

Eight: The Laws which govern the emergence of the quality or soul, through the medium of forms, are simply the mental purpose and life direction of the ray Lords, Whose purpose is immutable, Whose vision is perfect, and Whose justice is supreme.

Nine: The mode or method of development for humanity is self-expression and self-realisation. When this process is consummated the self expressed is the One Self or the ray Life, and the realisation achieved is the revelation of God as the quality of the manifested world and as the Life behind appearance and quality.

The seven ray Lives, or the seven soul types, are seen as the expression of one Life, and diversity is lost in the vision of the One and in identification with the One.

Ten: The method employed to bring about this realisation is experience, beginning with individualisation and ending with initiation, thus producing the perfect blending and expression of life-quality-appearance.

This is a brief statement of the Plan. Of this the Hierarchy of Masters in Its seven divisions (the correspondences of the seven rays) is the custodian, and with Them lies the responsibility in any century of carrying out the next stage of that Plan. (EP1–141/3)

What are the Rays?

• *A ray is but a name for a particular force or type of energy, with the emphasis upon the quality which that force exhibits and not upon the form aspect which it creates. This is a true definition of a ray.* (EP1–316)

• When we speak of ray energy we are in reality considering the quality and the will-purpose aspect of a certain great Life to Whom we give the name "Lord of a Ray".... His divine intention, will, purpose, or the determined projection of His mind, creates a radiation or stream of energy which – according to type and quality – plays upon all forms of manifested life within our planetary ring-pass-not. These Lords of the Rays are the creating and sustaining energies which implement the Will of the planetary Logos. They co-operate with Him in the defining and the expression of His supreme purpose. Their radiating emanations are cyclically objectified and are cyclically withdrawn. As they radiate forth into the three worlds, the impacting energies produce changes, disturbances, progress and unfoldment; they create the needed new forms and vitalise and qualify that through which the immediate divine intention is expressing itself; they intensify both the quality and the receptivity of consciousness.

At other times, during the process of being withdrawn "to

their own place", they cause the fading out or the dying of form aspects, of institutions, and the "organising organisms" (to use a peculiar phrase); they therefore produce cycles of destruction and of cessation and thus make room for those new forms and life expressions which an incoming ray will produce. (RI–568/9)

• All manifestation is of a septenary nature, and the Central Light which we call Deity, the one Ray of Divinity, manifests first as a Triplicity, and then as a Septenary. The One God shines forth as God the Father, God the Son, and God the Holy Spirit, and these three are again reflected through the Seven Spirits before the Throne, or the seven Planetary Logoi. The students of occultism of non-Christian origin may call these Beings the One Ray, demonstrating through the three major Rays and the four minor, making a divine Septenary. The Synthetic Ray which blends them all is the great Love-Wisdom Ray, for verily and indeed "God is Love". This Ray is the indigo Ray, and is the blending Ray. It is the one which will, at the end of the greater cycle, absorb the others in the achievement of synthetic perfection. It is the manifestation of the second aspect of Logoic life. It is this aspect, that of the Form-Builder, that makes this solar system of ours the most concrete of the three major systems. The Love or Wisdom aspect demonstrates through the building of the form, for "God is Love", and in that God of Love we "live and move and have our being", and will to the end of aeonian manifestation.

The seven planes of Divine Manifestation, or the seven major planes of our system, are but the seven sub-planes of the lowest cosmic plane. The seven Rays of which we hear so much, and which hold so much of interest and of mystery, are likewise but the seven sub-rays of one cosmic Ray. (IHS–3/4)

• One permanent cosmic Ray is the ray of our Logos Himself, and the subrays of this ray permeate His entire system. Six other cosmic Rays, animating other systems, influence ours, finding their reflections in the subrays of our logoic Ray. To these six cosmic influences our Heavenly Men respond. They absorb the influence, being centres in the body logoic, pass it through Their schemes, circulate it through Their own centres (chains), and transmit it on to other schemes, colouring it with Their own peculiar shade and qualifying it by Their own peculiar tone or note. The whole system of ray influence, or radiatory warmth, considered both physically and psychically, is one of an intricate circulation and interaction. The radiation or vibration passes in ordered cycles from its originating source, the One Ray, or systemic Logos, to the different centres in His body. Viewed from the physical standpoint this ray force is the energising factor in matter. Viewed from the psychical point of view it is the qualitative faculty. From scheme to scheme, from chain to chain, and from globe to globe, this force or quality passes and circulates, both adding, and at the same time abstracting, and returns to its focal point with two noticeable differences:

a.   The radiatory heat is intensified.
b.   The qualitative character or colour is increased.

The effect on the form side is equally noticeable, and the warmth or quality of a Ray not only affects the psyche of a man, a planetary Logos, and a solar Logos, but has a definite effect on material substance itself. (TCF–437/8)

• …There are divine attributes and ray characteristics which have hitherto never been revealed to the minds of men or sensed by them in their highest moments of inspiration; this is due to the lack of sensitivity of even the most advanced of the sons of men. Their apparatus remains inadequately developed and so unable to respond to these higher divine qualities. Even the Christ Himself and other Members of the Great White Lodge are preparing Themselves to register these divine attributes and consciously to merge Themselves in a still higher process or scale of evolution; it will be obvious to you that the little conclusions of the little minds are some of the most dangerous factors today in world affairs. (DN–40/1)

• This teaching anent the seven rays remains a profitless speculation unless it is susceptible of investigation, of eventual proof and of general as well as particular usefulness. Too much is written at this time which will have to be relegated to the discard as useless, as not warranting acceptance as a possible hypothesis and as not demonstrating a truth which can be proved. I am, therefore, seeking here to do two things:

1. Indicate, as you have seen, a new and powerfully efficient esoteric psychology, and also
2. Show the lines of development which are inevitable, for the reason that certain major potencies are coming into play at this time. Certain forces are becoming increasingly active whilst others are steadily becoming quiescent. (DN-4)

• We shall find, as we study, that words will greatly handicap our expression of the realities involved, and we must endeavour to penetrate beneath the surface meaning to the esoteric structure of truth. These rays are in constant movement and circulation, and demonstrate an activity which is progressive and cyclic and evidences increasing momentum. They are dominant at one time and quiescent at another, and according to the particular ray which is making its presence felt at any particular time, so will be the quality of the civilisation, the type of forms which will make their appearance in the kingdoms of nature, and the consequent stage of awareness (the state of consciousness) of the human beings who are carried into form life in that particular era. These embodied lives (again in all four kingdoms) will be responsive to the peculiar vibration, quality, colouring and nature of the ray in question. The ray in manifestation will affect potently the three bodies which constitute the personality of man, and the influence of the ray will produce changes in the mind content and the emotional nature of the man and determine the calibre of the physical body.

I am aware, therefore, that in giving out this relatively new teaching upon the rays I may, in my endeavour to shed fresh light, temporarily increase the complexity of the subject. But as experiment is made, as people are studied in the laboratories of the psychologists and the psychoanalysts in connection with their ray indications, and as the newer sciences come into wise use and their proper sphere, we shall gain much and the teaching will find corroboration. We shall see emerging a new approach to the ancient truths, and a new mode of investigating humanity. In the meantime let us concentrate upon the clear enunciation of the truth anent the rays, and seek to tabulate, outline and indicate their nature, purpose and effects.

The seven rays, being cyclic in appearance, have continuously passed in and out of manifestation and have thus left their mark down the ages upon mankind, and therefore hold the clue to any true historical survey. Such a survey still remains to be made. (EP1–3/4)

• Some of the points which I may seek to make clear will not be capable of substantiation and cannot be proved by you. These it would be wise to accept as working hypotheses, in order to understand that whereof I seek to speak. Some of the points I may make you may find yourself capable of checking up in your own life experience, and they will call forth from you a recognition coming from your concrete mind; or they may produce in you a reaction of the intensest conviction, emanating from your intuitively aware Self. In any case, read slowly; apply the laws of analogy and of correspondence; study yourself and your brethren; seek to link what I say to any knowledge you may possess of the modern theories, and remember that the more truly you live as a soul the more surely you will comprehend that which may be imparted.

As you study you must not forget the basic concept that in all occult work one is occupied with energy – energy units, energy embodied in forms, energy streams in flow; and that these energies are made potent and embody our purpose through the use of thought.... (EP1–9)

• [As a result of a study of these rays] we shall have a practical method of analysis whereby we can arrive at a right understanding of ourselves as ensouling entities, and at a wiser comprehension of our fellowmen. When, through our study, we ascertain for instance that the tendency of our soul ray is that of will or power, but that the ray governing the personality is that of devotion, we can more truly gauge our opportunity, our capacities and our limitations; we can more justly determine our vocation and service, our assets and our debits, our true value and strength. When we can add to that knowledge an analysis which enables us to realise that the physical body is reacting preeminently to the soul ray, whilst the emotional body is under the influence of the personality ray which is historically in manifestation at the time, we are then in a position to gauge our particular problem with judgment. We can then deal more intelligently with ourselves, with our children and with our friends and associates. We shall find ourselves able to co-operate more wisely with the Plan as it is seeking expression at any particular time. (EP1–8)

• Occult students must increasingly think and work in terms of energy. These energies are spoken of esoterically as "having impulsive effects, magnetic appeals, and focused activities". The streams or emanations of energy exist, as is well known, in seven major aspects or qualities. They carry the sons of men into incarnation and withdraw them from incarnation. They have their own specific qualities and characteristics, and these determine the nature of the forms constructed, the quality of the life which is expressed at any particular time or in any particular incarnation, the length of the life cycle, and the appearance and disappearance of any of the three form aspects. (EP2–79)

• This instruction on the rays is of deeper significance than can as yet be comprehended. Careful systematic study and a sane refraining from the forming of rapid deductions will be the wisest way in which to approach its consideration.... I am occupied with stating a general outline, with the impartation of ideas, with the grounding of a few basic concepts in the consciousness of the reader, and with an attempt to clothe this most abstruse and difficult subject in such a form that some new rhythm of thought may be set in motion, and some new realisations be grasped and held.... We begin with the universal and end with the particular, which is ever the truly occult method. (EP1–72/3)

• There has been for long in esoteric circles much idle and oft foolish talk anent the ray upon which a man may be found. People are as ignorantly excited over being told which is their ray as they are over the portrayal of their past incarnations. The "new teaching on the rays" vies with astrology in its interest. Like the Athenians, men are always searching for the novel and the unusual, forgetting that every new truth and every new presentation of an old truth carries with it the onus of increased responsibility.

However, it is interesting to trace parallels, and it is becoming obvious to the careful student that the emergence of the teaching on the rays has happened at a time when the scientist is announcing the fact that there is naught to be seen and known save energy, and that all forms are composed of energy units and are in themselves expressions of force. (EP1–315)

Apparent Contradictions

• ...I want to touch upon the apparent contradictions which occur (and which may continue to occur) in this treatise. Sometimes a ray will be spoken of as being in manifestation. At other times it may be referred to as being out of manifestation. We may speak about its influence upon a particular kingdom in nature, and then again still another ray may be regarded as of prime importance. These discrepancies are only apparent, and their cause lies hid in the right understanding of the Law of Cycles. Until this basic Law of Periodicity is comprehended (and this will not be possible until man has succeeded in developing fourth dimensional vision) it will not be easy to avoid what may look like contradictions. At one time a certain ray may be in incarnation and thus of paramount influence, and yet, at the same time, still another ray may govern the major cycle, – a cycle of which the ray under consideration may be only a temporary aspect. For instance, the seventh Ray of Ceremonial Organisation is now coming in, and the sixth Ray of Devotion is going out; yet this sixth ray is a major ray cycle and its influence will not entirely disappear for another 21,000 years. At the same time, this sixth ray might well be regarded as the sixth sub-ray of the fourth Ray of

Harmony through Conflict, which has been in manifestation for several thousand years and will remain operative for another 40,000 years. Yet at the same time, this fourth ray *is* out of manifestation as regards its minor and cyclic influence.

I fully realise that this information is of a most confusing nature to the beginner in occultism, and only those students who conform to the requirement of grasping the general outline and the broad basic propositions will be able to gather out of these instructions the true, intended perspective. If the reader loses himself in the mass of possible analyses and intricacies of the imparted detail, he will not emerge into the realm of that clear vision which is intended. When he eliminates the detail and deals with the general conformation of the solar Plan, he will then be enabled to co-operate with the needed intelligence. Read therefore constructively and not critically, knowing that it is not easy to see the Plan as it exists in the minds of the Builders, Who work in the closest co-operation, conforming to the initial Plan, and yet carrying forward Their individual efforts with concentration and sustained enterprise. (EP1–189/90)

• Apart from the cyclic impulses continuously going forth, overlapping and superseding, and intermingling with each other, there are many which we might call lesser impulses.... There are [also] vaster cycles, of 2500 years, of 7,000 years, of 9,000 years, of 15,000 years, and many others...; these can break in upon any of the lesser impulses, and can be seen appearing, unexpectedly, as far as average man's knowledge is concerned, and yet they are but the returning impulses set in cyclic motion perhaps thousands of years ago. (TCF–1038/9)

The Seven Rays

• The rays are the seven emanations from the "seven Spirits before the throne of God"; Their emanations come from the monadic level of awareness or from the second cosmic etheric plane. In a certain sense it could be said that these seven great and living Energies are in their totality the etheric vehicle of the planetary Logos. (TEV–161)

• They are called by many names in many different lands, but for our purposes the following seven names will be used:
1. The energy of Will, Purpose or Power, called in Christian lands the energy of the Will of God.
2. The energy of Love-Wisdom, called frequently the Love of God.
3. The energy of Active Intelligence, called the Mind of God.
4. The energy of Harmony through Conflict, affecting greatly the human family.
5. The energy of Concrete Knowledge or Science, so potent at this time.
6. The energy of Devotion or Idealism, producing the current ideologies.
7. The energy of Ceremonial Order, producing the new forms of civilisation. (DN–3/4)

• The seven Rays can be divided into the three Rays of Aspect and the four Rays of Attribute, as follows:

Rays of Aspect
> 1. The Ray of Will, or Power.
> 2. The Ray of Love-Wisdom.
> 3. The Ray of Activity or Adaptability.

Rays of Attribute

    4. The Ray of Harmony, Beauty, Art, or Unity.

    5. The Ray of Concrete Knowledge or Science.

    6. The Ray of Abstract Idealism or Devotion.

    7. The Ray of Ceremonial Magic, or Law.

The above names are simply some chosen from among many, and embody the different aspects of force by means of which the Logos manifests. (LOM–358/9) (IHS–223/4)

• Let us keep the numbering of the Rays clearly in mind. The numbers preceding the names have to do with the sevenfold manifestation, and the numbers succeeding the names concern the fivefold manifestation of Brahma.

Rays of Aspect:

    1. Will or Power.

    2. Love or Wisdom.

    3. Adaptability or active intelligence . . . . 1.

Rays of Attribute:

    4. Harmony, Beauty or Art . . . . 2.

    5. Concrete Knowledge or Science . . . . 3.

    6. Abstract Idealism . . . . 4.

    7. Ceremonial Magic . . . . 5.

                                    (TCF–427/8)

The Three Rays of Aspect

• The three great rays, which constitute the sum total of the divine manifestation, are aspect rays, and this for two reasons:

First, they are, in their totality, the manifested Deity, the *Word* in incarnation. They are the expression of the creative purpose, and the synthesis of life, quality and appearance.

Secondly, they are active in every form in every kingdom, and they determine the broad general characteristics which govern the energy, the quality and the kingdom in question; through them the differentiated forms come into being, the specialised lives express themselves, and the diversity of divine agents fulfil their destiny in the plane of existence allocated to them.

Along these three streams of qualified life-force the creative agencies of God make their presence powerfully felt, and through their activity every form is imbued with that inner evolutionary attribute which must eventually sweep it into line with divine purpose, inevitably produce that type of consciousness which will enable the phenomenal unit to react to its surroundings and thus fulfil its destiny as a corporate part of the whole. Thus intrinsic quality and specific type radiation become possible. The interplay of these three rays determines the outer phenomenal appearance, attracts the unity of life into one or other of the kingdoms in nature, and into one or other of the myriad divisions within that kingdom; the selective and discriminating process is repeated until we have the many ramifications within the four kingdoms, the divisions, groups within a division, families and branches. Thus the creative process, in its wondrous beauty, sequence and unfoldment, stands forth to our awakening consciousness, and we are left awestruck and bewildered at the creative facility of the Great Architect of the Universe.

Looking at all this beauty from a symbolic angle, and thereby simplifying the concept (which is ever the work of the worker in symbols), we might say that Ray I embodies the dynamic idea of God, and thus the Most High starts the work of creation.

Ray II is occupied with the first formulations of the plan upon which the form must be constructed and the idea materialised, and (through the agencies of this great second emanation) the blue prints come into being with their mathematical accuracy, their structural unity and their geometrical perfection. The Grand Geometrician comes thus to the forefront and makes the work of the Builders possible. Upon figure and form, number and sequences will the Temple be built, and so embrace and express the glory of the Lord. The second ray is the ray of the Master Builder.

Ray III constitutes the aggregate of the active building forces, and the Great Architect, with His Builders, organises the material, starts the work of construction, and eventually (as the evolutionary cycle proceeds upon its way) materialises the idea and purpose of God the Father, under the guidance of God the Son. Yet these three are as much a unity as is a human being who conceives an idea, uses his mind and brain to bring his idea into manifestation, and employs his hands and all his natural forces to perfect his concept. The division of aspects and forces is unreal, except for the purpose of intelligent understanding. (EP1–158/9)

The Four Rays of Attribute

• ...The work of the four minor rays (as they are called, though with no idea of there being lesser or greater) is to elaborate or differentiate the qualities of the life, and so produce the infinite multiplicity of forms which will enable the life to assume its many points of focus and express – through the process of evolutionary manifestation – its diverse characteristics. (EP1–70)

• The energies into which the three distribute themselves, thus becoming seven, in their turn produce the forty-nine types of force which express themselves through all the forms in the three worlds and the four kingdoms in nature. You have therefore:

a. Three monadic groups of energies. The essential Unity expresses, through these three, the qualities of Will, Love and Intelligence.

b. Seven groups of energies which are the medium through which the three major groups express the divine qualities.

c. Forty-nine groups of forces to which all forms respond and which constitute the body of expression for the seven, who in their turn are reflections of the three divine qualities. (EP1–7)

• The rays are sometimes considered as divided into three classes; the first ray by itself, the second ray by itself, and the other five in a group. When regarded in this way, they are spoken of as the three rays, and typify the various Trinities. (EP1–167)

Ray Purposes

• We shall now express the ray purpose in the form of an ancient teaching preserved on leaves that are so old that the writing is slowly fading. I now translate it into modern language though much is lost thereby.

THE FIRST PURPOSE OF DEITY

Ray I. Will or Power.

Behind the central sacred sun, hidden within its rays, a form is found. Within that form there glows a point of power which vibrates not as yet but shines as light electric.

Fierce are its rays. It burns all forms, yet touches not the life of God incarnate.

From the One who is the seven goes forth a word. That word reverberates along the line of fiery essence, and when it sounds within the circle of the human lives it takes the form of affirmation, an uttered fiat or word of power. Thus there is impressed upon the living mold the thought of . . . . . . (the hidden, inexpressible ray name.)

Let dynamic power, electric light, reveal the past, destroy the form that is, and open up the golden door. This door reveals the way which leads towards the centre where dwells the one whose name cannot be heard within the confines of our solar sphere.

His robe of blue veils his eternal purpose, but in the rising and the setting sun his orb of red is seen.

His word is power. His light, electric. The lightning is his symbol. His will is hidden in the counsel of his thought. Nought is revealed.

His power is felt. The sons of men, reacting to his power, send to the utmost bounds of light a question:

Why this blind power? Why death? Why this decay of forms? Why the negation of the power to hold? Why death, Oh Mighty Son of God?

Faintly the answer comes: I hold the keys of life and death. I bind and loose again. I, the Destroyer, am.

This ray Lord is not yet in full expression, except as He causes destruction and brings cycles to an end. The Monads of power are much fewer in number than any others. Egos upon the power ray are relatively not so few. They are characterised by a dynamic will, and their power within the human family works out as the force of destruction, but in the last analysis it is a destruction that will produce liberation. We shall see as we continue to study first ray egos and personalities that death and destruction are always to be found in their work, and hence the apparent cruelty and impersonality of their reactions.... The intent of the Lord of the first ray is to stand behind His six Brothers, and when They have achieved Their purpose, to shatter the forms which They have built.... The first ray purpose therefore is to produce death, and some idea of that purpose may be gleaned if we study some of the names by which the ray Lord is called:

> The Lord of Death
> The Opener of the Door
> The Liberator from Form
> The Great Abstractor
> The Fiery Element, producing shattering
> The Crystallizer of the Form
> The Power that touches and withdraws
> The Lord of the Burning Ground
> The Will that breaks into the Garden
> The Ravisher of Souls
> The Finger of God
> The Breath that blasts
> The Lightning which annihilates
> The Most High

The qualities and characteristics of this Lord Who brings release may be gathered from the following six aphorisms which, an ancient legend says, His six Brothers gave to Him, as They begged Him to hold His hand till They had had time to work out Their purposes:

1. Kill out desire when desire has fulfilled its work. Thou art the one who indicates fulfillment.

   Quality . . . . . clear vision.

2. Seek out the gentle way, Oh Lord of Power. Wait for thy brother on the path of Love. He builds the forms that can withstand thy power.

   Quality . . . . . dynamic power.

3. Withhold thy hand until the time has come. Then give the gift

of death, Oh Opener of the Door.

Quality . . . . . sense of time.

4. Stand not alone, but with the many join thyself. Thou art the One, the Isolated. Come forth unto thine own.

Quality . . . . . solitariness.

5. Lead thine own forth but learn to know thine own. Hate not attachment but see its plan and purpose.

Quality . . . . . detachment.

6. Through thee the life pulsates, the rhythm is imposed. The life is all. Love life in all its forms.

Quality . . . . . singleness of purpose. (EP1–62/5)

THE SECOND PURPOSE OF DEITY

Ray II. Love-Wisdom

The Word is issuing from the heart of God, emerging from a central point of love. That Word is love itself. Divine desire colours all that life of love. Within the human hierarchy, the affirmation gathers power and sound.

The Word in the beginning was. The Word hath dwelt and dwells with God. In Him was light. In Him was life. Within His light we walk.

His symbol is the thunder, the Word that cycles down the ages.

Some of the names of this ray Lord which convey his purpose are as follows:

The Displayer of Glory
The Lord of Eternal Love
The Cosmic Magnet
The Giver of Wisdom
The Radiance in the Form
The Master Builder
The Conferrer of Names
The Great Geometrician
The One Who hides the Life
The Cosmic Mystery
The Light Bringer
The Son of God Incarnate
The Cosmic Christ

The legend tells us that the six Brothers summarise His qualities in the following aphorisms:

1. Send forth the Word and speak the radiant love of God. Make all men hear.

    Quality . . . . . love divine.

2. Let the glory of the Lord shine forth. Let there be radiant light as well as radiant love.

    Quality . . . . . radiance.

3. Draw to thyself the object of thy search. Pull forth into the light of day from out the night of time the one thou lovest.

    Quality . . . . . attraction.

4. When light and love are shewn forth then let the power within produce the perfect flower. Let the word that heals the form go forth. That secret word that then must be revealed.

    Quality . . . . . the power to save.

5. Salvation, light, and love, with the magnetic power of God, produce the word of wisdom. Send forth that word, and lead the sons of men from off the path of knowledge on to the path of understanding.

    Quality . . . . . wisdom.

6. Within the radius of the love of God, within the circle of the solar system, all forms, all souls, all lives revolve. Let each son of God enter into this wisdom. Reveal to each the oneness of the many lives.

    Quality . . . . . expansion or inclusiveness. (EP1–65/7)

THE THIRD PURPOSE OF DEITY

Ray III. Active Intelligence or Adaptability

Let the Warden of the South continue with the building. Let him apply the force which will produce the shining living stone that fits into the temple's plan with right exactitude. Let him prepare the corner stone and wisely place it in the north, under the eye of God Himself, and subject to the balance of the triangle.

Let the Researcher of the past uncover the thought of God, hidden deep within the mind of the Kumaras of Love, and thus let him lead the Agnishvattvas, waiting within the place of darkness, into the place of light.

Let the Keeper of the sparks breathe with the breath divine upon the points of fire, and let him kindle to a blaze that which is hidden, that which is not seen, and so illumine all the spheres whereon God works. (EP1–67)

• Some of the names of the Lord of the third ray indicate His use of force and His real nature. They are as follows:

> The Keeper of the Records
> The Lord of Memory
> The Unifier of the Lower Four
> The Interpreter of That Which is seen
> The Lord of Balance
> The Divine Separator
> The Discriminating Essential Life
> The One Who Produces Alliance
> The Three-sided Triangle
> The Illuminator of the Lotus
> The Builder of the Foundation
> The Forerunner of the Light
> The One Who veils and yet reveals
> The Dispenser of Time
> The Lord of Space
> The Universal Mind
> The Threefold Wick
> The Great Architect of the Universe   (EP1–68)

• The qualities which characterise this ray Lord might be enumerated in the following phrases...:

1. Produce the dual form and veil the life. Let form appear, and prove itself divine. All is of God.
    Quality . . . . . the power to manifest.
2. Conform the shell to that which dwells within. Let the world egg appear. Let ages pass; then let the soul appear. Let life emerge within a destined time.
    Quality . . . . . the power to evolve.
3. Let mind control. Let the clear shining of the sun of life reveal the mind of God, and set the shining one upon his way. Then lead him to the central point where all is lost within the light supernal.
    Quality . . . . . mental illumination.
4. God and His form are one. Reveal this fact, Oh sovereign Lord of form. God and His form are one. Negate the dual concept. Lend colour to the form. The life is one; the harmony complete. Prove thus the two are one.

> Quality ..... the power to produce synthesis on the
> physical plane.

5. Produce the garment of the Lord; set forth the robe of many
    colours. Then separate that robe from That Which hides behind
    its many folds. Take off the veiling sheaths. Let God be seen.
    Take Christ from off the cross.

> Quality ..... scientific investigation.

6. Let the two paths converge. Balance the pairs of opposites and
    let the path appear between the two. God and the Path and man
    are one.

> Quality ..... balance.   (EP1–69/70)

THE FOURTH PURPOSE OF DEITY

Ray IV. Harmony, Beauty, Art

Colour, and yet no colour now is seen. Sound and the soundless
One meet in an infinite point of peace. Time and the timeless One
negate the thoughts of men. But time is not.

Form is there found, and yet the psychic sense reveals that which
the form is powerless to hide, – the inner synthesis, the all-embracing
prism, that point of unity which – when it is duly reached – reveals
a further point where all the three are one, and not the two alone.

Form and its soul are merged. The inner vision watches o'er the
fusion, knows the divine relation and sees the two as one. But from
that point of high attainment, a higher vision blazes forth before the
opened inner eye. The three are one, and not alone the two. Pass on,
O pilgrim on the Way. (EP1–70)

• The Lord of the fourth ray has many names which warrant
careful study and much consideration....

> The Perceiver on the Way
> The Link between the Three and Three
> The Divine Intermediary
> The Hand of God
> The Hidden One
> The Seed, that is the flower
> The Mountain whereon Form dies
> The Light within the Light
> The Corrector of the Form
> The One Who marks the parting of the Way
> The Master

The Dweller in the Holy Place
The Lower than the Three, the Highest of the Four
The Trumpet of the Lord

The aphorisms connected with this fourth ray are not easy of comprehension. They require an exercise of the intuition and are conveyed by six short and excessively brief commands...:

1. Speak low the Word. Speak low.
    Quality . . . . . power to penetrate the depths of matter.
2. Champion desire. Give what is needed to the seeker.
    Quality . . . . . the dual aspects of desire.
3. Lower the thread. Unfold the Way. Link man with God. Arise.
    Quality . . . . . power to reveal the path.
4. All flowers are thine. Settle the roots in mud, the flowers in sun. Prove mud and sun, and roots and flowers are one.
    Quality . . . . . power to express divinity. Growth.
5. Roll and return, and roll again. Cycle around the circle of the Heavens. Prove all is one.
    Quality . . . . . the harmony of the spheres.
6. Colour the sound. Sound forth the colour. Produce the notes and see them pass into the shades, which in their turn produce the sounds. Thus all are seen as one.
    Quality . . . . . the synthesis of true beauty.   (EP1–71/2)

THE FIFTH PURPOSE OF DEITY

Ray V. Concrete Knowledge or Science

The thunders crash around the mountain top; dark clouds conceal the form. The mists, arising from the watery sphere, serve to distort the wondrous . . . . . . found within the secret place. The form is there. Its note is sounding forth.

A beam of light illuminates the form; the hidden now appears. Knowledge of God and how He veils Himself finds consummation in the thoughts of man. The energies and forces receive their secret names, reveal their inner purpose, and all is seen as rhythm, a returning on itself. The great scroll can now be read. God's purpose and His plans are fixed, and man can read the form.

The plan takes form. The plan is form. Its purpose is the revelation of the mind of God. The past reveals the form, but the present indicates the flowing in of energy.

That which is on its way comes as a cloud which veils the sun. But hid behind this cloud of immanence is love, and on the earth is love and in the heaven is love, and this, – the love which maketh all things new – must stand revealed. This is the purpose back of all the acts of this great Lord of Knowledge. (EP1–75)

• Some of the names given to the Lord of this ray are as follows:

> The Revealer of Truth
> The Great Connector
> The Divine Intermediary
> The Crystallizer of Forms
> The Three-fold Thinker
> The Cloud upon the Mountain-top
> The Precipitator of the Cross
> The Dividing Sword
> The Winnower of the Chaff
> The Fifth great Judge
> The Rose of God
> The Heavenly One
> The Door into the Mind of God
> The Initiating Energy
> The Ruler of The Third Heaven
> The Guardian of the Door
> The Dispenser of Knowledge
> The Angel with the Flaming Sword
> The Keeper of the Secret
> The Beloved of the Logos
> The Brother from Sirius
> The Master of the Hierophants (EP1–77)

• [The following] six aphorisms were chanted by His six Brothers at that momentous crisis wherein the human family came into existence and the solar Angels sacrificed themselves....

1. God and His Angels now arise and see. Let the mountain-tops emerge from out the dense wet mist. Let the sun touch their summits and let them stand in light. Shine forth.
   Quality . . . . . emergence into form and out of form.
2. God and His Angels now arise and hear. Let a deep murmur rise

and let the cry of seeking man enter into their ears. Let man listen. Let man call. Speak loud.

> Quality ..... power to make the Voice of the Silence heard.

3. God and His Angels now arise and touch. Bring forth the rod of power. Extend it outward toward the sons of men; touch them with fire, then bring them near. Bring forth.

> Quality ..... initiating activity.

4. God and his Angels now arise and taste. Let all experience come. Let all the ways appear. Discern and choose; dissect and analyze. All ways are one.

> Quality ..... revelation of the way.

5. God and His Angels now arise and sense the odour rising from the burning-ground of man. Let the fire do its work. Draw man within the furnace and let him drop within the rose-red centre the nature that retards. Let the fire burn.

> Quality ..... purification with fire.

6. God and His Angels now arise and fuse the many in the One. Let the blending work proceed. Let that which causes all to be produce the cause of their cessation. Let one temple now emerge. Produce the crowning glory. So let it be.

> Quality ..... the manifestation of the great white light.

> (The Shekinah. A.A.B.)   (EP1–77/8)

THE SIXTH PURPOSE OF DEITY

Ray VI. Devotion or Idealism

The Crusade is on. The warriors march upon their way. They crush and kill all that impedes their way, and aught that rises on their onward path is trampled under foot. March towards the light.

The work goes forward. The workers veil their eyes from pity as from fear. The work is all that counts. The form must disappear so that the loving spirit may enter into rest. Naught must arrest the progress of the workers with the plan. They enter upon the work assigned with paean and with song.

The cross is reared on high; the form is laid thereon, and on that cross must render up its life. Each builds a cross which forms the cross. They mount upon the cross.

Through war, through work, through pain and toil, the purpose is achieved. Thus saith the symbol. (EP1–79/80)

• It will be noted how this purpose, when applied by man to himself, works his release. When applied by man to man, it has produced the corrupt and awful story of man's cruelty to man.... Some of the names for this beneficent yet somewhat violently energised Lord of a ray are as follows:

> The Negator of Desire
> The One Who sees the Right
> The Visioner of Reality
> The Divine Robber
> The Devotee of Life
> The Hater of Forms
> The Warrior on the March
> The Sword Bearer of the Logos
> The Upholder of the Truth
> The Crucifier and the Crucified
> The Breaker of Stones
> The Imperishable Flaming One
> The One Whom Naught can turn
> The Implacable Ruler
> The General on the Perfect Way
> The One Who leads the Twelve

Curiously enough, this sixth ray Lord has always been a loved enigma to His six Brethren. This comes out in the questions which They addressed to Him....

1. Why is desire red? Why red as blood? Tell us, Oh Son of God, why thy way is red with blood?

   Quality . . . . . power to kill out desire.

2. Why do you turn your back upon the sphere of earth? Is it too small, too poor? Why kick it as a ball upon a playing field?

   Quality . . . . . spurning that which is not desired.

3. Why set the cross from earth to heaven? But earth can be a heaven. Why mount the cross and die?

   Quality . . . . . self-immolation.

4. Why battle thus with all that is around? Seek you not peace? Why stand between the forces of the night and day? Why thus unmoved and calm, untired and unafraid?

   Quality . . . . . endurance and fearlessness.

5. See you not God in all, the life in all, and love in all? Why separate yourself and leave behind the loved and the well-known?

   Quality . . . . . power to detach oneself.

6.   Can you arrest the waters of the sixth great sphere? Can you stem the flood? Can you recover both the raven and the dove? Can you, the Fish, swim free?

        Quality . . . . . overcoming the waters of the emotional nature.   (EP1–80/1)

THE SEVENTH PURPOSE OF DEITY

Ray VII. Ceremonial Order or Magic

"Let the Temple of the Lord be built", the seventh great Angel cried. Then to their places in the north, the south, the west and east, seven great sons of God moved with measured pace and took their seats. The work of building thus began.

The doors were closed. The light shone dim. The temple walls could not be seen. The seven were silent and their forms were veiled. The time had not arrived for the breaking forth of light. The Word could not be uttered. Only between the seven Forms the work went on. A silent call went forth from each to each. Yet still the temple door stayed shut.

As time went on, the sounds of life were heard. The door was opened, and the door was shut. Each time it opened, the power within the temple grew; each time the light waxed stronger, for one by one the sons of men entered the temple, passed from north to south, from west to east and in the centre of the heart found light, found understanding and the power to work. They entered through the door; they passed before the Seven; they raised the temple's veil and entered into life.

The temple grew in beauty. Its lines, its walls, its decorations, and its height and depth and breadth slowly emerged and entered into light.

Out from the east, the Word went forth: Open the door to all the sons of men who come from all the darkened valleys of the land and seek the temple of the Lord. Give them the light. Unveil the inner shrine, and through the work of all the craftsmen of the Lord extend the temple's walls and thus irradiate the world. Sound forth the Word creative and raise the dead to life.

Thus shall the temple of the light be carried from heaven to earth. Thus shall its walls be reared upon the great plains of the world of men. Thus shall the light reveal and nurture all the dreams of men.

Then shall the Master in the east awaken those who are asleep. Then shall the warden in the west test and try all the true seekers after light. Then shall the warden in the south instruct and aid the blind. Then shall the gate into the north remain wide open, for there the

unseen Master stands with welcoming hand and understanding heart,
to lead the pilgrims to the east where the true light shines forth.

"Why this opening of the temple?" demand the greater Seven.
"Because the work is ready; the craftsmen are prepared. God has
created in the light. His sons can now create. What can else be done?"

"Naught!" came the answer from the greater Seven. "Let the work
proceed. Let the sons of God create." (EP1–83/4)

• The names whereby this ray Lord is known are many, and
their meaning is of prime significance today. The work of the
future can be seen from a study of these names.

> The Unveiled Magician
> The Worker in the Magical Art
> The Creator of the Form
> The Bestower of Light from the Second Lord
> The Manipulator of the Wand
> The Watcher in the East
> The Custodian of the Seventh Plan
> The Invoker of Wrath
> The Keeper of the Magical Word
> The Temple Guardian
> The Representative of God
> The One Who lifts to Life
> The Lord of Death
> The One Who feeds the Sacred Fire
> The Whirling Sphere
> The Sword of the Initiator
> The Divine Alchemical Worker
> The Builder of the Square
> The Orienting Force
> The Fiery Unifier
> The Key to the Mystery
> The Expression of the Will
> The Revealer of Beauty   (EP1–85/6)

• The aphorisms embodying His qualities run as follows, and
were esoterically whispered into His ears when He "left the
most high place and descended into the seventh sphere to carry

out the work assigned."

1. Take thy tools with thee, brother of the building light. Carve
    deep. Construct and shape the living stone.
      Quality . . . . . power to create.
2. Choose well thy workers. Love them all. Pick six to do thy will.
    Remain the seventh in the east. Yet call the world to enter into
    that which thou shalt build. Blend all together in the will of God.
      Quality . . . . . power to co-operate.
3. Sit in the centre and the east as well. Move not from there. Send
    out thy force to do thy will and gather back thy forces. Use well
    the power of thought. Sit still.
      Quality . . . . . power to think.
4. See all parts enter into the purpose. Build towards beauty,
    brother Lord. Make all colours bright and clear. See to the inner
    glory. Build the shrine well. Use care.
      Quality . . . . . revelation of the beauty of God.
5. Watch well thy thought. Enter at will into the mind of God.
    Pluck thence the power, the plan, the part to play. Reveal the
    mind of God.
      Quality . . . . . mental power.
6. Stay in the east. The five have given thee a friendly Word. I, the
    sixth, tell thee to use it on the dead. Revive the dead. Build
    forms anew. Guard well that Word. Make all men seek it for
    themselves.
      Quality . . . . . power to vivify.   (EP1–86/7)

Individualisation and the Seven Ray Types

• We will express the reaction of these seven ray types to the
process of Individualisation (which is the process of identification with form) by seven occult statements which can, if
properly understood, give the keynote of the new psychology.
They state the major impulse, the native quality, and the
technique of unfoldment.

Ray One
    "The Blessed One flies like an arrow into matter. He destroys (or
ruptures) the way by which he might return. He grounds himself
deeply in the depths of form.
    He asserts: 'I will return. My power is great. I will destroy all
obstacles. Nothing can stop my progress to my goal. Around me lies

that which I have destroyed. What must I do?'

The answer comes: 'Order from chaos, O Pilgrim on the way of death, this is the way for you. Love you must learn. Dynamic will you have. The right use of destruction for the furtherance of the Plan, must be the way for you. Adherence to the rhythm of the planet will release the hidden Blessed One and order bring.' "

Ray Two

"The Blessed One built him an ark. Stage by stage he built it, and floated upon the bosom of the waters. Deeply he hid himself, and his light was no more seen, – only his floating ark.

His voice was heard: 'I have built and strongly built, but am a prisoner within my building. My light is hidden. Only my word goes forth. Around me lie the waters. Can I return from whence I came? Is the word strong enough to open wide the door? What shall I do?'

The answer came: 'Build now an ark translucent, which can reveal the light, O Builder of the ark. And by that light you shall reveal the lighted way. The power to build anew, the right use of the Word, and the using of the light, – these will release the Blessed One, deep hidden in the ark.' "

Ray Three

"The Blessed One gathered force. He hid himself behind a veil. He rolled himself within that veil, and deeply hid his face. Naught could be seen but that which veiled, and active motion. Within the veil was latent thought.

The thought reached forth: 'Behind this veil of maya I stand, a Blessed One, but unrevealed. My energy is great, and through my mind I can display the glory of divinity. How can I, therefore, demonstrate this truth? What shall I do? I wander in illusion.'

The word went forth: 'All is illusion, O Dweller in the shadows. Come forth into the light of day. Display the hidden glory of the Blessed One, the glory of the One and Only. The glory and the truth will rapidly destroy that which has veiled the truth. The prisoner can go free. The rending of the blinding veil, the clear pronouncing of the truth, and practice right will render to the Blessed One that golden thread which will provide release from all the maze of earth existence.' "

Ray Four

"The Blessed One rushed forth to combat. He saw existence as two warring forces, and fought them both. Loaded with the panoply of war, he stood midway, looking two ways. The clash of battle, the many weapons he had learned to use, the longing not to fight, the thrill of finding those he fought were but brothers and himself, the anguish of defeat, the paean of his victory, – these held him down.

The Blessed One paused and questioned: 'Whence come the victory and whence defeat? Am I not the Blessed One Himself? I will invoke the angels to my aid.'

The trumpet sound went forth: 'Rise up and fight, and reconcile the armies of the Lord. There is no battle. Force the conflict to subside; send for the invocation for the peace of all; form out of two, one army of the Lord; let victory crown the efforts of the Blessed One by harmonising all. Peace lies behind the warring energies.' "

Ray Five

"The Blessed One came forth in ignorance. He wandered in a darkness deep of spirit. He saw no reason for this way of life. He sought among the many threads that weave the outer garment of the Lord, and found the many ways there be, leading to the centre of the web eternal. The forms that weave that web hide the divine reality. He lost himself. Fear entered in.

He asked himself: 'Another pattern must be woven; another garment formed. What shall I do? Shew me another way to weave.'

The Word for him came forth in triple form. His mind responded to the vision clear evoked: – 'The truth lies hidden in the unknown Way. The Angel of the Presence guards that Way. The mind reveals the Angel and the door. Stand in that Presence. Lift up thine eyes. Enter through that golden door. Thus will the Angel, who is the shadow of the Blessed One, reveal the open door. That Angel too must disappear. The Blessed One remains and passes through that door into the light sublime.' "

Ray Six

"The Blessed One caught the vision of the Way, and followed the Way without discretion. Fury characterised his efforts. The way led down into the world of dual life. Between the pairs of opposites, he took his stand, and as he swung pendent between them, fleeting glimpses of the goal shone forth. He swung in mid-heaven. He sought to swing into that radiant place of light, where stood the door upon the higher *Way*. But ever he swung between the pairs of opposites.

He spoke at last within himself: 'I cannot seem to find the Way. I try this way, and tread with force that way, and always with the keenest wish. I try all ways. What shall I do to find *The Way*?'

A cry went forth. It seemed to come from deep within his heart: 'Tread thou, O Pilgrim on the Way of sensuous life, the middle, lighted way. It passes straight between the dual worlds. Find thou that narrow, middle way. It leads you to your goal. Seek that perceptive steadiness which leads to proved endurance. Adherence to the chosen Way, and ignoring of the pairs of opposites, will bring this Blessed One upon the lighted way into the joy of proved success.'"

Ray Seven

"The Blessed One sought the pathway into form, but held with firmness to the hand of the Magician. He sought to reconcile the Pilgrim, who was himself, to life in form. he sought to bring the world of disorder in which he found himself into some kind of order. He wandered far into the deepest depths and became immersed in chaos and disorder. He could not understand, yet still held to the hand of the Magician. He sought to bring about that order that his soul craved. He talked with all he met, but his bewilderment increased.

To the Magician thus he spoke: 'The ways of the Creator must be good. Behind all that which seems to be, must be a Plan. Teach me the purpose of it all. How can I work, immersed in deepest matter? Tell me the thing that I must do?'

The Magician said: 'Listen, O Worker in the furthest world, to the rhythm of the times. Note the pulsation in the heart of that which is divine. Retire into the silence and attune yourself unto the whole. Then venture forth. Establish the right rhythm; bring order to the forms of life which must express the Plan of Deity.'

For this Blessed One release is found in work. He must display his knowledge of the Plan by the sounding of those words which will evoke the Builders of the forms and thus create the new."

It might be of value, if here were summarised in more simple and less occult terms, the significance of the above esoteric stanzas, to express their true meaning in a few succinct and terse phrases. The stanzas are of no use unless they convey to the ray types among the students of this Treatise some useful meaning, whereby they can live more truly.

The individualised Spirit expresses itself through the various ray types in the following manner:–

Ray One

> Dynamic one-pointedness.
> Destructive energy.
> Power realised selfishly.
> Lovelessness.
> Isolation.

A longing for power and authority.
Desire to dominate.
Expressed strength and self-will,

> leading to

A dynamic use of energy for the furtherance of the Plan.
The use of destructive forces in order to prepare the way
   for the Builders.
The will to power in order to co-operate.
Power realised as the major weapon of love.
Identification with the rhythm of the Whole.
The cessation of isolation.

Ray Two

The power to build for selfish ends.
Capacity to sense the Whole and to remain apart.
The cultivation of a separative spirit.
The hidden light.
The realisation of selfish desire.
Longing for material well-being.
Selfishness, and subordination of all soul powers to this
   end,

> leading to

Building wisely, in relation to the Plan.
Inclusiveness.
A longing for wisdom and truth.
Sensitivity to the *Whole.*
Renunciation of the great heresy of separativeness.
The revelation of the light.
True illumination.
Right speech through generated wisdom.

Ray Three

Force manipulation through selfish desire.
Intelligent use of force with wrong motive.
Intense material and mental activity.
The realisation of energy as an end in itself.

Longing for glory, beauty and for material objectives.
Submergence in illusion, glamour, and maya,

> leading to

The manipulation of energy in order to reveal beauty and
truth.
The use of forces intelligently for the furtherance of the
Plan.
Ordered rhythmic activity in co-operation with the
Whole.
Desire for right revelation of divinity and light.
Adherence to right action.
The revelation of glory and goodwill.

Ray Four

Confused combat.
The realisation of that which is high and that which is
low.
The darkness which precedes form expression.
The veiling of the intuition.
The sensing of inharmony, and co-operation with the
part and not the whole.
Identification with humanity, the fourth Creative
Hierarchy.
Undue recognition of that which is produced by speech.
Abnormal sensitivity to that which is the Not-Self.
Constant points of crisis,

> leading to

Unity and harmony.
The evocation of the intuition.
Right judgment and pure reason.
The wisdom which works through the Angel of the
Presence.

Ray Five

The energy of ignorance.
Criticism.

The power to rationalise and destroy.

Mental separation.

Desire for knowledge. This leads to material activity.

Detailed analysis.

Intense materialism and temporarily the negation of Deity.

Intensification of the power to isolate.

The implications of wrong emphasis.

Distorted views of truth.

Mental devotion to form and form activity.

Theology,

> leading to

A knowledge of reality.

The realisation of the soul and its potentialities.

Power to recognise and contact the Angel of the Presence.

Sensitivity to Deity, to light and to wisdom.

Spiritual and mental devotion.

The power to take initiation. (This is a point of real importance.)

Ray Six

Violence. Fanaticism. Wilful adherence to an ideal.

Short sighted blindness.

Militarism and a tendency to make trouble with others and with groups.

The power to see no point except one's own.

Suspicion of people's motives.

Rapid reaction to glamour and illusion.

Emotional devotion and bewildered idealism.

Vibratory activity between the pairs of opposites.

Intense capacity to be personal and emphasise personalities,

> leading to

Directed, inclusive idealism.

Steadiness of perception through the expansion of

consciousness.

Reaction to, and sympathy with, the point of view of others.

Willingness to see the work of other people progress along their chosen lines.

The choosing of the middle way.

Peace and not war. The good of the *Whole* and not the part.

Ray Seven

Black magic, or the use of magical powers for selfish ends.

The power to "sit upon the fence" till the selfish values emerge.

Disorder and chaos, through misunderstanding of the Plan.

The wrong use of speech to bring about chosen objectives.

Untruth.

Sex magic. The selfish perversion of soul powers,

leading to

White magic, the use of soul powers for spiritual ends.

The identification of oneself with reality.

Right order through right magic.

Power to co-operate with the *Whole*.

Understanding of the Plan.

The magical work of interpretation.

Manifestation of divinity.   (EP2–36/43)

Ray Qualities

• There is much of practical usefulness to the reader in a study of these qualities. When he believes himself to be upon a particular ray, they will indicate to him some of the characteristics for which he may look, and perhaps demonstrate to him what he has to do, what he has to express, and what he has to overcome. These qualities should be studied from two angles:

their divine aspect and their reverse aspect or the form side. [The fifth] ray, for instance, is shown to be the revealer of the Way, and it should be remembered therefore that this fifth ray reveals the way down into death or into incarnation (which is the death-like prison of the soul), or it reveals the way up and out of darkness into the pure light of God's day. I mention this as I am exceedingly anxious that all who read this treatise should make application of this teaching to their daily lives. I am not interested in imparting weird or unusual items of information anent these matters for the delectation of an unhealthy mental appetite. The stocking of the memory with occult detail which serves no useful purpose only strains the brain cells and feeds the pride. (EP1–78/9)

• It will...be apparent to you how the lower and the higher expressions of a ray are closely related to each other and how easily the higher loses its hold and the lower comes into manifestation – something that evolution itself must eventually adjust. (DN–41)

The First Ray of Will or Power

Special Virtues:
Strength, courage, steadfastness, truthfulness arising from absolute fearlessness, power of ruling, capacity to grasp great questions in a large-minded way, and of handling men and measures.

Vices of Ray:
Pride, ambition, wilfulness, hardness, arrogance, desire to control others, obstinacy, anger.

Virtues to be acquired:
Tenderness, humility, sympathy, tolerance, patience.

This has been spoken of as the ray of power, and is correctly so called, but if it were power alone, without wisdom and love, a destructive and disintegrating force would result. When however the three characteristics are united, it becomes a creative and governing ray. Those on this ray have strong will power, for either good or evil, for the former when the will is directed by wisdom and made selfless by love. The first ray man will always "come to the front" in his own line. He may be the burglar or the judge who condemns him, but in either case he will be at the head of his profession. He is the born leader in any and every public career, one to trust and lean on, one to defend the weak and put down oppression, fearless of consequences and utterly indifferent to comment. On the other hand, an unmodified first ray can produce a man of unrelenting cruelty and hardness of nature.

The first ray man often has strong feeling and affection, but he does not readily express it; he will love strong contrasts and masses of colour, but will rarely be an artist; he will delight in great orchestral effects and crashing choruses, and if modified by the fourth, sixth or seventh rays, may be a great composer, but not otherwise; and there is a type of this ray which is tone-deaf, and another which is colour-blind to the more delicate colours. Such a man will distinguish red and yellow, but will hopelessly confuse blue, green and violet.

The literary work of a first ray man will be strong and trenchant, but he will care little for style or finish in his writings. Perhaps examples of this type would be Luther, Carlyle and Walt Whitman. It is said that in attempting the cure of disease the best method for the first ray man would be to draw health and strength from the great fount of universal life by his will power, and then pour it through the patient. This, of course, presupposes knowledge on his part of occult methods.

The characteristic method of approaching the great Quest on this ray would be by sheer force of will. Such a man would, as it were, take the kingdom of heaven "by violence". We have seen that the born leader belongs to this ray, wholly or in part. It makes the able commander-in-chief, such as Napoleon or Kitchener. Napoleon was first and fourth rays, and Kitchener was first and seventh, the seventh ray giving him his remarkable power of organisation. (EP1–201/2)

• Souls on this ray are spoken of occultly as "crashing their way into incarnation". They appropriate dynamically that which they require. They brook no hindrance in the satisfaction of their desires. They stand alone in a proud isolation, glorying in their strength, and their ruthlessness. These qualities have to be transmuted into that intelligent use of power which makes them powerful factors in the Plan, and magnetic centres of force, gathering workers and forces around them. An illustration of this can be seen in the work of the Master Morya, Who is the centre, the magnetic attractive centre, of all esoteric groups, conferring on them, by His power, the capacity to destroy that which is undesirable in the life of the disciples. Forget not that the work of stimulating that which is needed is one of the major tasks of a Master, and the power of a disciple to destroy that which limits him is greatly needed. Souls of this ray, as they come into incarnation through desire, *grasp*. This expresses the nature of the force demonstration employed. There is a measure of violence in their technique. They eventually "take the kingdom of heaven by force". (EP2–80)

• …The outstanding quality of the first ray…is loneliness, isolation, [and] the ability to stand alone and unmoved. (DNA1–320)

• It is easy for first ray people to resist the tendency to identify themselves with others. To have true understanding involves an increased ability to love all beings and yet, at the same time, to preserve personality detachment. This detachment can be so easily founded on an inability to love, in a selfish concern for one's own comfort – physical, mental or spiritual, and above all, emotional. First ray people dread emotion and despise it, but sometimes they have to swing into an emotional condition before they can use emotional sensitivity in the right manner. (GWP–4)

• First ray people belong to what is called the "Destroyer Ray" and the power of the first aspect, which is the power to bring to an end, flows through them. They will have a tendency to destroy, as they build, through a wrong direction of energy, through over-emphasis of energy in some particular direction, or through misuse of energy in work with themselves or others. Many first ray people have the tendency to pride themselves on this and hide behind a plea that, being upon the first ray, a destructive tendency is unavoidable. Such is not the case. Builders, such as second ray people always are, have to learn to destroy, when prompted by group love and acting under the Will or first ray aspect. Destroyers have to learn to build, acting ever under the impulse of group love and utilising the power of attachment in a detached manner. Both groups, builders and destroyers, must ever work from the standpoint of reality, from the inner nucleus of truth and must "take their stand at the centre". (GWP–6)

• The will of Deity coloured the stream of energy units which we call by the name of the Ray of Will or Power, the first ray, and the impact of that stream on the matter of space insured that the hidden purpose of Deity would inevitably and eventually be revealed. It is a ray of such dynamic intensity that we call it the ray of the Destroyer. It is not as yet functioning actively. It will come into full play only when the time comes for the purpose to be safely revealed. Its units of energy in manifestation in the human kingdom are very few. As I earlier said, there is not a true first ray type in incarnation as yet. Its main potency is to be found in the mineral kingdom, and the key to the mystery of the first ray is to be found in radium. (EP1–44)

The Second Ray of Love-Wisdom

Special Virtues:
Calm, strength, patience and endurance, love of truth, faithfulness, intuition, clear intelligence, and serene temper.

Vices of the Ray:
Over-absorption in study, coldness, indifference to others, contempt of mental limitations in others.

Virtues to be acquired:
Love, compassion, unselfishness, energy.

This is called the ray of wisdom from its characteristic desire for pure knowledge and for absolute truth – cold and selfish, if without love, and inactive without power. When both power and love are present, then you have the ray of the Buddhas and of all great teachers of humanity, – those who, having attained wisdom for the sake of others, spend themselves in giving it forth. The student on this ray is ever unsatisfied with his highest attainments; no matter how great his knowledge, his mind is still fixed on the unknown, the beyond, and on the heights as yet unscaled.

The second ray man will have tact and foresight; he will make an excellent ambassador, and a first-rate teacher or head of a college; as a man of affairs, he will have clear intelligence and wisdom in dealing with matters which come before him, and he will have the capacity of impressing true views of things on others and of making them see things as he does. He will make a good business man, if modified by the fourth, fifth and seventh rays. The soldier on this ray would plan wisely and foresee possibilities; he would have an intuition as to the best course to pursue, and he would never lead his men into danger through rashness. He might be deficient in rapidity of action and energy. The artist on this ray would always seek to teach through his art, and his pictures would have a meaning. His literary work would always be instructive.

The method of healing, for the second ray man, would be to learn thoroughly the temperament of the patient as well as to be thoroughly conversant with the nature of the disease, so as to use his will power on the case to the best advantage.

The characteristic method of approaching the Path would be by close and earnest study of the teachings till they become so much a part of the man's consciousness as no longer to be merely intellectual knowledge, but a spiritual rule of living, thus bringing in intuition and true wisdom.

A bad type of the second ray would be bent on acquiring knowledge for himself alone, absolutely indifferent to the human needs of others. The foresight of such a man would degenerate into suspicion, his calmness into coldness and hardness of nature. (EP1–202/4)

• Souls on this ray use the method of "gathering in", or "drawing into". The soul sets up a vibration (little as we may yet grasp the real significance of that word) and that vibration affects its environment, and atoms of substance on all three planes are attracted to the central point of energy. The method is relatively gentle, when compared to the method of the first ray, and the process is somewhat longer whilst the overshadowing (carried forward prior to entering into the three worlds for purposes of appearance) is very much longer. This refers to that overshadowing of the substance to be built into form, and not to the overshadowing of the completed form, i.e. the child in the mother's womb. In the first case, it might be said that souls on the first ray are sudden and rapid in their desire to incarnate, and in the methods employed. Souls on the second ray are slower in coming to that "impulsive" action (in the sense of impulse to action and not impulse in time) which leads to the occult manufacture of an appearance with which to manifest.

Souls on this ray, as they come into incarnation through desire, *attract.* They are magnetic more than they are dynamic; they are constructive, and they work along the line which is, for all lives and forms, the line of least resistance within our universe. (EP2–80/1)

• Teaching is an expression of second ray energy. (DNA1–216)

• *The Energy of Love-Wisdom*…always has an effect upon every type of human being in the world. Its effect is to stimulate the tendency towards goodwill and to produce a mental development which can transmute the knowledge – garnered down the ages – into wisdom. It is wisdom which is needed today. Those who are now attempting to foster goodwill in themselves and others will be stimulated into wise action. You can see, therefore, that the outpouring of this energy is the first and greatest need. It *can* reach mankind because the Founders of all the world religions (I refer not to their many diversifications) are banded together in unison with the Christ, Their Lord and Master; through Their united and directed effort, these energies will flow. Forget not that Christ represents the energy of love and the Buddha that of wisdom. (EXH–644/5)

• Those upon the second ray fall...into two groups, generally speaking; there are, naturally, numerous exceptions. Souls on the wisdom aspect of the second ray go to Shamballa and join the Great Council in some capacity or another. Such a one was the Buddha. Those on the love aspect of the second ray tread one or other of the various paths, primarily that of the World Saviours; They become the divine Psychologists and World Teachers. The Christ combined in Himself all these three great traits.

Those in this second group of souls upon the second ray likewise fall into two groups: They follow the way of specialised detail and of a comprehensive inclusiveness, and are the outstanding occultists; the other group is distinguished by pure love. Of the group which finds its way into Shamballa a developed simplicity will be found to govern all relations.

Simplicity and unity are related; simplicity is one-pointedness of outlook, free from glamour and the intricacies of the thoughtform-making mind; simplicity is clarity of purpose and steadfastness in intention and in effort, untrammelled by questioning and devious introspection; simplicity leads to simple loving, asking nothing in return; simplicity leads to silence – not silence as an escape mechanism, but as an "occult retention of speech". (DNA2–518)

The Third Ray of Activity and Adaptability

Special Virtues:
Wide views on all abstract questions, sincerity of purpose, clear intellect, capacity for concentration on philosophic studies, patience, caution, absence of the tendency to worry himself or others over trifles.

Vices of Ray:
Intellectual pride, coldness, isolation, inaccuracy in details, absent-mindedness, obstinacy, selfishness, overmuch criticism of others.

Virtues to be acquired:
Sympathy, tolerance, devotion, accuracy, energy and common-sense.

This is the ray of the abstract thinker, of the philosopher and the metaphysician, of the man who delights in the higher mathematics but who, unless modified by some practical ray, would hardly be troubled to keep his accounts accurately. His imaginative faculty will be highly developed, i.e., he can by the power of his imagination grasp the essence of a truth; his idealism will often be strong; he is a dreamer and a theorist, and from his wide views and great caution he sees every side of a question equally clearly. This sometimes paralyses his action. He will make a good business man; as a soldier he will work out a problem in tactics at his desk, but is seldom great in the field. As an artist his technique is not fine, but his subjects will be full of thought and interest. He will love music, but unless influenced by the fourth ray he will not produce it. In all walks of life he is full of ideas, but is too impractical to carry them out.

One type of this ray is unconventional to a degree, slovenly, unpunctual and idle, and regardless of appearances. If influenced by the fifth ray as the secondary ray, this character is entirely changed. The third and the fifth rays make the perfectly balanced historian who grasps his subject in a large way and verifies every detail with patient accuracy. Again the third and the fifth rays together make the truly great mathematician who soars into heights of abstract thought and calculation, and who can also bring his results down to practical scientific use. The literary style of the third ray man is too often vague and involved, but if influenced by the first, fourth, fifth or seventh rays, this is changed, and under the fifth he will be a master of the pen.

The curing of disease by the third ray man would be by the use of drugs made of herbs or minerals belonging to the same ray as the patient whom he desires to relieve.

The method of approaching the great Quest, for this ray type, is by deep thinking on philosophic or metaphysical lines till he is led to the realisation of the great Beyond and of the paramount importance of treading the Path that leads thither. (EP1–204/5)

• Just as the grasping and attracting are terms applicable to the methods of the two first rays, so a process of "selective manipulation" is characteristic of this third ray. This method is totally different in its technique to that of the two mentioned above. It might be said that the note which generates the activity set up by souls on this ray, is such that atoms of the different planes are moved as if consciously responding to a selective process. The vibratory activity of the soul makes itself felt, and atoms collect from widely different points in response to a certain quality in the vibration. It is far more selective than in the case of the second ray.

Just as souls in the first case seem to *grasp* indiscriminately what they need, and force the substance thus grasped into the form or appearance required, enduing it with the quality needed in a dynamic and forceful way, and just as souls on the second ray set up a motion which gathers material out of the immediately surrounding environment, and imposes on it, through *magnetic attraction*, the desired quality, so in the case of souls on the third ray the required material is chosen here and there, but that chosen already has the needs quality (note this difference) and nothing whatever is imposed. (EP2–81/2)

• ...If [the student] is using third ray force, in a *personal* manner, he will be devious in his propositions, subtle and elusive in his arguments, using manipulation in his relations with his fellowmen, or be an interfering busybody, actively engaged in running the world, in managing other people's lives for them, or in grasping so firmly the reins of government in his own self-interest that he will sacrifice everything and everybody in the work of furthering his own busy ends. If he is, however, a true disciple and aspirant, he will work with the Plan and will wield third ray force to bring about the loving purposes of the spiritual Reality. He will be busy and active and his words will carry truth, and will lead to the helping of others, for they will be detached and true. (TWM–574/5)

• ...The third ray...finds its expression through the third major centre on the planet; this centre, we call Humanity. (DN–21)

The Fourth Ray of Harmony, Beauty and Art

Special Virtues:
Strong affections, sympathy, physical courage, generosity, devotion, quickness of intellect and perception.

Vices of Ray:
Self-centredness, worrying, inaccuracy, lack of moral courage, strong passions, indolence, extravagance.

Virtues to be acquired:
Serenity, confidence, self-control, purity, unselfishness, accuracy, mental and moral balance.

This has been called the "ray of struggle" for on this ray the qualities of rajas (activity) and tamas (inertia) are so strangely equal in proportion that the nature of the fourth ray man is torn with their combat, and the outcome, when satisfactory, is spoken of as the "Birth of Horus", of the Christ, born from the throes of constant pain and suffering.

Tamas induces love of ease and pleasure, a hatred of causing pain amounting to moral cowardice, indolence, procrastination, a desire to let things be, to rest, and to take no thought of the morrow. Rajas is fiery, impatient, ever urging to action. These contrasting forces in the nature make life one perpetual warfare and unrest for the fourth ray man; the friction and the experience gained thereby may produce very rapid evolution, but the man may as easily become a ne'er-do-well as a hero.

It is the ray of the dashing cavalry leader, reckless of risks to himself or his followers. It is the ray of the man who will lead a forlorn hope, for in moments of excitement the fourth ray man is entirely dominated by rajas; of the wild speculator and gambler, full of enthusiasm and plans, easily overwhelmed by sorrow or failure, but as quickly recovering from all reverses and misfortunes.

It is pre-eminently the ray of colour, of the artist whose colour is always great, though his drawing will often be defective. (Watts was fourth and second rays.) The fourth ray man always loves colour, and can generally produce it. If untrained as an artist, a colour sense is sure to appear in other ways, in choice of dress or decorations.

In music, fourth ray compositions are always full of melody, and the fourth ray man loves a tune. As a writer or poet, his work will often be brilliant and full of picturesque word-painting, but inaccurate, full of exaggerations, and often pessimistic. He will generally talk well and have a sense of humour but he varies between brilliant conversations and gloomy silences, according to his mood. He is a delightful and difficult person to live with.

In healing, the best fourth ray method is massage and magnetism, used with knowledge.

The method of approaching the Path will be by self-control, thus gaining equilibrium amongst the warring forces of the nature. The lower and extremely dangerous way is by Hatha Yoga. (EP1–205/7)

• The fourth Ray of Harmony through Conflict is a controlling factor in human affairs at all times, and peculiarly today. (RI–639)

• This fourth ray is, in the last analysis, the ray which teaches the art of living in order to produce a synthesis of beauty. There is no beauty without unity, without embodied idealism and the resultant symmetrical unfoldment. This ray is *not* the ray of art, as it is often claimed, but is the energy which brings about the beauty of those living forms which embody the ideas and the ideals which are seeking immediate expression. Many people claim to be on the fourth ray because they dream of the artistic expressive life. As I have told you before, creative art expresses itself upon all the rays. (DN–143)

• [This ray] will work out in the following ways:

In the development of the intuition by the means of the knowledge of sound vibration, and the higher mathematics.

This is being already touched upon exoterically.

Music, as a means to be employed in building and destroying, will be recognised, and the laws of levitation and of rhythmic movement in all forms, from an atom to a solar system, will be studied. The manipulation of matter of all kinds by the means of sound will be practised on the two lower planes, and when the synthesis of the four rays into the third is in process of accomplishment, then a similar knowledge will be displayed on the mental plane.

The laws of fire will be gradually permitted exoteric publication; there are twenty-seven occult laws which are only revealed after initiation at this stage of evolution. In them are summed up the basic laws of colour and of music and rhythm. When music produces warmth or stimulation, and when pictures, for instance, glow or reveal the subjective within the objective, then will this fourth Ray of Harmony be coming to fruition. (TCF–427)

• [The] fourth Ray of Harmony gives to all forms that which produces beauty and works towards the harmonising of all effects emanating from the world of causes, which is the world of the three major rays. The ray of beauty, of art and harmony is the producer of the quality of *organisation through form.* It is in the last analysis the ray of mathematical exactitude and is not the ray of the artist, as so many seem to think. The artist is found on all rays, just as is the engineer or the physician, the home-maker or the musician. I want to make this clear, for there is much misunderstanding on this matter. (EP1–49)

The Fifth Ray of Concrete Knowledge or Science

Special Virtues:
Strictly accurate statements, justice (without mercy), perseverance, common-sense, uprightness, independence, keen intellect.

Vices of Ray:
Harsh criticism, narrowness, arrogance, unforgiving temper, lack of sympathy and reverence, prejudice.

Virtues to be Acquired:
Reverence, devotion, sympathy, love, wide-mindedness.

This is the ray of science and of research. The man on this ray will possess keen intellect, great accuracy in detail, and will make unwearied efforts to trace the smallest fact to its source, and to verify every theory. He will generally be extremely truthful, full of lucid explanation of facts, though sometimes pedantic and wearisome from his insistence on trivial and unnecessary verbal minutiae. He will be orderly, punctual, business-like, disliking to receive favours or flattery.

It is the ray of the great chemist, the practical electrician, the first-rate engineer, the great operating surgeon. As a statesman, the fifth ray man would be narrow in his views, but he would be an excellent head of some special technical department, though a disagreeable person under whom to work. As a soldier, he would turn most readily to artillery and engineering. The artist on this ray is very rare, unless the fourth or seventh be the influencing secondary ray; even then his colouring will be dull, his sculptures lifeless, and his music (if he composes) will be uninteresting, though technically correct in form. His style in writing or speaking will be clearness itself, but it will lack fire and point, and he will often be long-winded, from his desire to say all that can possibly be said on his subject.

In healing, he is the perfect surgeon, and his best cures will be through surgery and electricity.

For the fifth ray, the method of approaching the Path is by scientific research, pushed to ultimate conclusions, and by the acceptance of the inferences which follow these. (EP1–207/8)

• …This ray concerns itself with the building of form, with the utilisation of matter, with the embodying of ideas, or of entities, whether cosmic, systemic, lunar, or subhuman. (TCF–433)

• The fifth ray…works actively on the plane of the greatest moment to humanity [the mental plane], being, for man, the plane of the soul, and of the higher and the lower mind. It embodies the principle of knowledge, and because of its activity and its close relation to the third Ray of Active Intelligence might be regarded as a ray having a most vital relation to man at this time in particular. It is the ray which – when active, as it was in Lemurian times, – produces individualisation, which is literally the shifting of the evolving life of God into a new sphere of awareness. This particular transference into higher forms of awareness tends, at the beginning, to separativeness.

The fifth ray has produced what we call science. In science we find a condition which is rare in the extreme. Science is separative in its approach to the differing aspects of the divine manifestation which we call the world of natural phenomena, but it is non-separative in actuality, for there is little warring between the sciences and little competition between scientists. In this the workers in the scientific field differ profoundly from those of the religious. (EP1–51)

The Sixth Ray of Abstract Idealism and Devotion

Special Virtues:
Devotion, single-mindedness, love, tenderness, intuition, loyalty, reverence.

Vices of Ray:
Selfish and jealous love, over-leaning on others, partiality, self-deception, sectarianism, superstition, prejudice, over-rapid conclusions, fiery anger.

Virtues to be acquired:
Strength, self-sacrifice, purity, truth, tolerance, serenity, balance and common sense.

This is called the ray of devotion. The man who is on this ray is full of religious instincts and impulses, and of intense personal feeling; nothing is taken equably. Everything, in his eyes, is either perfect or intolerable; his friends are angels, his enemies are very much the reverse; his view, in both cases, is formed not on the intrinsic merits of either class, but on the way the persons appeal to him, or on the sympathy or lack of sympathy which they show to his favourite idols, whether these be concrete or abstract, for he is full of devotion, it may be to a person, or it may be to a cause.

He must always have a "personal God", an incarnation of Deity to adore. The best type of this ray makes the saint, the worst type, the bigot or fanatic, the typical martyr or the typical inquisitor. All religious wars or crusades have originated from sixth ray fanaticism. The man on this ray is often of gentle nature, but he can always flame into fury and fiery wrath. He will lay down his life for the objects of his devotion or reverence, but he will not lift a finger to help those outside of his immediate sympathies. As a soldier, he hates fighting but often when roused in battle fights like one possessed. He is never a great statesman nor a good business man, but he may be a great preacher or orator.

The sixth ray man will be the poet of the emotions (such as Tennyson) and the writer of religious books, either in poetry or prose. He is devoted to beauty and colour and all things lovely, but his productive skill is not great unless under the influence of one of the practically artistic rays, the fourth or seventh. His music will always be of a melodious order, and he will often be the composer of oratorios and of sacred music.

The method of healing for this ray would be by faith and prayer.

The way of approaching the Path would be by prayer and meditation, aiming at union with God. (EP1–208/10)

• Idealism is the major gift of the sixth ray force. (DNA1–216)

• The sixth Ray of Devotion embodies the principle of recognition. By this I mean the capacity to see the ideal reality lying behind the form; this implies a one-pointed application of desire and of intelligence in order to produce an expression of that sensed idea. It is responsible for much of the formulation of the ideas which have led man on, and for much of the emphasis on the appearance which has veiled and hidden those ideals. (EP1–52)

• Pure religion, undefiled and spiritually focused, is the higher expression of the sixth ray....

In the same connection, among the *lower aspects* of the sixth ray are to be found all forms of dogmatic, authoritative religion as expressed by the organised and orthodox churches. All formulated theologies are the lower expression of the higher spiritual truths because they embody the mind reactions of the religious man, his confidence in his own personal mind deductions and the surety that he is obviously right. They do not embody the spiritual values as they truly exist. Consequently the dreadful nature of the lower expressions of the sixth ray and the control by the forces of separativeness (which are ever the outstanding characteristic of the lower sixth ray activity) can be seen nowhere more potently than in religious and Church history with its hatreds and bigotry, its pomp and luxurious appeal to the outer ear and eye, and its separativeness from all other forms of faith as well as its internal dissensions, its protesting groups and its cliques and cabals. The Church has wandered far from the simplicity which is in Christ. (DN–39/40)

• The sixth ray devotee is far more abstract and mystical in his work and thought [than the seventh ray disciple], and seldom has any real understanding of the right relation between form and energy. He thinks almost entirely in terms of quality and pays little attention to the material side of life and the true significance of substance as it produces phenomena. He is apt to regard matter as evil in nature and form as a limitation, and only lays the emphasis upon soul consciousness as of true importance. (DN–126/7)

• One is apt to recognise with ease that the sixth ray, working through Mars, rules Christianity. It is a religion of devotion, fanaticism, of high courage, of idealism, of the spiritual emphasis upon the individual and his worth and problem, of conflict and of death. All those characteristics are familiar to us in the presentation of Christian theology. (EA–212)

• ...Put no sixth ray people in positions of influence; they know not how to co-operate and are frequently points of dissension and dislike. (DNA2–86)

The Seventh Ray of Ceremonial Law or Magic

Special Virtues:
Strength, perseverance, courage, courtesy, extreme care in details, self-reliance.

Vices of Ray:
Formalism, bigotry, pride, narrowness, superficial judgments, self-opinion over-indulged.

Virtues to be acquired:
Realisation of unity, wide-mindedness, tolerance, humility, gentleness and love.

This is the ceremonial ray, the ray which makes a man delight in "all things done decently and in order", and according to rule and precedent. It is the ray of the high priest and the court chamberlain, of the soldier who is a born genius in organisation, of the ideal commissary general who will dress and feed the troops in the best possible way. It is the ray of the perfect nurse for the sick, careful in the smallest detail, though sometimes too much inclined to disregard the patients' idiosyncrasies and to try and grind them in the iron mill of routine.

It is the ray of form, of the perfect sculptor, who sees and produces ideal beauty, of the designer of beautiful forms and patterns of any sort; but such a man would not be successful as a painter unless his influencing ray were the fourth. The combination of four with seven would make the very highest type of artist, form and colour being both *in excelcis*. The literary work of the seventh ray man would be remarkable for its ultra-polished style, and such a writer would think far more of the manner than of the matter in his work, but would always be fluent both in writing and speech. The seventh ray man will often be sectarian. He will delight in fixed ceremonials and observances, in great processions and shows, in reviews of troops and warships, in genealogical trees, and in rules of precedence.

The bad type of seventh ray man is superstitious, and such a man will take deep interest in omens, in dreams, in all occult practices, and in spiritualistic phenomena. The good type of the ray is absolutely determined to do the right thing and say the right word at the right moment; hence great social success.

In healing, the seventh ray man would rely on extreme exactness in carrying out orthodox treatment of disease. On him the practices of yoga would have no physical bad results.

He will approach the Path through observance of rules of practice and of ritual, and can easily evoke and control the elemental forces. (EP1–210/1)

• The prime...function of the seventh ray is to perform the magical work of blending spirit and matter in order to produce the manifested form through which the life will reveal the glory of God. (EP1–369)

• ...It would be wise if students would ponder the significance of the coming in of the present Ray of Ceremonial Law or Magic. It is the ray that deals with the building forces of nature, that concerns itself with the utilisation of the form intelligently by the life aspect. It is largely the ray of executive work, with the object of building, co-ordinating and producing cohesion in the four lower kingdoms of nature. It is distinguished largely by the energy which manifests itself in ritual, but this word ritual must not be narrowed down to its present use in connection with Masonic, or religious ritual. Its application is far wider than this, and includes the methods of organisation which are demonstrated in all civilised communities, such as in the world of commerce and of finance, and the great business organisations everywhere to be seen. Above all, its interest lies for us in the fact that it is the ray which brings opportunity to the occidental races, and through the medium of this life force of executive organisation, of government by rule and order, by rhythm and by ritual, will come the time wherein the occidental races (with their active, concrete mind, and their vast business capacity) can take initiation, – an initiation, we must remember, upon a ray which is temporarily recognised as a major ray. A large number of the initiates and those who have obtained adeptship in the last cycle, have been orientals and those in Hindu bodies. This cycle has been dominated by the sixth ray, which is just passing out, and the two preceding. In the preservation of equilibrium the time now comes when a period of attainment by occidentals will be seen, and this upon a ray suited to their type of mind. It is interesting to note that the oriental type attains its objective through meditation, with a modicum of executive organisation and ritual, and that the occidental will achieve largely through the organisation which lower mind produces, and a type of meditation of which intense business concentration might be considered an illustration. The one-pointed application of the mind by a European or American business man might be regarded as a type of meditation. In the purification of motive lying back of this application will come, for the occidental, his day of opportunity. (IHS–182/3)

• …The higher and more living energy of the seventh ray is the most active at this time and its resultant idealism and consequent New Age concepts are playing upon the sensitive minds of the race and preparing humanity for a great and much needed change. The work of the Ray of Ceremonial Order is to "ground" or make physically visible the results of bringing spirit and matter together. Its function is to clothe spirit with matter, producing form. (DN–46/7)

• The powers of the magical age are many and one of the reasons why the seventh ray is now making its appearance is that, owing to the rapid perfecting and integration of the human personality, the higher integration between soul and personality is today more possible and more easily accomplished than ever before. The new forms, through which that much desired consummation can be affected, must be consequently gradually and scientifically developed. This, as you may well conceive, will be achieved through the intensification of the forces, functioning through the etheric body, through the coordination of the seven major centres, and the establishing of their rhythmic relationship. The seventh ray governs predominantly upon the etheric levels of the physical plane. It does not govern the dense physical form which is under the control of the third ray.

It is the vital or the etheric body which is responsive to and developed by the incoming seventh ray influences. (DN–117/8)

• ...The seventh ray is spoken of as governing the mineral kingdom and also as manifesting through its mediumship that significant soul characteristic and quality which we call *radiation*. That word effectively describes the result of soul stimulation upon and within every form. The life of the soul eventually radiates beyond the form and this radiation produces definite and calculated effects. (DN–123)

• The seventh Ray of Ceremonial Order or Magic embodies a curious quality which is the outstanding characteristic of the particular Life which ensouls this ray. It is the quality or principle which is the co-ordinating factor unifying the inner quality and the outer tangible form or appearance. This work goes on primarily on etheric levels and involves physical energy. This is the true magical work. I should like to point out that when the fourth ray and the seventh ray come into incarnation together, we shall have a most peculiar period of revelation and of light-bringing. It is said of this time that then "the temple of the Lord will take on an added glory and the Builders will rejoice together". (EP1–52)

The Seventh Ray and Ritual

• It might be wise here to elucidate somewhat the idea underlying ceremonial and ritual. There is so much revolt at this time against ceremonial, and so many good and well-meaning people regard themselves as having outgrown and transcended ritual. They pride themselves on having attained that so-called "liberation", forgetting that it is only the sense of individuality that permits this attitude, and that no group work is ever possible without some form of ritual. The refusal therefore to participate in uniformity of action is no sign of a liberated soul.

The Great White Brotherhood has its rituals, but they are rituals which have for their objective the inauguration and the assistance of various aspects of the Plan, and of the varying cyclic activities of that Plan. Where these rituals exist, but where the meaning (inherently present) remains hidden and unrealised, there must as a consequence be demonstrated a spirit of deadness, of uselessness, and of weariness of interest over forms and ceremonies. But where it is demonstrated that ritual and organised ceremonies are but the evidence of a custody of forces and energies, then the idea is constructive in its working out, co-operation with the Plan becomes possible, and the aim of all the divine service begins to demonstrate. All service is governed by ritual. (EP1–363)

• One of the first lessons that humanity will learn under the potent influence of the seventh ray is that the soul controls its instrument, the personality, through ritual, or through the imposition of a regular rhythm, for rhythm is what really designates a ritual. When aspirants to discipleship impose a rhythm on their lives they call it a discipline, and they feel happy about it. What groups do who are gathered together for the performance of any ritual or ceremony whatsoever (Church ritual, the Masonic work, the drill of the army or navy, business organisations, the proper functioning of a home, of a hospital, or of an entertainment, etc.) is of an analogous nature, for it imposes on the participants a simultaneous performance, an identical undertaking, or a ritual. No one on this earth can evade ritual or ceremonial, for the rising and the setting of the sun imposes a ritual, the cyclic passing of the years, the potent movements of the great centres of population, the coming and the going of trains, of ocean liners and of mails, and the regular broadcasting of the radio organisations, – all of these impose a rhythm upon humanity, whether this is recognised or not. Of these rhythms the present great experiments in national standardisation and regimentation are also an expression, as they demonstrate through the masses in any nation.

There is no evading the process of ceremonial living. It is unconsciously recognised, blindly followed, and constitutes the great discipline of the rhythmic breathing of life itself. The Deity works with ritual and is subjected to the ceremonials of the universe. The seven rays come into activity and pass out again under the rhythmic and ritualistic impulse of the divine

Life. Thus is the temple of the Lord built by the ceremonial of the Builders. Every kingdom in nature is subjected to ritualistic experience and to the ceremonials of cyclic expression. These only the initiate can comprehend. Every ant hill and every beehive is equally impelled by instinctive rituals and by rhythmic impulses. (EP1–365/6)

The Rays and Their Colours

• ...The one Ray of which all the others are but sub-rays, might be regarded as a circle of sevenfold light. Too apt is the student to picture seven bands, striking down athwart the five lower planes till they contact the earth plane and are absorbed into dense matter. Not so is it in fact. The seven colours may be regarded as a band of seven colours circling and continuously shifting and moving through the planes back to their originating source.... These seven bands of colour emanate from the synthetic Ray. The indigo sub-ray of the indigo Ray forms the path of least resistance from the heart of densest matter back again to the source. The bands of colour form a circulating ring which, moving at different rates of vibration, passes *through* all the planes, circling down and up again. What I seek to bring out specially here is that these seven bands do not all move at the same rate, and herein lies hid the key to the complexity of the matter. Some move at a swifter rate of vibration than do some of the others. Hence – as they carry their corresponding monads with them – you have here the answer to the question as to why some egos seem to make more rapid progress than do some others.

These coloured rings do not follow a straight unimpeded course, but interweave in a most curious manner, blending with each other, absorbing each other in stated cycles, and grouping themselves in groups of threes or fives, yet ever moving onwards. This is the real foundation to the diamond pattern upon the back of the serpent of wisdom. Three major lines of colour should be portrayed as forming the lattice work on the serpent's skin, with the four other colours interweaving. (LOM–211/12)

• ...*Colour is but the form assumed by force, of some kind, when that force is moving at a certain measure, and when its action and movement is impeded or unimpeded by the material through which it plays.* In this sentence lies the key to the solution of the problem as to the colour differences on the higher planes and on the lower. The resistance of matter to the downflow of force or life, and its relative density or rarity accounts for much of the colour distinction. (LOM–232)

• ...The colours as seen in the aura of a savage and in those of the average developed man are extraordinarily dissimilar. Why? because one is moving or vibrating at a slow rate and the other with greatly increased rapidity. One has a rhythm slow, sluggish and heavy, the other is pulsating and moving with a tremendous velocity, permitting consequently a more rapid play of the material of which those bodies are constructed.

Therefore, I would like to point out that as the race progresses as a collective unit, Those Who gaze upon it from a higher plane are aware of the steady improvement in the colours seen, and of a greater purity and clarity of hue in the aura of the race, which aura is composed of the composite auras of the units of the race. (LOM—233)

• ...These influences (which show forth as colours when they contact matter) move in their own ordered cycles. These cycles we describe as the coming in or the going out of a ray. In this fourth round usually four rays are in flux at any one given time; by this I seek to impress upon you that though all rays manifest in the solar system, at certain stages of manifestation more or less of them will be dominating simultaneously. These rays, forces, influences, or co-ordinations of qualities, when expressed in terms of light, colour the matters they impinge upon with certain recognisable hues, and these give the *tone* to the life of the personality or to the Ego. They are recognized by you as the composite character and are seen by the clairvoyant as colour.

Groups, therefore, of units who converge through similarity of vibration will be seen as having approximately the same basic hue, though with many lesser differentiations in colour and tone. As stated before, the colour of large masses of people can be gauged and judged. It is in this way that the members of the Hierarchy in Whose Hands is placed evolutionary development in the three worlds, judge of the stage attained and the progress made.

Different rays come in bearing units coloured by that ray. Other rays pass out carrying with them units of a different basic hue. In the period of transition the blending of colour is of deep complexity, but of mutual helpfulness and benefit. Each ray imparts somewhat to the other rays in incarnation at the same time, and the rate of rhythm will be slightly affected. This from the standpoint of the present and of time in the three worlds, may be almost inappreciably small, but through the frequent meeting and interplay of the forces and colours, and their constant action and interaction upon each other, will come a steady, general levelling up, and an approximation in vibration. You will see, therefore, how synthesis is achieved at the end of a greater maha-manvantara. The three rays absorb the seven and lead eventually to a merging in the synthetic ray.

In the microcosm the three rays of the Monad, the Ego, and the Personality will likewise dominate and absorb the seven, and in time also lead to a merging in the synthetic ray of the Monad. The correspondence will be found perfect. (LOM–233/5)

• Every individual vibrates to some particular measure. Those who know and who work clairvoyantly and clairaudiently find that all matter sounds, all matter pulsates, and all matter has its own colour. Each human being can therefore be made to give forth some specific sound; in making that sound he flashes into colour, and the combination of the two is indicative of some measure which is peculiarly his own.

Every unit of the human race is on some one of the seven rays; therefore some one colour predominates, and some one tone sounds forth; infinite are the gradations and many the shades of colour and tone. Each ray has its subsidiary rays which it dominates, acting as the synthetic ray. These seven rays are linked with the colours of the spectrum. There are the rays of red, blue, yellow, orange, green and violet. There is the ray that synthesises them all, that of indigo. There are the three major rays – red, blue and yellow – and the four subsidiary colours which, in the evolving Monad, find their correspondence in the spiritual Triad and the lower quaternary. The Logos of our system is concentrating on the love or blue aspect. This – as the synthesis – manifests as indigo. This matter of the rays and their colours is confusing to the neophyte. I can but indicate some thoughts, and in the accumulation of suggestion light may eventually come. The clue lies in similarity of colour, which entails a resemblance in note and rhythm. When, therefore, a man is on the red and yellow rays, with red as his primary ray, and meets another human being who is on the blue and yellow rays, with a secondary resemblance to the yellow, there may be recognition. But when a man on the yellow and blue rays, with yellow as his primary colour, meets a brother on the yellow and red rays, the recognition is immediate and mutual, for the primary colour is the same. When this fundamental cause of association or dissociation is better understood, the secondary colours will be made to act as the meeting ground, to the mutual benefit of the parties concerned.

Of the colours, red, blue and yellow are primary and irreducible. They are the colours of the major rays.

    a. Will or Power . . . . Red

    b. Love-Wisdom . . . . Blue

    c. Active Intelligence . . . . . . Yellow

We have then the subsidiary rays:

    d. Orange.

    e. Green.

    f. Violet.

and the synthesising ray, Indigo. (EP1–126/8)

Ray Combinations or Relationships

• The first and the second rays work closely together; love and will are closely identified on the higher levels of consciousness and service; the two basic energies in reality constitute one great expression of divine planning and purpose. (DNA2–517)

• There is an aspect of the relationship between the first and second rays which is very apt to be overlooked. The second ray is outgoing, inclusive, friendly and prone to attachment; the first ray is isolated, exclusive, antagonistic and prone to detachment. It is the conflict between these two energies – brought together in one incarnation – which has brought about the distorted and unhappy life conditions which have characterised you, which you recognise, and which cause you so much real distress. It is time that this clashing of the two forces should end, and the conflict can only be determined *by the subjugation of your first ray personality by your second ray soul.* (DNA2–698/9)

• I would have you bear in mind in connection with the five rays which we have seen are influencing or beginning to influence humanity at this time (the first, second, third, sixth and seventh rays) that their effect varies according to the ray type or ray quality of the individual concerned and according to his position upon the ladder of evolution. Such points are often forgotten. If a man is, for instance, upon the second Ray of Love-Wisdom, it may be expected that the influence of that ray and of the sixth (which is along the second ray line of power) will be easily effective and will necessarily constitute the line of least resistance. This situation may, therefore, produce undue sensitivity and an unbalanced unfoldment of characteristics. It is our characteristics which influence our conduct and our reactions to circumstance. It will mean also that the influence of the first, third and seventh rays will be fundamentally unsettling and will call out resistance or – at the very least – an attitude of non-receptivity. In the world today, the rays which are along the line of energy which is that of the first Ray of Will or Power (including the third and the seventh) are in the ratio of three to two (as regards present manifestation) and, therefore, we can look for a fuller expression of the first ray attributes and happenings than would otherwise be the case. This will be particularly so because the sixth ray is fast going out of manifestation. (DN–135/6)

• …The characteristics of any given ray find closer correspondence with one of the other rays than with the rest. This is a fact. The only one which stands alone and has no close relationship with any of the others is the fourth.…

Between the third and the fifth rays there is a close relationship. In the search after knowledge, for example, the most laborious and minute study of detail is the path that will be followed, whether in philosophy, the higher mathematics or in the pursuit of practical science.

The correspondence between the second and the sixth rays shews itself in the intuitive grasp of synthesised knowledge, and in the common bond of faithfulness and loyalty.

Masterfulness, steadfastness, and perseverance are the corresponding characteristics of the first and the seventh rays. (EP1–211/2)

• …There is a close relation between the third and the sixth rays, just as there is between the first and the second rays, and the second and the fourth. The fourth, fifth, sixth and seventh rays have no such paralleling relations. 1 added to 1 equals 2, 2 added to 2 equals 4, 3 added to 3 equals 6. Between these pairs of rays there is a line of special energy flowing which warrants the attention of disciples who are becoming conscious of their relationships. This relation and interplay only becomes active at a relatively high stage of evolution. (EP2–373)

Cyclic Manifestation of the Rays

• It is not easy for us to do more than grip as a mental concept the fact that the rays, schemes, planets, chains, rounds, races and laws form a unit; seen from the angle of human vision the confusion seems unimaginable, and the key of its solution to be so hidden as to be useless; yet, seen from the angle of logoic sight, the whole moves in unison, and is geometrically accurate. In order to give some idea of the complexity of the arrangement, I would like here to point out that the Rays themselves circulate, the Law of Karma controlling the interweaving. For instance, Ray I may pass around a scheme (if it is the paramount Ray of the scheme) with its first subray manifesting in a chain, its second in a round, its third in a world period, its fourth in a root race, its fifth in a subrace, and its sixth in a branch race. I give this in illustration, and not as the statement of a fact in present manifestation. This gives us some idea of the vastness of the process, and of its wonderful beauty. It is impossible for us, sweeping through on some one Ray, to visualise or in any way to apprehend this beauty; yet, to those on higher levels and with a wider range of vision, the gorgeousness of the design is apparent.

This complexity is for us very much increased because we do not yet understand the principle governing this mutation. Nor is it possible for even the highest human mind in the three worlds to do more than sense and approximate that principle. By mutation I mean the fact that there is a constant changing and shifting, an endless interweaving and interlocking, and a ceaseless ebb and flow, in the dramatic interplay of the forces that stand for the dual synthesis of Spirit and matter. There is constant rotation in the Rays and planes, in their relative importance from the standpoint of time, which is the standpoint most closely associated with us. But we can rest assured that there is some fundamental principle directing all the activities of the Logos in His system, and by wrestling to discover the basic principle on which our microcosmic lives rest, we may discover aspects of this inherent logoic principle. This opens to our consideration a wide range of vision, and though it emphasises the complexity of the subject, it also demonstrates the divine magnitude of the scheme, with its magnificent intricacies. (TCF–597/9)

• It should be borne in mind by all students when considering the planes, plane substance and energy that they are in a condition of flux and change all the time. The matter of all planes circulates, and cyclically certain portions become more energised than others; the matter of the planes is thus under a threefold influence, or – to word it otherwise – deva substance is subjected to a threefold cyclic stimulation:

1. *Ray stimulation,* dependent upon any Ray being in or out of power. It is inter-systemic and planetary.
2. *Zodiacal stimulation,* which is an extra-systemic stimulation, and is also cosmic and cyclic.
3. *Solar stimulation,* or the impact of direct solar force or energy upon the substance of a plane; this emanates from the "Heart of the Sun" and is peculiarly potent. (TCF–678)

• ...Regarding the rays as the channels through which all being flows, we must recognise them as influences operating on the world in turn. Each ray has its period of greatest influence, to which all are subject to a considerable extent, not merely those belonging by nature to that particular ray, but those on all the other rays as well. The long period of influence of each is divided into seven stages, each of which is qualified by the influence of the greater ray period, being intensified when its own sub-ray period is reached (i.e. the sixth ray influence is greatest during the period of the sixth sub-ray). We must carefully note that the term "sub-ray" is used merely for convenience to designate the shorter period of influence, not as indicating any difference in the nature of the ray. (EP1–164/5)

• ...We may perhaps conclude that the time during which each sub-ray exerts its modifying influence is between one hundred and fifty and two hundred years.

We do not know how often (perhaps seven times?) the sub-rays are repeated successively within the cycle of the great ray. It must manifestly be more than once.... (EP1–166)

• The rays stream forth in:
1. A solar cycle, such as the present one, in which the second Ray of Love-Wisdom is the major ray, and all the others are but subsidiary to it.
2. A planetary cycle...in connection with the races....
3. Cycles connected with the twelve signs of the zodiac.

These are primarily two in number:

a.   Those which are connected with a complete zodiacal round, about 25,000 years.

b.   Those which are connected with each of the twelve signs, and which come in and out of manifestation approximately every 2,100 years.

4.   Those cycles when certain rays are in power for a period of racial evolution, such as the five major racial periods to which we have referred.

5.   The lesser cycling in and out of manifestation....

6.   Cycles of ray activity which are determined by their numerical figures.

The first ray, for instance, governs all cycles such as those of one million years, one hundred thousand years, one thousand years, one hundred years and one year. The seventh ray controls such similar cycles as seven thousand years, and seven million years. The interchange and interplay of these ray cycles is so intricate and so great that it would serve only to confuse should I further elaborate. Remember, however, that all of the seven rays are forever functioning, and functioning simultaneously, but that cyclically and under the directed plan of the Minds (who are embodied by the rays), certain of these influences and forces are more dominant at one time than at another, and certain lines of activity and certain results of this activity are demonstrated under one ray influence more than under another. These influences pour through all forms in all kingdoms, producing specific effects, definite and different forms of life, peculiar types of realisation, and particular expressions of consciousness in form which are, for that period, the product of the united and concerted plan of the building forces, working in complete harmony, but temporarily under one or another of their number. They enter into constructive activity; they pass through that particular cycle; they then pass out, or die to that activity, and are then "raised into heaven", until such time as their cycle again comes round. This process they constantly enact and re-enact, repeating the drama of birth, death and resurrection.

In this ray activity will be found the true significance of the Law of Rebirth, and it lies behind the process of incarnation and of reincarnation. Upon this I may not here dwell, beyond pointing out that men's ideas and teaching anent reincarnation are as yet childish and inaccurate. Much readjustment must be made, and much re-arrangement of ideas is necessitated, before a true understanding of this basic cyclic law will be possible.

Cyclic appearance, therefore, governs the rays as well as the kingdoms in nature and the forms contained therein. It determines the activity of God Himself. Races incarnate, disappear and reincarnate, and so do all lives in form. Reincarnation or cyclic activity lies behind all phenomenal activity and appearance. It is an aspect of the pulsating life of Deity. It is the breathing out and the breathing in of the process of divine existence and manifestation. (EP1–265/7)

• The rays of aspect have longer cycles than the rays of attribute, and their measure is occultly slow, cumulative in effect, and – as the ages pass away – their momentum steadily increases. The rays of attribute have briefer cycles, and produce a steady heart-beat and a regular rhythm in the solar system. (EP1–351/2)

• Only one ray is today really out of manifestation altogether and functioning entirely behind the scenes, and that is the first ray. Where humanity is concerned, the first ray makes its presence felt, and its potency dominates, when the stage of accepted discipleship is reached. It increases in power as progress on the Path is gained. Thus there is beginning to be gathered on the subjective side of life a steadily growing group of those who can function under the influence of this first ray. When enough of the sons of men can thus function, their united responsiveness will constitute a channel through which this first ray can come into manifestation. This is one of the main activities and objectives of the Hierarchy. (EP1–350/1)

• [The first] ray is still out of physical manifestation but is beginning to have a definite effect upon the mental plane; there it influences the minds of disciples everywhere and lays the stage for the appearance of a certain group of disciples from Shamballa. Two thousand years from today, the influence of this ray will be felt powerfully upon the physical plane. One hundred years hence its potency will be noted upon the astral plane. (DN–142)

• Ray two has a rapidly recurring cycle. This is due to its excessive potency. Being the major ray of our solar system (of which all the other rays are but aspects), it might be said that this ray is really never out of incarnation. There are nevertheless constant cycles of waxing and waning potency.... The cycles of the second ray are dynamic and recur in a regular rhythm at this time and during the twenty-five thousand years of a zodiacal cycle in sequences of five hundred years.... In 1825 the potency of this ray began to decline as the peak of its two hundred fifty years emergence was reached. (EP1–349)

• [The second] ray is always in subjective manifestation and very potent because it is the ray of our solar system and particularly so at this time as the Hierarchy is approaching closer to humanity in preparation for the "crisis of love", and an imminent major planetary initiation. At this time, however, the second ray is becoming objective in its influence upon the physical plane. It will become increasingly so for the next two thousand two hundred years when it will gradually withdraw into the background. (DN–142)

• [The third] ray will remain in objective incarnation from the point of view of humanity for a very long time – so long a time that it is needless for us to anticipate its waning influence. That planetary centre which is Humanity itself still needs the intensified application of these forces so as to stimulate even the "lowest of the sons of men". (DN–142)

• ...The third Ray of Active Intelligence...has been in objective manifestation since 1425 A.D. and will remain in incarnation throughout the Aquarian Age. Its cycles are the longest of any of the ray cycles. However, within these major cycles there are periods of intensified activity which are like the beat or pulsation of the heart and these periods last approximately three thousand years. They are, when out of incarnation, called "cycles of withdrawal but not of abstraction". They are three thousand years also in incarnation. One of these three thousand year periods of expression is now here and we can look for much development of the intellectual faculty and a marked increase of creative work during this time. This particular cycle of expression marks a climaxing point in the larger cycle. During the coming age, the intelligence of the race and its active development will assume real proportions and this with much speed. (DN–36/7)

• Ray three has been the longest in incarnation, but in 1875 it occultly "completed its outgoing, and began to curve upon itself, and thus return"[1]. It is therefore just beginning to wane. When this event occurs in connection with any type of energy, the effect produced is always of a crystallising nature and is apt to produce "set forms which warrant prompt destruction". This causes mental conditions of a set and static nature. The inference is therefore clear that in the later stages of this ray's activity we have the demonstration of those dogmatic, sectarian and theological attitudes, for instance, which mark the decline and consequent uselessness of the various schools of thought which have in their time embodied man's ideas and sufficed for his helping during the period of their growth. (EP1–348/9)

• [The fourth] ray…begins to come into incarnation early in the [21st] century and – in collaboration with the developing Saturnian influence – will lead many on to the path of discipleship. When the peculiar energy, to which we give the somewhat unsatisfactory name of "harmony through conflict" and the forces of that planet which stage opportunity for the aspirant are working in combination and an ordained synthesis, we can then look for a very rapid adjustment in human affairs, particularly in connection with the Path. (DN–142/3)

---

[1] For comment on the paradoxes contained in these extracts, please refer to "Apparent Contradictions" on page 9.

• Ray five is the latest of the rays to come into activity and is only in process of "coming forth to power". It is steadily increasing in potency, and the result of its influence will be to guide humanity into increasing knowledge. Its energy beats upon the minds of men at this time and produces that stimulation which lies behind all the scientific approach to truth in all departments of human thought. Being also the ray which governs the personality aspect of the fourth kingdom in nature, and being one of the rays determining or conditioning our Aryan race, its present potency is excessive. This is a point to be remembered with care, for it accounts for much that we can see happening in the world of thought. (EP1–350)

• [The fifth] ray has been in manifestation for nearly seventy years. It will pass out (by special and unique arrangement) in another fifty years [published 1949], thus breaking into its own normal cycle, because it is deemed that the needed special impulse has been adequate and that the impetus given to the human "spirit of discovery" has served its purpose. Any further intensification of the mental processes just now (except through the general pervasive effect of the third ray) might prove disastrous. The ray cycles are usually set and determined, but, in collaboration with each other and because of the imminent spiritual Crisis of Approach, the Lord of the Fifth Ray and the Lord of the World have decided temporarily to withdraw this type of force. It will take about fifty years to do this. (DN–143)

• The sixth ray began to pass out of manifestation in 1625.... (DN–29)

• ...The seventh Ray of Ceremonial Order began to come into manifestation in 1675. (DN–29)

• ...The main problem of today is brought about by the fact that two rays of great potency are functioning simultaneously. As yet their effects are so equally balanced that a situation is brought about which is described in the ancient archives in the following terms: "A time of rending, when the mountains, which have sheltered, fall from their high places, and the voices of men are lost in the crash and thunder of the fall".

Such periods come only at rare and long intervals, and each time they come a peculiarly significant period of divine activity is ushered in; old things pass entirely away, yet the ancient landmarks are restored. The seventh Ray of Ceremonial Order or Ritual is coming into manifestation. The sixth Ray of Idealism or of Abstract Visioning is slowly passing out. The seventh ray will bring into expression that which was visioned and that which constituted the ideals of the preceding cycle of sixth ray activity. One ray prepares the way for another ray, and the reason for the manifestation of one ray or another is dependent upon the Plan and divine Purpose. It is not often that two rays follow each other in a regular numerical sequence, such as is now happening. When this does happen, there eventuates a rapid following of effect upon cause, and this today can provide the basis for an assured hope. (EP1–358)

Astrology
and the Rays

• I would here call your attention to the fact that the astrology which I am emphasising is that which is concerned with the effective energies – what they are and from whence they come. I would repeat here as I have often done before that I am not concerned with predictive astrology. The coming emphasis in astrology will be upon the available energies and the use the subject makes of them and the opportunity which they present at any given time. (DN–75)

• ...I would like to emphasise...that we are considering esoteric influences and not astrology, per se. *Our subject is the seven rays and their relationship to the zodiacal constellations* or – in other words – the interaction of the seven great Lives which inform our solar system with the twelve constellations which compose our zodiac. (EA–26/7)

• It might here be asked: What are the differences between the influences which are ray influences and those which are of an astrological nature, such as the rising sign, or the governing planets?

The energies which astrologically affect a human being are those which play upon him as a result of the apparent progress of the sun through the heavens, either once every twenty-five thousand years or once every twelve months. Those that constitute the ray forces do not come from the twelve constellations of the zodiac, but emanate primarily from a world of being and of consciousness which lies behind our solar system, and which themselves come from the seven constellations which form the body of manifestation of the One About Whom

Naught May Be Said. Our solar system is one of these seven constellations. This is the world of Deity Itself, and of it a man can know nothing until he has passed through the major initiations. When we come later to study the zodiac and its relation to the rays we shall work this out more carefully and so make the idea clearer. (EP1–332/3)

• Astrology now deals primarily with the personality for whom the horoscope may be cast and with the events of the personality life. When, through meditation and service, plus the discipline of the lunar bodies, a man comes consciously and definitely under his soul ray, then he comes as definitely under the influence of one or other of the seven solar systems, as they focus their energy through one or other of the constellations and subsequently one or other of the seven sacred planets. Eventually, there will be twelve sacred planets, corresponding to the twelve constellations, but the time is not yet. Our solar system, as you know, is one of seven. When a man has arrived at this point in evolution, birth months, mundane astrology, and the influences which play upon the form aspect become of less and less importance. This circle of solar systems affects paramountly the soul and it becomes the focal point of spiritual energies. This is the problem of the soul on its own plane, – responsiveness to these types of energy, and, of them, the personality is totally unaware.

The signs which fall therefore into the four categories of earth, water, fire and air, concern primarily the man who lives below the diaphragm, and who utilises the lower four centres:– the centre at the base of the spine, the sacral centre, the solar plexus and the spleen. The inner group of seven major or systemic energies produce their effect upon the man who is living above the diaphragm, and work through the seven representative centres in the head. Four of them focus through the throat centre, the heart centre, the ajna and head centres. Three are held latent in the region of the head centres (the thousand petalled lotus) and only enter into functioning activity after the third initiation. It will be evident therefore how complicated from the standpoint of the horoscope (as well as of the individual problem) is this meeting of the energies of two types of constellations in the case of the man who is neither purely human nor purely spiritual. The ordinary horoscope is negated. The horoscope is not possible as yet of delineation. The only horoscope, which is basically and almost infallibly correct is that of the entirely low grade human being who lives entirely below the diaphragm and is governed by his animal nature alone. (TWM–437/8)

• Seven stars of the Great Bear are the originating Sources of the seven rays of our solar system. The seven Rishis (as They are called) of the Great Bear express Themselves through the medium of the seven planetary Logoi Who are Their Representatives and to Whom They stand in the relation of prototype. The seven Planetary Spirits manifest through the medium of the seven sacred planets.

Each of these seven Rays, coming from the Great Bear, are transmitted into our solar system through the medium of three constellations and their ruling planets. (EA–85/6, –422, –589)

• …The united energies of the three constellations which control and energise our solar system: The Great Bear, the Pleiades and Sirius; these work through the medium of the seven rays and these in turn express themselves through the twelve constellations which form the great zodiacal wheel. The Lords or ruling Powers of these twelve sources of light and life "step down" the potency of these three major energies so that our solar Logos can absorb them; they "tune out" those aspects of these three Potencies which are not suited to our systemic life at this point in the evolutionary process, just as the Hierarchy upon our little planet tunes out or steps down the energies from Shamballa. These three major energies in a mysterious manner express themselves through the seven rays just as all triplicities subdivide into septenates, yet preserve their identity. These seven energies, emanating from the major three and transmitted via the twelve constellations, are embodied in the seven sacred planets and are represented on our Earth by the seven Spirits before the throne of God (the symbol of synthesis). This tremendous inter-relation is embodied in one great process of: *Transmission. Reception. Absorption. Relation and Living Activity. The method is one of Invocation and Evocation.* In these two sentences, you have one of the most important clues to the whole evolutionary process; the key to the mystery of time and space, and the solution of all problems. But the factor which is of major importance is that the whole matter is an expression of focused Will. (EA–595/6)

• All the Lords of the rays create a body of expression, and thus the seven planets have come into being.… The energies of these seven Lives however are not confined to their planetary expressions, but sweep around the confines of the solar system just as the life impulses of a human being – his vital forces, his desire impulses, and his mental energies – sweep throughout his body, bringing the various organs into activity and enabling him to carry out his intent, to live his life, and to fulfil the objective for which he created his body of manifestation.

Each of the seven kingdoms in nature reacts to the energy of some particular ray Life. Each of the seven planes similarly reacts; each septenate in nature vibrates to one or another of the initial septenates, for the seven rays establish that process which assigns the limits of influence of all forms. They are that which determines all things, and when I use these words I indicate the necessity of Law. Law is the will of the seven Deities, making its impression upon substance in order to produce a specific intent through the method of the evolutionary process. (EP1–62)

The Ray of the Solar System

• We are told that seven great rays exist in the cosmos. In our solar system only one of these seven great rays is in operation. The seven sub-divisions constitute the "seven rays" which, wielded by our solar Logos, form the basis of endless variations in His system of worlds. These seven rays may be described as the seven channels through which all being in His solar system flows, the seven predominant characteristics or modifications of life, for it is not to humanity only that these rays apply, but to the seven kingdoms as well. In fact there is nothing in the whole solar system, at whatever stage of evolution it may stand, which does not belong and has not always belonged to one or other of the seven rays. (EP1–163)

• It must be remembered that the dominating ray, the outstanding influence in our solar system, is the great cosmic second Ray of Love-Wisdom, a dual ray, – that is, a ray combining two great cosmic principles and energies. It is the ray which governs the "personality" of our solar Logos, if such an expression may be used, and (because it is dual) it indicates both His personality and soul rays, which in Him are now so balanced and blended that, from the angle of humanity, they constitute the major ray, the one ray. This major ray determines both His quality and His purpose.

Every unit of life and every form in manifestation is governed by this second ray. Basically speaking, the energy of love, expressed with wisdom, is the line of least resistance for the manifested lives in our solar system. This ray qualifies the life of all the planets, and the attractive magnetic love of God pours through His created universe; it emerges in the consciousness and determines the objective of all evolving forms. Each human being, as a whole, therefore, lives in a universe and on a planet which is constantly the objective of God's love and desire, and which constantly (as a result of this love) is itself attracted and attractive. For this we do not make adequate allowance. Teachers, parents and educators would do well to recognise the potency of this ray force, and trust to the Law to make all things good. (EP1–334)

The Rays and the Planets

• All parts of the solar system are interdependent; all the forces and energies are in constant flux and mutation; all of them sweep in great pulsations, and through a form of rhythmic breathing, around the entire solar atom; so that the qualities of every solar life, pouring through the seven ray forms, permeate every form within the solar ring-pass-not, and thus link every form with every other form. Note therefore the fact that each of the seven rays or creative Builders embodies the energy, will, love and purpose of the Lord of the solar system, as that Lord in His turn embodies an aspect of the energy, will, love and purpose of the "One About Whom Naught May Be Said". Therefore the first proposition to be grasped by the student of the rays is as follows:

I. *Every ray Life is an expression of a solar Life, and every planet is consequently...*
1. Linked with every other planetary life in the solar system.
2. Animated by energy emanating from one or other of the seven solar systems.
3. Actuated by a triple stream of life forces coming from:
   a. Solar systems outside our own.
   b. Our own solar system.
   c. Its own planetary Being.

It is impossible for the average thinker to grasp the significance of this statement, but he can understand somewhat the statement that every planet is a focal point through which forces and energies circulate and flow ceaselessly, and that these energies emanate from the outer cosmos or universe itself, from the solar system of which his own planet is a part, and of which our sun is the centre, and from that Being Who constitutes our own particular planetary Lord or Life....

The complexity of the subject is very great, and only the broad general outline of the system, and the basic principles governing the law of evolution, can be dimly sensed and grasped. The sweep of the subject is so vast that the concrete mind and the rationalising nature lose themselves in the realised complexities and problems. But the illumined intuition, with its power to synthesise (which is the emerging characteristic of the disciples and initiates under training), can and does lead them into a measured sequence of expansions of consciousness which eventually land them at last on the summit of the Mount of Transfiguration. From that eminence the disciple can gain the vision which will enable him to see the whole world scheme in a moment of time.... He can then descend from that mountain with his personality transfigured and radiant. Why? Because he now knows that spirit is a fact and the basis of immortality; he knows, past all controversy, that there is a Plan, and that the love of God is the basic law of all manifestation and the origin of all evolutionary momentum; and he can rest back upon the knowledge that the fact of spirit, the immediacy of love and the synthetic scope of the Plan provide a foundation upon which he can place his feet, take his stand with assurance, and then go forward in certain confidence of an assured goal.

Our second statement of fact is therefore:

II. *Each one of the rays is the recipient and custodian of energies coming from*

1. The seven solar systems.
2. The twelve constellations.

    Each ray passes these energies through its body of manifestation (a planet), and thereby imparts them to the planetary form, and to all forms upon and within it. These differentiated forms are therefore animated by energy coming from the cosmic Life, from the solar Deity, and from the planetary Life, and are consequently coloured by qualities from the seven solar systems and the twelve constellations. This blend of energies, working on substance, produces the forms, and each subjective form, in its turn, produces the outer appearance. (EP1–151/4)

• The energies of the various signs are attracted by the different planets according to their stage of development and by what is esoterically called "ancient relationship" between the informing entities of the planets and of the constellations. This relation exists between beings and is founded on a Law of Affinity. It is this law of affinity which produces the magnetic pull and the dynamic response between constellations and planets within the solar system. (EA–266/7)

• The rays use the planets as transmitting agencies and we know which rays – in this world cycle – are related to the different planets. ...They are as follows:

Sacred Planets		*Non-Sacred Planets*	
1. Vulcan	1st ray	1. Mars	6th ray
2. Mercury	4th ray	2. The Earth	3rd ray
3. Venus	5th ray	3. Pluto	1st ray
4. Jupiter	2nd ray	4. The Moon	4th ray
5. Saturn	3rd ray	(veiling a hidden planet)	
6. Neptune	6th ray	5. The Sun	2nd ray
7. Uranus	7th ray		(EA–513)

The Zodiac

• ...Each of the seven rays [expresses] itself through the medium of three constellations or through a triangle of energies. This relation is the basis of the entire Science of Triangles and, therefore, of astrology itself; it is also related to the rays, the constellations, their ruling planets and our Earth in a great synthesis of energies; it relates our solar system to the larger whole and our tiny non-sacred planet to the solar system. Let me repeat that statement and thus indicate to you some vital facts anent this world of interweaving energies. The Rays pour through, are expressed by and are transmitted through the following constellations:

Ray I	Aries	Leo	Capricorn
Ray II	Gemini	Virgo	Pisces
Ray III	Cancer	Libra	Capricorn
Ray IV	Taurus	Scorpio	Sagittarius
Ray V	Leo	Sagittarius	Aquarius
Ray VI	Virgo	Sagittarius	Pisces
Ray VII	Aries	Cancer	Capricorn (EA–489)

• Today, the following points of the triangles of energy or the following constellations in the triangles are the controlling factors:

Ray I. Aries: This constellation, as might be expected, is the source of the initial energy, producing the New Age.

Ray II. Virgo: This constellation produces the increased activity of the Christ principle in the heart of humanity.

Ray III. Cancer: The mass movement towards liberty, release and light, so dominant today, is caused by the energy of this sign.

Ray IV. Scorpio: Through this constellation comes the testing of humanity, the world disciple.

Ray V. Leo: This sign produces the growth of individualism and of self-consciousness, so prevalent today on a world scale.

Ray VI. Sagittarius: This sign produces the focused one-pointed effort of the world aspirant.

Ray VII. Capricorn: This Capricornian energy produces initiation and the overcoming of materialism. (EA–490)

Planetary Rulers

• The constellations and the planets which govern them may, and do, have one effect upon the mass and another upon the average individual man, and still a third effect upon the disciple or the initiate. As the various energies and forces circulate throughout the etheric body of our solar system, their reception and effect will depend upon the state of the planetary centres and upon the point of unfoldment of the centres in individual man. That is why the various charts and tabulations can differ so widely and different planets can appear as ruling the constellations. There seems to be no fixed rule and the student gets bewildered. Orthodox astrology posits one set of planetary rulers, and they are correct as far as the mass of humanity are concerned. But the disciple, who lives above the diaphragm, responds to another combination.... That is why the three charts here given do not appear to coincide. They are drawn up to express the situation in regard to three groups:

1. The mass of people who conform to orthodox and recognised astrological conclusions.

2. Disciples and advanced individuals, conforming to the conclusions of esoteric astrology.
3. The Creative Hierarchies, giving the interim situation in this world cycle.

3 TABULATIONS

THE ORTHODOX ASTROLOGICAL RELATIONSHIP IN CONNECTION WITH ORDINARY MAN

	Constellation	*Ruler*	*Ray*	*Related to*		
1.	Aries	*Mars*	6th ray	Scorpio	Same ruler	
2.	Taurus	Venus	5th ray	Libra	"	"
3.	Gemini	Mercury	4th ray	Virgo	"	"
4.	Cancer	*Moon*	4th ray	none		
5.	Leo	*The Sun*	2nd ray	none		
6.	Virgo	Mercury	4th ray	Gemini	"	"
7.	Libra	Venus	5th ray	Taurus	"	"
8.	Scorpio	*Mars*	6th ray	Aries	"	"
9.	Sagittarius	Jupiter	2nd ray	Pisces	"	"
10.	Capricorn	Saturn	3rd ray	none		
11.	Aquarius	Uranus	7th ray	none		
12.	Pisces	Jupiter	2nd ray	Sagittarius	"	"

a. The non-sacred planets are italicised.
b. All the rays are represented except the first. This is interesting, as the mass of the people move within their horoscopes and the will aspect is latent but unexpressed.

THE UNORTHODOX ASTROLOGICAL RELATIONSHIP IN CONNECTION WITH DISCIPLES AND INITIATES

	Constellation	*Ruler*	*Ray*	*Related to*		
1.	Aries	Mercury	4th ray	Virgo	Same ruler	
2.	Taurus	Vulcan	1st ray	Pisces	"	"
3.	Gemini	Venus	5th ray	none		
4.	Cancer	Neptune	6th ray	Scorpio	"	"
5.	Leo	*The Sun*	2nd ray	Aquarius	"	"
6.	Virgo	*The Moon*	4th ray	Aries	"	"

	Constellation	Ruler	Ray	Related to		
7.	Libra	Uranus	7th ray	none		
8.	Scorpio	*Mars*	6th ray	Cancer	Same ruler	
9.	Sagittarius	*The Earth*	3rd ray	Capricorn	"	"
10.	Capricorn	Saturn	3rd ray	Sagittarius	"	"
11.	Aquarius	Jupiter	2nd ray	Leo	"	"
12.	Pisces	Pluto	1st ray	Taurus	"	"

Note: In connection with disciples and the zodiacal signs, *Gemini and Libra* are two constellations which – through their rulers – express 5th ray and 7th ray energy. For some occult reason, they remain unrelated to any other of the signs.

The relation between the other constellations through the planets, as expressing the rays, is as follows:

1. *Taurus and Pisces*, through Vulcan and Pluto, are related to *Ray 1*. Transmutation of desire into sacrifice and of the individual will into the divine will.
   The World Saviour

2. *Leo and Aquarius*, through the Sun and Jupiter, are related to *Ray 2*. Development of the individual consciousness into world consciousness. Thus a man becomes a world server.
   The World Server

3. *Sagittarius and Capricorn*, through the Earth and Saturn, are related to *Ray 3*. The one-pointed disciple becomes the initiate.
   The Initiate

4. *Aries and Virgo*, through Mercury and the Moon, are related to *Ray 4*. Harmonising the cosmos and the individual through conflict, producing unity and beauty. The birth pangs of the second birth.
   The Cosmic and Individual Christ

5. *Cancer and Scorpio*, through Neptune and Mars, are related to *Ray 6*. Transformation of the mass consciousness into the inclusive consciousness of the disciple.
   The Triumphant Disciple

THE UNORTHODOX ASTROLOGICAL RELATIONSHIP
IN CONNECTION WITH THE HIERARCHIES

Constellation	*Ruler*	*Ray*	*Related to*		
1. Aries	Uranus	7th ray	none		
2. Taurus	Vulcan	1st ray	Pisces	Same ruler	
3. Gemini	*The Earth*	3rd ray	Libra	"	"
4. Cancer	Neptune	6th ray	Sagittarius	"	"
5. Leo	*The Sun*	2nd ray	Virgo	"	"
6. Virgo	Jupiter	2nd ray	Leo	"	"
7. Libra	Saturn	3rd ray	Gemini	"	"
8. Scorpio	Mercury	4th ray	Aquarius	"	"
9. Sagittarius	*Mars*	6th ray	Cancer	"	"
10. Capricorn	Venus	5th ray	none		
11. Aquarius	*The Moon*	4th ray	Scorpio	"	"
12. Pisces	*Pluto*	1st ray	Taurus	"	"

Note: Aries and Capricorn in conjunction with 7th and 5th ray energy stand alone. The other constellations and rays are related in every case.

a. Ray 1 – Taurus and Pisces, through Vulcan and Pluto.

b. Ray 2 – Leo and Virgo, through the Sun and Jupiter.

c. Ray 3 – Gemini and Libra, through the Earth and Saturn.

d. Ray 4 – Scorpio and Aquarius, through Mercury and Moon.

e. Ray 6 – Cancer and Sagittarius, through Neptune and Mars.

(EA–65/8)

The Twelve Constellations

Aries

• In connection with Aries, which expresses or is the agent primarily of the first Ray of Will or Power, the ray of the destroyer, it should be stated that first ray energy comes from the divine Prototype in the Great Bear, that it becomes transmuted into the force and activity of the planetary Logos of the first ray, and works out as His triple activity under the guidance of the three ruling planets – Mars, Mercury and Uranus.

Mars embodies sixth ray force which leads to idealism, destructive fanaticism frequently, struggle, strife, war, effort and evolution.... *Mercury*, embodying the energy of the fourth ray, eventually carries the man around the wheel of life and through the medium of conflict enables him to achieve harmony.... *Uranus* embodies the energy of the seventh ray and its work is analogous to that of Mercury, for the seventh ray is the ray which relates spirit and matter and brings together electric fire and fire by friction, thus producing manifestation. (EA–99/100)

• Experience leads to rulership and in this sign the man who is embodied first ray force develops the power of organisation, of control over forces, particularly over the energy of death, over the power of destruction applied with love, of dominance over multitudes, of co-operation with the plan and the practice of the Will in rightly and correctly guiding and directing planetary affairs. (EA–108)

Taurus

• The two rays which directly affect [this] sign are...the fifth (through Venus) and the first (through Vulcan). These two when viewed in combination with the Earth (which is an expression of the third ray) demonstrate a most difficult combination of rays, for all are along the line of the first Ray of Energy.... This combination tremendously increases the already difficult task of the Taurian subject. Only indirectly does the second Ray of Love-Wisdom and its subsidiary line of energies appear and, therefore, love and wisdom are often noticeably lacking in the person born in this sign. (EA–393/4)

• [Taurus] is governed by only two planets. Venus is its exoteric ruler and Vulcan its esoteric and hierarchical ruler. We touch upon one of the mysteries of the Ageless Wisdom. Venus holds a unique relation to the Earth, different to that of any other planet and this, therefore, brings about a much closer relation between Taurus and the Earth than perhaps exists in any other zodiacal relation where our planet is concerned. (EA–382/3)

• The esoteric ruler of Taurus is Vulcan, the forger of metals, the one who works in the densest, most concrete expression of the natural world.... He is the one who goes down into the depths to find the material upon which to expend his innate art and to fashion that which is beautiful and useful. Vulcan is, therefore, that which stands for the soul, the individual, inner, spiritual man; in his activity we find the key to the soul's task upon the eternal round of the wheel of life. (EA–385/6)

• Hierarchically also the ruler is Vulcan, conditioning the planet and determining the fact that man is the macrocosm of the microcosm and that the fourth kingdom fashions or conditions all subhuman kingdoms. (EA–387)

Gemini

• ...The exoteric ruler [is] given as Mercury and the esoteric ruler as Venus, for they embody between them the energies of the fourth Ray of Harmony through Conflict and the fifth Ray of Concrete Knowledge or Science which is embryonic under-standing of causes and conditions resulting therefrom and also of the Plan. (EA–354)

• ...The hierarchical ruler of Gemini is the Earth itself, which is a non-sacred planet.... A slight study will show you that you have in these three rulers a most interesting sequence of forces, for Rays 3, 4, and 5 produce a synthesis of activity and of eager potencies which are essential for the development of humanity. (EA–356/7)

Cancer

• It will...be clear to you why the Moon and Neptune, trans-mitting the energies of the psychic nature and of form, plus the tendency to achieve through the medium of conflict, rule Cancer so potently, both directly and indirectly. They control the form and the lower psychic nature and produce the battle ground (later to be transmuted into the burning ground) whereon these two "face in the final conflict" their higher correspondence, the soul and spirit, for matter is spirit at its lowest point and spirit is matter at its highest. (EA–340)

• It is because – speaking in parables – the light of Cancer is only diffused, vague and inchoate that the influences of the first

Ray of Focused Intention and of purposeful Will and of the second Ray of Love-Wisdom (recognised duality and gained experience) are found to be missing. Their influences are not present, except in so far that love and purpose underlie all manifestation. But they are not focused in this sign. (EA–330/1)

Leo

• As you have been told, the Sun veils certain hidden planets, and in the case of Leo, the two planets through which the Sun focuses its energy or influences (like a lens) are Neptune and Uranus…. The activity of Uranus is, however, only registered at a very advanced stage of development upon the Path…. (EA–296)

• Neptune, being the sign of the Deity of the waters, is related to the sixth ray which governs the astral or emotional plane of desire. When Neptune is thus active in the advanced Leo subject, then emotion-desire have been transmuted into love-aspiration and are dedicated to and oriented to the soul…. (EA–297/8)

• …The Sun, as it veils Neptune, produces a potent effect upon the personality, symbolised for us here by the astral body, whilst Uranus (which is also veiled by the Sun) symbolises the effect of the soul upon the personality. Hence the activity of the seventh ray, which is – from one angle – the lowest aspect of the first ray. (EA–300)

Virgo

• Through these three planetary rulers [Mercury, the Moon, Jupiter] the energies of the fourth ray pour, governing the mind through Mercury and the physical form through the Moon; the energies of the first ray, expressive of the will of God, begin their control of the self-conscious man (unfolded in Leo) and the energies of the second ray, embodying the love of God, pour through into manifestation. Will, love and harmony through conflict – such are the controlling forces which make man what he is and such are the governing and directing energies which use the mind (Mercury), the emotional nature, love (in Jupiter) and the physical body (the Moon, or esoteric will) for purposes of divine expression and manifestation. (EA–263/4)

Libra

• From the angle of orthodox astrology, Venus rules Libra, whilst – esoterically speaking – Uranus rules. Saturn is the ruler in this sign of that stupendous Creative Hierarchy which is one of the three major groups of Builders, forming part of the third aspect of divinity.... (EA–243)

• These three planets are (through the rays of which they are the medium) all to be found upon the first major line of force, the line of will or power and of purpose and visioned goal.

1. Uranus. – 7th Ray of Ceremonial Magic. *God the Father*. He who relates. The Source of Duality. He who perceives the end from the beginning. Spiritual consciousness.
    Intuition to Inspiration.

2. Venus. – 5th Ray of Mind. *God the Son*. The Son of Mind. He who includes. Egoic consciousness.
    Intellect to Intuition.

3. Saturn. – 3rd Ray of Intelligence. *God the Holy Spirit*. He who knows. Mind. Human Consciousness.
    Instinct to Intellect.

• It is for this basic reason – founded upon the above triple relationship – that Libra is the "point of balance" in the zodiac. (EA–247/8)

Scorpio

• We come now to a consideration of the Rulers which govern the sign, Scorpio [Mars and Mercury].... Through these Rulers, two rays are brought into a potent controlling position in Scorpio; they are the sixth Ray of Devotion and the fourth Ray of Harmony through Conflict, the latter having a peculiar relation to the *mode* of human development and the former to the *methods* of the Piscean age which is just passing. Mars and Mercury control and Mars is particularly active, owing to the fact that Mars is both the orthodox planet controlling the personality in Scorpio and also the esoteric planet conditioning the unfoldment of the disciple. (EA–209)

Sagittarius

• The ruler of Sagittarius from the orthodox angle is Jupiter, and from the standpoint of the path of discipleship it is the Earth itself. Mars governs this sign from the standpoint of the Hierarchies involved. (EA–184)

• An analysis of this will show that the "forces of conflict" are powerful in this sign, primarily in the life of the disciple. Harmony through Conflict is ceaselessly active and appears in both the orthodox and the esoteric assignments. The destructive power of the first ray, focused in Pluto, brings change, darkness and death. To this intensity and potency of Pluto must be added the forceful and dynamic energy of the planet Mars. This brings the entire human family, as well as the individual, under the law of strife, based this time upon sixth ray devotion to an ideal, high or low. (EA–187)

Capricorn

• The exoteric and the esoteric planetary rulers of Capricorn are the same, and Saturn rules the career of the man in this sign, no matter whether he is on the ordinary or the reversed wheel, or whether he is on the Mutable or the Fixed Cross. When he has taken the third initiation and can consciously mount the Cardinal Cross, he is then released from the ruling of Saturn and comes under the influence of Venus.... On the Mutable Cross and on the Fixed Cross we have the so-called green ray, controlling not only the daily life of karmic liability upon the path of evolution, but also controlling the experiences and processes of evolution. The reason for this is that Capricorn is an earth sign and because the *third* and *fifth* rays work pre-eminently through this sign, embodying the third major aspect of divinity, active intelligence plus that of its subsidiary power, the fifth Ray of Mind. These pour through Capricorn to Saturn and to Venus and so reach our planet, the Earth. (EA–163/4)

Aquarius

• The rulers of Aquarius [Uranus, Jupiter and the Moon] are of a peculiar interest. They constitute an effective group of planets and bring in the influences of the seventh, second and fourth rays. These are pre-eminently the rays which determine the final stages of man's progress as well as the initial stages, being more potent at the beginning of the involutionary path and the end of the evolutionary path than they are in the middle period. They determine the final stages and happenings of the Path of Initiation. The seventh ray brings into expression upon the physical plane the major pairs of opposites – spirit and matter – and relates them to each other, producing eventually one functioning whole. The second ray gives soul expression and spiritual consciousness and also the power to pour out love and wisdom upon earth whilst the fourth ray indicates the field of service and the mode of attaining the goal. This mode or method is that of conflict and struggle in order to reach harmony and thus express all truly human characteristics, for the fourth ray and the fourth Creative Hierarchy constitute essentially one expression of truth. (EA–137)

• …The third ray expresses itself powerfully through this sign, reaching our planet through Uranus and the Moon which hides or veils Uranus symbolically in this case. There is, therefore, to be found the double influence of Uranus, expressing the quality and bringing in the energies of the seventh ray, in one case, and the third ray in the other. The seventh ray is, in the last analysis, the focused differentiated energy of Ray One as it expresses the will of the first aspect of divinity on earth through the power to relate and bring into objective manifestation – by an act of the will – both spirit and matter. This it brings about through the activity of Ray Three, expressing itself through humanity and its individual units, though combining with the energy of the three rays which are released through the ruling planets:

1. Uranus – Ray Seven – The will to be and to know simultaneously on all planes of manifestation.

2. Jupiter – Ray Two – The fusion of heart and mind, which is the subjective purpose of manifestation. This is brought about through the third and the seventh ray activity on the exoteric wheel.

3. The Moon – Ray Four – The will to be and to know plus the fusion of heart and mind is the result of the work carried forward in the fourth Creative Hierarchy under the influence of that energy which produces harmony through conflict. (EA–138/9)

Pisces

• As regards the rays which express themselves through the planetary rulers and which absorb or collaborate with the influences of the sign Pisces and thus influence our planet and humanity, we find a most interesting situation. Two major rays express themselves through the rulers of Pisces, orthodox and esoteric: The first Ray of Will or Power, focused through Pluto, and the second Ray of Love-Wisdom. It is the interplay of these dual potencies which:

1. Produces the duality of his sign.
2. Brings about the major problem of Pisces – psychic sensitivity.
3. Causes the lure of the Path, in the first instance the path of evolution and later the lure of the probationary path....
4. Precipitates the process of transmutation and eventual escape through death.
5. Unfolds the significance, activity and beauty of death and of the work of the destroyer.

From this it will be apparent how important and powerful is this sign. Through its orthodox ruler, Jupiter, that force is brought to bear which "brings all together" and – in this case – relates the two fishes and binds them together in a functioning relationship. It is the activity consequently of the second ray force which relates soul and form and brings the two together, and this magnetic potency is peculiarly descriptive of the activity of Pisces. (EA–125/6)

The Rays and World Affairs

• It is of major interest for us to know something about the energies and forces which are producing the present international situation.... In the last analysis, all history is the record of the effects of these energies or radiations (rays, in other words) as they play upon humanity in its many varying stages of evolutionary development. These stages extend all the way from those of primeval humanity to our modern civilisation; all that has happened is the result of these energies, pouring cyclically through nature and through that part of nature which we call the human kingdom.

To understand what is today taking place we must recognise that...[the energies of the seven rays] are ceaselessly playing on humanity, producing changes, expressing themselves through successive civilisations and cultures, and fashioning the many races and nations.

This in no way infringes upon man's freewill; these forces have both their higher and their lower aspects and men respond to them according to their mental and spiritual development, and so do nations and races as a whole. Humanity has reached a point today where there is a most sensitive response to that which is higher and better. (DN–3/4)

• In the early days of the present cycle of hierarchical effort (between 1925 and 1936), the ray at work upon humanity was the first ray. The activity of this ray culminated in the declaration of war by Great Britain in 1939, when the destructive force of that ray – misapplied and misdirected – led Germany to invade Poland. In 1932, the influence of the second ray began to assert itself and will continue to do so until 1945 when the seventh ray will swing slowly into activity. You will then have three rays producing simultaneous effects upon mankind:

1. The first Ray of Will or Power, expending its force.
2. The second Ray of Love-Wisdom, reaching its meridian and holding the centre of the stage until 1957.
3. The seventh Ray of Ceremonial Order, coming into activity in combination with the other two – the will-to-love and the will-to-order – producing beauty out of the present chaos. (DNA1–730)

• It should be remembered that each ray embodies an idea which can be sensed as an ideal. The rays in time produce the world pattern which moulds all planetary forms and thus bears witness to the inner potency of the evolutionary processes. This pattern-forming tendency is being recognised today by modern psychology in connection with the human being and his emotional or thought patterns are being charted and studied. *So it is with the nations and races also.* Every ray produces three major patterns which are imposed upon the form nature, whether it be that of a man, a nation or a planet. These three patterns are: *the emotional pattern,* embodying the aspiration of a man, a nation or a race; it is the sumtotal of the desire tendency at any one time; *the mental pattern,* emerging later in time and governing the thought processes of a man, a nation or a race. The emotional and mental patterns are the negative and positive aspects of the personality of a man, a nation or a race. *The soul pattern* is the pre-disposing and spiritual goal, the ring-pass-not or destiny which the spiritual principle succeeds eventually in imposing upon the personality of a man, a nation or a race. This soul pattern eventually supersedes and obliterates the two earlier pattern-producing processes. (DN–57/8)

• I would like to…point out that these forces come into play either cyclically or through demand. This is an interesting point for students to remember. The work done through the Great

Invocation is not then necessarily invalid. It might perhaps clarify the subject if I pointed out that there are five energies (and there are usually five dominant ray energies active at any time) coming into play:

1. Those energies which are passing out of manifestation, as the sixth Ray of Devotion is at this time passing out.
2. Those energies which are coming into manifestation or incarnation, as the seventh Ray of Ceremonial Order is at this time emerging into expression.
3. Those energies which are – at any given time – expressing the ray type of the bulk of the manifesting humanity. Today these ray types are predominantly the second and the third. Relatively large numbers of first ray egos are also to be found acting as focal points for certain first ray forces.
4. Those energies which are today being invoked as the result of human need and human demand for succour. This demand curiously enough remains largely in the realm of the first ray influence for the desperate need of humanity is evoking the will aspect and that ray embodies the divine will-to-good and remains immutable and is – for the first time in the history of humanity – being invoked on a large scale. This statement is definitely encouraging, if you study its implications.

You have, therefore, in the present field of divine expression the following energies manifesting:

1. The energy of idealism, of devotion or of devoted attention, embodied in the sixth ray.
2. The energy whose major function it is to produce order, rhythm and established, sequential activity – the seventh Ray of Ceremonial Ritual.
3. The energy of the second ray, which is always basically present in our solar system, that of love-wisdom, to which many of the egos now in incarnation belong and will increasingly belong. The next one hundred and fifty years will see them coming into incarnation. The reason is that

it is to this type of human being that the work of reconstruction, and of re-building is naturally committed.

4.   The energy of intelligence, actively displayed in creative
activity. The creative ability of the future will emerge on
a relatively large scale in the realm of creative living and
not so much in the realm of creative art. This creative
living will express itself through a new world of beauty
and of recognised divine expression; through the outer
form, the "light of livingness" (as it is esoterically called)
will shew. The symbol and that for which it stands will be
known and seen. This is the energy of the third Ray of
Active Intelligence, working towards the manifestation of
beauty.

5.   The energy of the will aspect of divinity. This has been
but little expressed and understood by humanity up to the
present, but the time has now come when it must be better
comprehended. The demand from our innumerable planetary forces has not hitherto been adequate to invoke it and
for its invocation the great Lord of the World has patiently
waited. The call has now gone forth. Its first faint notes
were heard two hundred years ago and the sound and
demand has increased in volume and potency until today
this great energy is making its presence unmistakably felt.

I am anxious to have you realise the potency and the effect
of these five energies as they play upon our planet, evoke
response – good and bad – and produce the turmoil and chaos,
the warring forces and the beneficent influences. They,
therefore, account in their totality for all that we see happening
around us at this time. In the books which are being written
today in an effort to solve the problems of the why and the
wherefore of present world conditions, the writers are
necessarily dealing only with effects. Few there are that can
penetrate into the distant world of causes or look back into that
ancient past and see past and present in their true perspective.
I, however, seek to deal with causes – predisposing, effective,
determining, and productive of those events which cause the
present state of affairs. I deal with energies; they are concerned

with resultant forces. I would remind you here that these effects which are producing so much fear, foreboding and concern are but temporary and will give place to that ordered, rhythmic imposition of the needed idealism which will be applied eventually by love, motivated by wisdom in co-operation with intelligence. All will be actuated by a dynamic (not a passive) will-to-good....

It is a truism to remark that the history of the world is based on the emergence of ideas, their acceptance, their transformation into ideals, and their eventual superseding by the next imposition of ideas. It is in this realm of *ideas* that humanity is not a free agent. This is an important point to note. Once an idea becomes an ideal, humanity can freely reject or accept it, but ideas come from a higher source and are *imposed* upon the racial mind, whether men want them or not. Upon the use made of these ideas (which are in the nature of divine emanations, embodying the divine plan for planetary progress) will depend the rapidity of humanity's progress or its retardation for lack of understanding. (DN–4/8)

• I suggest...that you endeavour to see the three major ideologies with which you have perforce to deal in terms of the three efforts which are emanating from the three major planetary centres at this time: Shamballa, the Hierarchy and Humanity. You will thus gain a more synthetic viewpoint, and a deeper understanding of the slowly emerging world picture.

Is it not possible that the ideologies...are the response – distorted and yet a definite and determined, sensitive reaction – to the energies playing upon humanity from the two higher major centres? I would like to suggest that the ideology which is embodied in the vision of the totalitarian states is an erroneous but clearcut response to the Shamballa influence of *will*; that the ideology behind the democratic ideal constitutes a similar response to the universality which the *love* of the Hierarchy prompts it to express, and that communism is of human origin, embodying that ideology which humanity has formulated in its own right. Thus the three aspects of God's nature are beginning to take form as three major ideas and what we see upon the planet at this time are the distorted human reactions to spiritual impulses, emanating from three different centres, but all equally divine in their essential natures, and in their essences. (DN–21/2)

• Nothing can stop or truly impede [the united effect of the five controlling rays to which I have referred above]. This is a point I would have you remember. Modern man is apt to condemn the ideology which is not familiar to him and for which he has no use. He repudiates those ideas which do not lie at the back of his national and personal life or tradition and which would not suit him as an individual nor meet the need of the nation to which he belongs.

The recognition of these facts would lead to two results if correctly applied: first, the individual who accepts and is devoted to a particular ideology would cease fighting other ideologies for he would remember that the accident of birth and of background is largely responsible for making him – as an individual – what he is and determining his beliefs. And, secondly, it would bring to an end the attempt to impose a personally or nationally accepted ideology (political or religious) on other nations and persons. These are basic steps towards eventual peace and understanding and hence I emphasise them today....

These five energies together will determine the trend of world affairs. The problem before the Hierarchy at this time is so to direct and control these powerful activities that the Plan can be rightly materialised and the close of this [20th] century and the beginning of the next see the purposes of God for the planet and for humanity assume right direction and proportion. In this way, the new culture for the relatively few and the new civilisation for the many during the coming age will start in such a manner that the peoples of the earth can go forward into an era of peace and true development – spiritual and material. I would like to remind you that the fact that you see the world picture as one of outstanding chaos, of striving ideologies and warring forces, of the persecution of minorities, of hatreds which are working out into a furious preparation for war, and of world anxiety and terror does not really mean that you are seeing the picture as it is in reality. You are seeing what is superficial, temporal, ephemeral and entirely concerned with the form aspect. The Hierarchy is primarily occupied, as you know well, with the consciousness aspect and with the unfoldment of awareness, using form as a means only for the accomplishment of its designs. (DN–10/11)

The Three Planetary Centres

• It will be of value next if I connect up the three major planetary centres of energy with the five rays which are today working towards the consummation of the Plan for the race at this time. Three of these streams of energy are working powerfully in the world at this time and two others are struggling for expression. Of these latter, one is struggling towards domination and the other is struggling to hold on to that which it has so long controlled. This refers to the incoming seventh ray and the outgoing sixth ray. They constitute, in their duality, the reactionary and the progressive forces which are seeking to govern human thought, to determine natural and human evolution and to produce widely divergent civilisations and culture – one of which would be the perpetuation and crystallisation of that which now exists and the other would be so entirely new, as an outgrowth of the present world upheaval, that it is difficult for the average student to conceive of its nature. (DN–10/11)

• At the heart of this vast sea of energies is to be found that cosmic Consciousness to Whom we give the name of Sanat Kumara, the Lord of the World, the Ancient of Days....

This great Centre of Existence works through a triangle of energies or through lesser centres, each of which is brought into active expression by one of the three major Rays or Energies. The Centre which is created by the Ray of Will or Power is called Shamballa and its major activity is bequeathing, distributing and circulating the basic principle of life itself to every form which is held within the planetary ring-pass-not of the planetary Life or Logos. This energy is the dynamic

incentive at the heart of every form and the sustained expression of the intention of Sanat Kumara – an intention working
out as the planetary Purpose which is known only to Him.

The second Centre is created by the Ray of Love-Wisdom;
this is the basic energy which brought into being the entire
manifested universe, for it is the energy of the Builder Aspect.
To it we give – as far as humanity is concerned – the name of
Hierarchy, for it is the controlling factor of the great chain of
Hierarchy. The prime activity of this Centre is related to the
unfolding consciousness of the planet, and therefore of all
forms of life within or upon the planet; it is not related to the
life aspect in any sense.

...This consciousness is progressively developed, and the
Members of this second Centre, the Hierarchy, have the major
and important task, in this particular solar systemic cycle, of
bringing all the units in each kingdom of nature to an understanding of place, position, responsibility and relationships.
This probably sounds entirely meaningless in relation to those
conditions where the units of life are, for instance, in the
vegetable or the animal kingdom, but a glimmering of understanding may come when you remember that the seed or germ
of all states of consciousness is latent in every form, and of this
the instinct to perpetuate and the instinct to mate are the major
incubating areas.

The third Centre is that of the Human Kingdom, which is
brought into being by means of the energy of the third Ray of
Active Intelligence. Its major function is intelligent creation;
but it has nevertheless a secondary activity which is to relate
the second and the third Centres to each other and to assume
progressive control of the subhuman kingdoms and relate them
to each other. This secondary function is only now assuming
proportions which can be recognised and noted. (TEV–183/5)

• Just as the rapport between the Hierarchy and Humanity is
established via aspirants, disciples and initiates in physical
existence who are responding to the love-wisdom of the
universe in some measure and who work via the intelligent
people in incarnation primarily, so rapport between Shamballa

and the Hierarchy is being more closely established via the senior Ashrams, and not via the secondary ones. You have, therefore, a situation which might be depicted somewhat as follows:

I.   First Planetary Centre . . . .   Shamballa
                    working through
     1. The seven Rays or the seven Spirits before the Throne.
     2. Certain great Intermediaries.
     3. The Council Chamber of the Lord of the World.

II. Second Planetary Centre . . . .   Hierarchy
                    working through
     1. The seven major Chohans and Their Ashrams.
     2. The forty-nine Masters of the secondary Ashrams.
     3. The sumtotal of the secondary Ashrams.

III. Third Planetary Centre . . . .   Humanity
                    working through
     1. Disciples in manifestation – of the seven ray types.
     2. The New Group of World Servers.
     3. The sumtotal of humanitarians, educators and men of
        goodwill.

This is but a rough picture and one which is not totally correct; it will, however, show you certain direct lines of contact and of relationship which *are* true and which will suffice to give you a vague and general idea of the new alignment being set up between the three major planetary centres, requiring new adjustments.   (EXH–528/9)

• Within the solar system, as you know, are to be found the seven sacred planets, which are the custodians or the expression of these seven rays, of these seven qualities of divinity; within our planet, the Earth (which is not a sacred planet), there are likewise seven centres which become, as evolution proceeds, the recipients of the seven ray qualities from the seven sacred planets, thus providing (within the solar ring-pass-not) a vast interlocking system of energies. Three of these centres, representing the three major rays, are well known to you:

1. Shamballa	The ray of power or purpose. The first aspect. The energy of will.
2. The Hierarchy . . .	The ray of love-wisdom. The second aspect. The energy of love.
3. Humanity	The ray of active intelligence. The third aspect. The energy of mind or thought.

There are four other centres, and these, with the above three, constitute the seven centres, or the seven planetary focal points of energy, which condition the bodily manifestation of our planetary Logos. Through them the Lord of the World, working from His Own level on a cosmic plane and through His divine Personality, Sanat Kumara, carries out His purposes upon our planet.

Similarly, within the microcosm, man, the correspondences to these seven centres are to be found. Therein likewise are seven major centres, and they are the recipients of the energy emanating from the seven planetary centres, the custodians of the seven aspects of ray force; these seven energies – at various stages of potency – condition the man's expression in the three worlds, make him what he is at any given moment whilst in incarnation, and indicate (by their effect or lack of effect upon the centres) his point in evolution. (EH–619/20)

• A closer study of the forces which are producing the outer turmoil may serve to clarify your vision and restore confidence in God's plan and its divine love and loveliness. Let us, therefore, consider these forces and their originating centres, and thus acquire perhaps a new vision and a more constructive point of view. (DN–11/12)

The First Ray

• ...The most obvious and powerful force in the world today is that of the *first Ray of Will and Power*. It works out in two ways:

1. As the will of God in world affairs, which is ever the will-to-good. Steadily – if you study human history intelligently – you will see that there has been a regular and rhythmic progression toward unity and synthesis in all departments of human affairs. This unity in multiplicity is the Eternal Plan – a unity in consciousness, a multiplicity in form.

2. As the destructive element in world affairs. This refers to man's use of this force of will which is seldom as yet the will-to-good in active expression, but something which leads to self-assertion (of the individual or the nation) and to war with its accompaniments – separation, selfish diplomacy, hate and armaments, disease and death.

This is the force which pours into the world from the major world centre, *Shamballa.*...

Only twice before in the history of mankind has this Shamballa energy made its appearance and caused its presence to be felt through the tremendous changes which were brought about:

1. When the first great human crisis occurred at the time of the individualisation of man in ancient Lemuria.

2. At the time of the great struggle in Atlantean days between the "Lords of Light and the Lords of Material Expression".

This little known divine energy now streams out from the Holy Centre. It embodies in itself the energy which lies behind the world crisis of the moment. It is the *Will* of God to produce certain radical and momentous changes in the consciousness of the race which will completely alter man's attitude to life and his grasp of the spiritual, esoteric and subjective essentials of living. It is this force which will bring about (in conjunction with second ray force) that tremendous crisis – imminent in the human consciousness – which we call the second crisis, *the initiation* of the race into the Mystery of the Ages, into that which has been hid from the beginning.

The first crisis...was the crisis of individualisation wherein man became a living soul. The second crisis is the immediate one of racial initiation, made possible (if you will but believe it) by the many individual initiations which have lately been undergone by those members of the human family who had vision and a willingness to pay the price.

This particular and somewhat unusual ray energy is expressing itself in two ways. Perhaps it would be more correct to say in two ways that are recognisable by man, because it should be remembered that these ray forces express themselves as potently in other kingdoms in nature as they do in the human. For instance, one phase of the destructive aspect of first ray force has been the organised and scientific destruction of forms in the animal kingdom. This is the destroying force, as manipulated by man. Another phase of the same force (which can be noted in relation to the unfoldment of consciousness in subtle and powerful ways) can be seen in the effect which human beings have upon the domestic animals, hastening their evolution, and stimulating them into forms of advanced instinctual activity. I mention these two phases as illustration of the effect of first ray energy in the animal kingdom, as expressed through human activity.

The ways in which humanity itself is affected by this ray energy, as it expresses itself in a twofold manner, producing a twofold result, are as follows:

1. There is, at this time, an emergence of certain powerful and dominating first ray personalities into the theatre of world activity. These people are in direct contact with this Shamballa force and are sensitive to the impact of the will energy of Deity. According to their type of personality and their point in evolution will be their reaction to this force and their consequent usefulness to the Lord of the World as He works out His plans of world unfoldment. The energy of the will of God works through them, though stepped down and often misused and misapplied, by their differing and limited personalities, and interpreted unsatisfactorily by their undeveloped consciousnesses. These people are found in every field of human affairs. They are the dominant persons, and the dictators in every

aspect of human living – political, social, religious and educational. Who shall say (until at least a century has gone by) whether their influence and their efforts have been good or bad. Where they flagrantly infringe the Law of Love, their influence may be powerful, but it is passing and undesirable, at least where that phase of their activities is concerned. Where they meet human emergency and need, and work along lines of basic restoration and the preservation of "units of synthesis", their influence is good and constructive.

I would here point out that real group love never demonstrates as hatred of the individual. It may work out as the arresting of the individual's activities or enterprises where that is deemed desirable in the interests of the whole and if what he is doing is estimated as harmful to the good of the group. But the arresting will not be destructive. It will be educational and developing in its results.

The true first ray personality who works in response to this Shamballa influence will have the ultimate good of the group deeply enshrined in his consciousness and heart; he will think in terms of the whole and not in terms of the part. That is the thing which he will endeavour to impress upon the racial consciousness. This may lead at times to ruthlessness and cruelty if the personality of the individual is not yet controlled by soul impulse. Such cases can frequently be seen.... The sword is ever the symbol of the first ray force just as the pen is of the second ray influence.

I wish to remind you that I use the word "energy" in reference to the spiritual expression of any ray and the word "force" to denote the use which men make of spiritual energy as they seek to employ it and usually, as yet, misapply it.... It might be apposite here to point out that such first ray exponents of force are often misunderstood and hated. They may and often do misuse the energy available but they also use it constructively within the desired limits of the immediate plan. I would also like to state that the lot of a first ray disciple is hard and difficult. There are disciples of Shamballa just as there are disciples of the Hierarchy and this is a fact hitherto not recognised and never as yet referred to in the current writings on occult subjects. It is wise and valuable to remember this. They are powerful, these disciples of Shamballa, headstrong and often cruel; they impose their will and dictate their desires; they make mistakes but they are nevertheless true disciples of Shamballa and are working out the Will of God as much as the disciples and Masters of the Hierarchy are working out the Love of God.

This is a hard saying for some of you but your failure to recognise this truth and to respond to it does not affect the issue. It simply makes your individual lot and difficulties harder.

I would also remind you that the use of first ray energy inevitably means destruction in the early stages but fusion and blending in the later and final results. If you study the nations of the world today from this angle, you will see this Shamballa energy of will working out potently through the agency of certain great outstanding personalities. The Lord of Shamballa in this time of urgency, from love of the life aspect and from understanding of the Plan as well as from love of humanity, is sending forth this dynamic energy. It is form destroying and brings death to those material forms and organised bodies which hinder the free expression of the life of God, for they negate the new culture and render inactive the seeds of the coming civilisation.

From this display of energy, unthinking humanity draws back in fear and likes it not. When full of personality hate and self-will, human beings seek often to turn this energy to their own selfish ends. If human beings (even the best of them) were not so undeveloped and so superficial in their judgments and their vision, they would be able to penetrate behind what is going on in the key countries in the world and see the gradual emergence of new and better conditions, and the passing away of the loved, but slowly decaying forms. The energy of Shamballa is, however, so new and so strange that it is hard for human beings to know it for what it is – the demonstration of the Will of God in new and potent livingness.

2. The second way in which this dominant will impulse makes itself felt is through the voice of the masses of the people throughout the world. This will express itself through *sound,* as consciousness or love does through *light.* The sound of the nations has been heard as a mass sound for the first time. That voice today is unmistakably expressive of the values which embody human betterment; it demands peace and understanding between men and it refuses – and will steadily refuse – to permit certain drastic things to happen. This "voice of the people", which is in reality the voice of public opinion is, for the first time and with no recognition of the fact, being determined by the Will of God. (DN–12/18)

• According…to the condition of the sensitive [etheric] bodies of the planet, of nations and of individuals, so will be their reaction to the five kinds of inflowing forces. The Shamballa force, for instance, in making its impact upon first ray types, and upon the other ray types on that line of major energy – the third, fifth and seventh ray types – evokes widely differing results than when it makes an impact upon the second ray line of energy; the results of the impact of Shamballa energy upon the first ray individuals and nations can be potent in the extreme. This impact, being relatively a new one to humanity, evokes in the world today all the political and organisational changes which are so prevalent and so disturbing. There is little that humanity can do about this except endeavour to balance this first ray display of energy with second ray or hierarchical force. This latter energy – working through the world religions and the men and women who respond to the love influence – can change methods (though not the purpose or the direction) by pouring in the love force. (EXH–86)

• …From day to day more and more intelligent men and women are coming (or are being brought) into touch with the emerging ideas of the Hierarchy. We can look, therefore, for the steady appearance, gradually and cautiously applied, of the will energy of the highest centre (Shamballa) which is to be found upon our planet.... Today, so many members of the human family – in incarnation or out of incarnation – have taken the first two initiations that the attention of Shamballa is being increasingly turned to humanity, via the Hierarchy, whilst simultaneously the thoughts of men are being turned to the Plan, to the use of the will in direction and guidance, and to the nature of dynamic force. The quality, for instance, of the explosive and dynamic nature of war in this century is indicative of this, for the will energy in one of its aspects is an expression of death and destruction; the first ray is the ray of the destroyer. What can, therefore, be seen occurring is the effect of the Shamballa force upon the forms in nature, due to the misuse of the incoming energy by man. War in the past, speaking generally and esoterically, has been based consistently upon the attractive power of possessions and this has led to the aggressive and grasping character of the motives which have led to war. Gradually there has been a change coming about and war has lately been founded upon somewhat higher motives and the acquisition of more land and territorial possessions has not been the true and the main motive. War has been prompted by economic necessity, or it has been in the nature of the imposition of the will of some nation or group of nations and their desire to impose some ideology or other upon some nation or to rid itself of a worn out system of thought, of government, of religious dogma which is holding back racial development. This is being now consciously done and is an expression of the Shamballa or will force and is not so definitely the desire force of the past.

The seventh ray is one of the direct lines along which this first ray energy can travel and here again is another reason for its appearance at this time, because, in the releasing of the life into the new and improved forms, the old ways of living, of culture and of civilisation have to be destroyed or modified. This is, all of it, the work of the first Ray of Will expressing itself predominantly at this present time through the seventh Ray of Organisation and Relationship. (DN–120/l)

• This Shamballa energy now for the first time is making its impact upon humanity directly and is not stepped down, as has hitherto been the case, through transmission via the Hierarchy of Masters. This change of direction constituted a somewhat dangerous experiment as it necessarily stimulated the personalities of men, particularly those whose personalities were along the line of will or power and in whom the love aspect of divinity was not sufficiently expressing itself; it was, however, permitted because it was realised that it would not affect the man in the street or the masses who would remain unresponsive to it, though it might greatly stimulate and intensify the mental and more potent type of man.

The effects of this widespread stimulation have been all that was anticipated and the so-called "evil results" of the Shamballa force upon ambitious and powerful personalities in all countries and all schools of thought have, nevertheless, been offset to some extent by the growth of the sense of relationship everywhere and by the spread of the Christ energy which generates at-one-ment, loving understanding and goodwill.

...The Hierarchy is guided in its conclusions by the mass light and by the inner subjective oft unexpressed reactions of the multitude and never by the outer happenings upon the physical plane. The fate of the form life and of outer organisations is deemed of small importance compared with the sensed inner spiritual development. That development must necessarily outrun the outer manifestation. Humanity is today further advanced spiritually and mentally than might appear from external happenings. The first result of such development is eventually the destruction of the outer form because it is proving inadequate to the pulsing, inner, spiritual life; then, secondly, comes the building of the new and more adequate outer expression. This accounts for the world crisis at this time. (EXH–107/8)

• From [Shamballa], the will of God goes forth and the power of God becomes the messenger of His will. Hitherto that highest form of spiritual energy has only reached humanity (as I have before told you) via the Hierarchy. Today, it is deemed desirable that it should be ascertained whether there are enough selfless and group-conscious people upon the planet to warrant a direct inflow of that higher energy to humanity, thus producing upon the physical plane a hastening of the divine plan and a more rapid working out of that which is to be. This direct contact can be produced if the Great Invocation is used by the world aspirants and disciples in collaboration with the Hierarchy. Hence the emphasis I have laid upon all of you using this Great Invocation as souls and as those who are in touch in some small measure with the Hierarchy. When the note of humanity and the note of the Hierarchy are synchronised by the use of the Great Invocation, there will come a dynamic and immediate response from Shamballa, and that will rapidly take place which the Hierarchy and the world disciples desire to see. (EXH–151/2)

• The Forces which are contacted by the use of this Great Invocation, in conjunction with trained hierarchical effort, are thereby attracted or magnetically impelled to respond and then potent energies can be sent direct to the waiting planetary centre, Humanity. Two effects of an immediate nature are consequently induced over a specific period of time:

a.   The energy of the Will of God serves to awaken the illumined but latent will-to-good in men and this, once dynamically awakened, will flower forth as goodwill. There is so much of this which remains latent and unexpressed because the will to demonstrate goodwill activity has not been aroused; it will be automatically aroused in the general public once the world disciples have invoked and evoked the inflow of this higher dynamic energy. Humanity awaits this and its arrival is dependent upon the efforts of those who know what should be done and who should now make their spiritual theories facts in outer expression. Nothing can arrest the eventual progress of this will-to-good and its planned activity any more than a bud which has started to unfold its petals in the light of the sun.... The expression of what has been potential will be the result of the impact of first ray force, of the will-to-good at this time, induced by the efforts of the world disciples.

b.   The second effect will be the forming or constitution of a planetary triangle or recognisable triad which will be the correspondence between the three planetary centres to the spiritual triad of Monad, Soul and Personality (the atma-buddhi-manas of the theosophical literature). Hitherto the word *alignment* has best described the planetary situation; there has been a straight line along which energy has poured from Shamballa to the Hierarchy and from the Hierarchy to Humanity, but this has meant no direct interplay between Humanity and Shamballa. If the Great Invocation can be rendered effective, humanity can then set up a direct relationship with Shamballa. The resultant triangle of force-relationship will promote the circulation of spiritual energies between the three centres from point to point so that there will be a triple relation. A planetary process of give and take between all three will then be established, and the emphasis upon *giving* will be far more pronounced. (EXH–153/4)

• One of the most beneficent results of the inflow of the Shamballa force through the focused demand of the aspirants and world disciples will be the intelligent recognition of the uses of pain and suffering. It is this truth – distorted and selfishly misapplied and interpreted – which has led certain types of people and certain types of governing bodies among the nations to take the position that the greater the suffering inflicted (as, for instance, in war time) and the greater the process of terrorism, the quicker the end which is desirable and right; they hold often that the more dire the effects of planned conditions, the more rapidly will the correct consummation be achieved. It is not, however, the duty or right of man to turn first ray force to selfish ends or material objectives; responsibility cannot be veiled behind specious and distorted half truths and evil cannot be done in order that good may come. What is applied by the Lord of the World in Shamballa under the motivation of love, wisdom and selflessness with a sure touch and a judgment as to times and seasons cannot be so used by those motivated by personality objectives, either on an individual or a personality scale (for nations as well as individuals have personalities). Ponder on this and seek enlightenment from the soul. (EXH–154/5)

• [The inflow of the energy of Will or Power] will…serve to bring about a "fixed intention" on the part of many to work ceaselessly for true peace and understanding. These people will therefore aid in the task of implementing goodwill. It will, nevertheless, strengthen the will of the selfish, ambitious and obstinate men who are in positions of power and influence, and produce increased trouble – at least temporarily. The salvation of the world and the production of the needed security will be brought about in the long run by the mass of men everywhere, in all lands; it will be the result of an intensified educational process. Humanity, as yet, does not know how to handle wisely the energy of the will-to-power, and it is largely this that has handicapped the manifestation of the will-to-good. The Shamballa force is too strong for those who are naturally will-ful. In the case of certain potent men, this energy reaches them directly, and is not stepped down for them through contact with the Hierarchy of Love; it naturally expresses itself in the political fields and in the realm of governments, through rulers, officials, statesmen and politicians. When the "little wills" of the intelligentsia, of those who serve the public in some capacity or other, and those above all who are working in some connection with the United Nations, become strengthened, stimulated and focused on goodwill, the union of the two energies of Love-Wisdom and of Will can bring about the needed changes in the planetary life. This is not an immediate happening, but it is not a visioning of the impossible. (EXH–645)

• This energy of the will is the most potent energy in the whole scheme of planetary existence. It is called the "Shamballa Force", and it is that which holds all things together in life. It is, in reality, life itself. This life force or divine will (implementing divine intention) is that by means of which Sanat Kumara arrives at His goal. On a tiny scale, it is the use of one of the lowest aspects of the will (human self-will) which enables a man to carry out his plans and attain his fixed purpose – if he has one. Where the will is lacking, the plan dies out and the purpose is not achieved. Even in relation to self-will, it is veritably the "life of the project". The moment Sanat Kumara has attained His planetary purpose, He will withdraw this potent energy, and (in this withdrawing) destruction will set in. This Shamballa force is steadily held in leash for fear of too great an impact upon the unprepared kingdoms in nature. This has reference to its impact also upon humanity.

You have been told that this force has – during this century – made its first direct impact upon humanity; heretofore, it reached mankind in the three worlds after being stepped down and modified by transit through the great planetary centre to which we give the name of the Hierarchy. This direct impact will again take place in 1975, and also in the year 2000, but the risks will then not be so great as in the first impact, owing to the spiritual growth of mankind. Each time this energy strikes into the human consciousness some fuller aspect of the divine plan appears. It is the energy which brings about synthesis, which holds all things within the circle of the divine love. Since its impact during the past few years, human thinking has been more concerned with the production of unity and the attainment of synthesis in all human relations than ever before, and one result of this energy has been the forming of the United Nations. (RI–715/6)

The Second Ray

● ...The next great energy which is making its potent contribution to the present world situation is that of the *second Ray of Love Wisdom, Christ's ray*. This energy is poured into the world through the second great planetary centre which we call The Hierarchy. The energy which is concentrated in this centre and which is manipulated by the initiates and the Masters is making one of its cyclic impacts upon the Earth and...is also making one of its major cyclic Approaches to humanity.

The energy flowing through the Hierarchy at this time – the energy of love – is seeking to blend with that which is flowing out of Shamballa and is needed in order to make the desired application of it. The problem of the Hierarchy at this time is to produce a wise and adequate fusion of the Shamballa and the hierarchical energies and thus temper destruction and bring to the fore the spirit of construction, setting in motion the building and re-habilitating forces of the second ray energy. The Shamballa energy prepares the way for the energy of the Hierarchy. Thus it has been from the beginning of time, but the cycles of the Hierarchy, though relatively frequent, have not coincided with those of Shamballa, which are rare and infrequent. As time progresses, the impact of the Shamballa force will be more frequent because men will develop the power to stand and withstand it. Hitherto it has been too dangerous an energy to apply to mankind, for the results have worked out destructively, except in the first great Lemurian crisis. Its work has, therefore, been confined almost entirely to the Hierarchy Whose Members are equipped to handle it and to assimilate it correctly and also to use it for the benefit of humanity. Now the experiment is being attempted of permitting man to receive it and its impact, free from the mediation of the Hierarchy. It may prove a premature and abortive effort, but the issues are not yet determined and the Lord of Shamballa, with His assistants and with the aid of the watching Members of the Hierarchy, are not discouraged over the initial results. Humanity is responding unexpectedly well. There has been much success along this line but the results do not appear with clarity to intelligent human beings because they refuse to see anything except the destructive aspect and the disappearance of the forms to which they have hitherto anchored their emotions, their desire, and their mental perceptions. They fail, as yet, to see the irrefutable evidence of constructive activity and of true creative work. The temple of humanity in the New Age is rising rapidly but its outlines cannot be seen because men are occupied entirely with their individual or national selfish point of view and with their personal or national instincts and impulses. I would here like to call your attention to the fact that the instinctual life of nations is something which remains to be studied scientifically and is a phase which leads inevitably to the individualistic life of nations – a matter of more immediate interest.

The new forms are, however, being built and the Shamballa potencies, plus hierarchical guidance, are working towards ends which are definitely planned and which are working out favourably. The potency of love-wisdom, transmitted by the Hierarchy, is playing upon modern humanity in a more intimate and close manner than ever before. The Directors of the Hierarchy are seeking to evoke an intelligent response from men and an indication that they are *conscious* of what is happening. Most of the response to the Shamballa activity is characterised by fear and terror, by sensitivity and distressingly developed reactions to the forces of hate and separation. Only a few, here and there, really grasp the vision of the future and realise what is going on, seeing truly the beauty of the emerging plan. It is with these few that the Members of the Hierarchy can work because they (even when lacking understanding) bear no ill-will or hatred to others. Love is a great unifier and interpreter.

This energy of love is primarily concentrated (for purposes of hierarchical activity) in the New Group of World Servers. This group has been chosen by the Hierarchy as its main channel of expression. This group, composed as it is of all world disciples and all working initiates, finds its representatives in every group of idealists and servers and in every body of people who express human thought, particularly in the realm of human betterment and uplift. Through them, the potency of love-wisdom can express itself. These people are frequently misunderstood, for the love which they express differs widely from the sentimental, affectionate personal interest of the average worker. They are occupied mainly with the interests and the good of the whole group with which they may be associated; they are not primarily concerned with the petty interests of the individual – occupied with his little problems and concerns. This brings such a server under the criticism of the individual and with this criticism they must learn to live and to it they must pay no attention. True group love is of more importance than personal relationships, though those are met as need (note, I say, *need*) arises. Disciples learn to grasp the need of group love and to amend their ways in conformity with group good, but it is not easy for the self-interested individual to grasp the difference. Through the medium of those disciples who have learned the distinction between the petty concerns of the individual plus his interest in himself and the necessities and urgencies of group work and love, the Hierarchy can work and so bring about the needed world changes, which are primarily *changes in consciousness*. (DN–18/21)

• The efforts of the disciples coming from the [second ray] Ashram of K.H. will be largely directed towards the general public, but they will work primarily through educators in all countries and through those concerned with the teaching of religion. Educators touch those preparing for all types of activity. The task will be necessarily slow, particularly at first, but the second ray endowment of these disciples (as that of all disciples on this ray) is a steady persistence which brooks no discouragement, even when discouragement makes its appearance. Such disciples refuse to discontinue their effort or to change the spiritually-ordained plans, even when the obstacles to accomplishment seem insuperable. Disciples will come deliberately into incarnation and will take office in institutions of higher learning and in the churches, and will exert such pressure that old and obsolete methods, ancient outworn theologies and selfish and competitive techniques will be ended and the sciences of co-operation, of right human relations and of correct adjustment to life through meditation and right vision will supersede the present methods of learning; this will lead to no damage to the acquisition of academic knowledge or the right apprehension of spiritual truth. The vision will be different and the goals of a higher order, but the best that is now taught along the lines of art, religion and science will still be available; they will, however, be presented with a greater enlightenment and a better emphasis. They will meet the people's need. The churches, being today headed towards failure and lacking vision, will eventually and inevitably crash upon the rocks of unwarranted and abused authority, yet out of the wreckage will emerge those true and spiritually enlightened churchmen who – with vision and sure knowledge, free from dogmatism and hating ecclesiastical authority – will develop the new world religion. (EXH–577/8)

• The agents of the second ray started their preparation around the year 1825 and moved outward in force soon after 1860. From that date on, great concepts and new ideas, and the modern ideologies and arguments for and against aspects of the truth, have characterised modern thought and produced the present mental chaos and the many conflicting schools and ideologies, with their attendant movements and organisations; out of all these, order and truth and the new civilisation will emerge. (EXH–678/9)

The Third Ray

• ...The major energy upon which we shall touch here is that of *intelligent activity* – the potency of the third ray. This finds its expression through the third major centre on the planet; this centre, we call Humanity. The evocation of a loving intelligent response to the Shamballa impulse, stepped down by the Hierarchy, is that to which this world centre should respond. This is rapidly and, as I have told you, satisfactorily happening. A definite world effect is being produced and the New Group of World Servers has given much aid in this. (DN–21)

• The energy of Active Intelligence...is the easiest one for modern humanity to receive – which is perhaps a sad comment-ary upon man's aspirations. The proof of this lies in the fact that much of this type of energy (through the selfish perception and desires of mankind) has been *crystallised into money*. Human intelligence has served on the side of materialism and not on the side of the spiritual values. Money is the concretised expression of the third type of spiritual energy. This particular expression appeared first in the ancient and equally materialistic system of barter and exchange; then, in later civilisations (predominantly including ours) we have the appearance of money, made first from the products of the mineral kingdom, and then later came paper money, made from the products of the vegetable kingdom. This has culminated in the modern preoccupation with money. There is very deep occult meaning to be found in the statement in the *New Testament* that "the love of money is the root of all evil". It is largely money and selfishness which lie behind the present disastrous economic situation. Great financiers are in reality those in whom the receipt of money, or of this type of energy, constitutes the line of least resistance, plus the will to make vast fortunes, which cannot be gainsaid. They will to make a fortune; they bring their intelligence to bear upon their goal, and naught can stop them. Many of them are purely selfish; some regard their money as a trust to be used for others and are amazingly generous in a philanthropic and humanitarian sense. These men are receptive to the first type of energy, and frequently all the three types find a channel through them, and the world is greatly benefited; such men are nevertheless very rare. It still remains for the crystallised aspect of this third energy – money – to be used on a large scale for the furtherance of the work of the Hierarchy. It is at this point and in connection with money that the great test of goodwill should demonstrate. (EXH–645/6)

The Passing out of the Sixth Ray

• The sixth ray began to pass out of manifestation in 1625.... (DN–29)

• The sixth ray is, as you know, the most powerful in manifestation in this time and a very large number of people are responsive to its influence. It is still the line of least resistance for the majority, particularly in the Aryan race, for the reason that when in process of time and through evolution the influence of a ray has become potent, it is groups that are primarily affected and not just individuals. A rhythm and a momentum is then set up which lasts a long time and which gains power through the very force of organised numbers.... Suffice it to say that the sixth ray people are the reactionaries, the conservatives, the die-hards and the fanatics, who hold on to all that is of the past and whose influence is potent to hinder the progress of humanity into the new age. Their name is legion. They provide, however, a needed balance and are responsible for a steadying process which is much needed in the world at this time. (DN–29)

• Under the influence of the Piscean cycle which is now in process of termination, the sixth Ray of Idealism or Devotion was predominantly active. This is the ray of one-pointed determination and – from one angle – it is *the ray of blind procedure*. The individual, the group or humanity, sees only one aspect of reality at any one time, and (because of man's present point in the evolutionary process) usually the least desirable aspect. All else is sealed to them; they vision only one picture; their horizon is limited to only one point of the compass (speaking esoterically). To the mass of humanity, the aspect of reality which was visioned and for which men lived and died was *the material world, material comfort, material possessions and material enterprises;* to this the labour movement today and the tendencies already apparent in the United Nations [written 1949] bear incontrovertible testimony. (RI–676)

• This out-going ray of devotion to the ideal, and the incoming ray of magical order or organisation are largely responsible for the type of man's consciousness today. Man is essentially devoted (to the point of fanaticism) to whatever may be the goal of his life's attention. This goal may be to achieve discipleship, or to raise a family, or to get money, or to achieve popularity, or any other objective to which he consecrates his time and energy; but whatever it may be, to it he devotes all that he is or has. Man also is essentially and inherently a producer of law and order, though this quality is only just beginning to make its presence felt. This is because mankind is, at last, becoming mentally centred, and hence we have in the world at this time the many and varied attempts to straighten out affairs along business, national, economic, social and other lines, to produce some system and order, and to bring about the re-arranging of all energies with the objective (unrealised consciously as yet) of inaugurating the New Age. Owing, however, to defective mental control and to an almost universal ignorance as to the laws of thought, and in addition, to a profound lack of knowledge as to man's own nature, man works blindly. The ideals sensed are not correctly interpreted by the mind nor applied in such a way that they are of general and appropriate application. Hence the confusion and the chaotic experimentation going on, and hence also the imposition of personal authority to enforce an individual's idea of the ideal. (EP1–81/2)

• Under the immediate expression of the sixth ray, the divine principle of desire has shifted potently away from the desire for material form into the realm of higher desire. Though materialism is still rampant, there are few people who are not animated by certain definite idealistic aspirations for which they are ready, when needed, to make sacrifices. This is a relatively new phenomenon and one that should be carefully noted. Down the ages, great sons of God have ever been ready to die for an idea; today, whole masses of men are equally ready and have done so, whether it is the idea of a superhuman state, empire or nation, or some response to a major world need, or some potent adherence to some current ideology. This indicates phenomenal racial achievement and the pronounced success of the Hierarchy to shift human attention into the world from whence ideas emerge and on to the higher and the less material values.

The instinct which has characterised this passing sixth ray period and which has been noticeably fostered under its influence is that of *taste* – taste in food, in human intercourse, in colour, in form, in art and architecture and in all branches of human knowledge. This discriminating taste has reached a relatively high stage of development during the past two thousand years and "good taste" is a highly cherished mass virtue and objective today. This is a totally new thing and one which has been hitherto the prerogative of the highly cultured few. Ponder on this. It connotes evolutionary achievement. For the disciples of the world, this sense of taste has to be transmuted into its higher correspondence – a discriminating sense of values. Hence the clear emphasis laid in all textbooks on discipleship upon the need to develop *discrimination.* Desire – taste – discrimination; these are the values, under the sixth ray, for all evolutionary unfoldment and peculiarly the goal of all disciples. (DN–113/4)

• It is [the] failure [of the sixth ray devotee] to work intelligently, and I would like to add, lovingly with substance and so bring it into right relation with the dense outer form that has made the last two thousand years produce so disastrously a mismanaged world and which has brought the population of the planet into its present serious condition. The unintelligent work upon the physical plane, carried forward by those influenced by the sixth ray force, has led to a world which is suffering from cleavage in as true a sense as an individual person can suffer from a "split personality". The lines of demarcation between science and religion are a striking instance of this and have been clearly and forcefully drawn. The cleavage to which I refer has been drawn by the churchmen of the past and by no one else; the lines have been determined by the mystics, impractical and visionary, and by the fanatical devotees of some idea who were, nevertheless, unable to see the broad implications and the universal nature of these recognised ideas. I am generalising. There have been many devoted and holy sons of God who have never been guilty of the above stupidities and separative tendencies. At the same time as we recognise this, we must also recognise that orthodox religion has temporarily separated the two great concepts of spirit and matter in their thought and teaching, thereby pushing apart religion and science.

The task of the new age workers is to bring these two apparent opposites together, to demonstrate that spirit and matter are not antagonistic to each other and that throughout the universe there is only spiritual substance, working on and producing the outer tangible forms. (DN–126/7)

The Incoming Seventh Ray

• The seventh ray has sometimes been called a peculiar name by Knowers. It is regarded as the "Ray of Ritualistic Decency". It aids and inaugurates the appearing of a new world order, based on a spiritual drive and on aspiration, mental freedom, loving understanding and a physical plane rhythm which provides opportunity for full creative expression. To bring this about, energy from Shamballa (embodying the will-to-good) is fused and blended with the organising energy of the seventh ray and then carried to humanity along the stream of love which emanates from the Hierarchy itself. (EA–445)

• The seventh ray is steadily gaining momentum and has for a long time been stimulating and enhancing the activity of all fifth ray nations. If you bear in mind that one of the major objectives of seventh ray energy is to bring together and to relate spirit and matter and also substance and form (note this distinction) you can see for yourself that the work of science is closely connected with this endeavour and that the creation of the new forms will definitely be the result of a working interaction between the rulers of the fifth, the second and the seventh rays, aided by the help – on demand – of the ruler of the first ray. A large number of seventh ray egos or souls and also of men and women with seventh ray personalities are coming into incarnation now, and to them is committed the task of organising the activities of the new era and of ending the old methods of life and the old crystallised attitudes to life, to death, to leisure and to the population.

The result of the increasing flow of seventh ray energy plus the decreasing influence of the sixth ray – which shows itself as a pronounced crystallisation of the standardised and accepted forms of belief, religious, social and philosophic – is to throw the millions of people who do not respond to either of the above influences through egoic or personality relation, into a state of bewilderment. They feel entirely lost, are gripped by the idea that life holds for them no desirable future, all that they have learnt to cherish and to hold dear is rapidly failing. (DN–29/30)

• ...This [seventh] ray is only in process of manifestation and we know not as yet what its major expressions will be, either higher or lower. Human reactions have their place and – as I have earlier pointed out – even the Masters Themselves do not and cannot foretell what the results of the impacts of force may be nor what may eventuate as a result, though They can frequently determine the probable happenings. If I say to you that the higher expression of the seventh ray is white magic, do you really understand what I mean? I question it. Have you any true idea of what is intended by these two words? I doubt it. White magic is realistically the power of the trained worker and executive to bring together into a constructive synthesis the "within and the without" so that that which is below may be recognisably patterned upon that which is above....

All, therefore, that is conducive to human sensitivity and to increased awareness is the work of the white magician; all that tends to produce better forms through which the living principle of deity can express itself is the work of the white magician; all that serves to thin or tear away the veil between the worlds wherein those who have no physical bodies live and move and work and the worlds of outer form is the work of the white magician. Of all this type of work there is always much, but never more so than at this time owing to the coming into manifestation of this ray of the magician (black and white), the seventh ray. Hence the rapid growth of the sense of omnipresence and the recognition of the non-existence of time in relation to reality. This has taken place through the discovery and use of the radio and of the many means of communication and through the steady growth of telepathic interplay; hence also the spread of education, enlarging man's horizon and opening up to him new worlds for investigation and adventure; hence also the breaking down of the old and limiting forms through the invoked force of the first ray, which has hitherto always worked through the medium of the seventh ray, because the kingdoms in nature cannot yet stand pure first ray energy; hence also the keen interest in the life after death and the appearance of all the many groups which are today investigating the nature of survival and the probability of immortality; hence again the appearance of the modern spiritualistic movement. This is a direct effect of the coming into manifestation of the seventh ray. Spiritualism was the religion of old Atlantis and the seventh ray dominated that ancient civilisation for a very long period of time, particularly during the first half of its existence, just as the fifth ray is of such dominant potency in our Aryan age and race.

It is through the correct development of spiritualism along psychological lines and the withdrawal of its emphasis upon phenomena (which is its outstanding characteristic and emphasis today) that the true nature of death and of the hereafter will be revealed. But it is in connection with spiritualism that I can best illustrate the lower expression of the incoming seventh ray influences. The work of the seventh ray is, as you know, the relating of life and of form, but when the emphasis is laid upon the form aspect then the wrong procedure eventuates and the work of the black magician can begin, and his objectives come unduly into play. This is what has happened in the spiritualistic movement; its investigators are occupied with the form side of life and its adherents with the satisfaction of their emotional desires (again related to the form side) so that the true import of the movement is in danger of being lost. (DN–41/4)

• We live today in a period of the world's history wherein three events of major importance are taking place, mostly unrealised and unobserved by the majority of people.

The seventh Ray of Law and Order is coming into manifestation; we are transitting into a new sign of the zodiac [Aquarius], and the "coming of Christ" is imminent. These three great happenings are the cause of much of the present upheaval and chaos; at the same time they are responsible for the universal turning to spiritual realities which all true workers at this time recognise, and for the growth of understanding, of welfare movements and of the tendency to co-operation, of religious unity and of internationalism. Types of energy which have hitherto been latent are now becoming potent. The consequent world reaction is, in the initial stages, material in its manifestation; in its final stages, divine qualities will manifest and change history and civilisation. The interest being shown today in the so-called cosmic rays indicates a scientific recognition of the new incoming seventh ray energies. These rays, pouring through the sacral centre of the planetary etheric body, have necessarily an effect upon the sacral centres of humanity, and hence the sex life of mankind is temporarily over-stimulated, and hence also the present over-emphasis upon sex. But hence also (and this must be remembered) the keen impetus now being mentally expressed which will eventually result in man's thinking through to a solution of this problem of sex.

The coming in of the Aquarian age also stimulates in man a spirit of universality and a tendency towards fusion. This can be seen working out in the present trend towards synthesis in business, in religion and in politics. It produces an urge towards union, and among other unions, towards religious understanding and tolerance. But these influences, playing upon the sensitive bodies of the undeveloped and the over-psychic, lead to a morbid tendency towards unions, legitimate and illegitimate; they produce an extreme aptitude to sexual intercourse in many directions, and to relations and fusions which are not along the intended or the evolutionary line, and which outrage oft the very laws of nature itself. Energy is an impersonal thing, and is dual in its effect, – the effect varying according to the type of substance upon which it plays.

The incoming seventh ray expresses the power to organise, the ability to integrate and to bring into synthetic relation the great pairs of opposites, and thus produce the new forms of spiritual manifestation. But it will also produce the new forms of what, from the standpoint of spirit, may be regarded as material evil. It is the great impulse which will bring into the light of day all that is to be found clothed with matter, and will thus eventually lead to the revelation of spirit and of the hidden glory, when that which has been revealed of the material form has been purified and sanctified. This it was to which Christ referred when He prophesied that, at the end of the age, the hidden things would be made plain, and secrets be shouted from the housetops.

By means of this process of revelation, within the human family as well as elsewhere in nature, we shall have the development of the power of thought. This will come about through the development of the faculty of discrimination, which will offer choices to man, and thus develop a truer sense of values. False and true standards will emerge in man's con-sciousness, and those choices will be made which will lay the foundation of the new order, which will inaugurate the new race, with its new laws and novel approaches, and so usher in the new religion of love and brotherhood, and that period wherein the group and the group-good will be the dominant note. Then separateness and hatreds will fade out and men will be merged in a true unity.

The third factor under consideration, the coming of the Christ as it is called, must also be noted. Everywhere we find the spirit of expectancy, and the demand for a manifestation and a symbolic happening which we call by various names but which is usually referred to as the advent of Christ. This, as you know, may be an actual physical coming, as before in Palestine, or it may connote a definite over-shadowing of His disciples and lovers by the Great Lord of Life. This over-shadowing will call forth a response from all those who are in any way spiritually awakened. Or again, the coming may take the form of a tremendous inflow of the Christ principle, the Christ life and love, working out through the human family. Perhaps all three possibilities may be found simultaneously on our planet very shortly. It is not for us to say. It is for us to be ready, and for us to work at preparing the world for that significant series of events. The immediate future will show. The point I seek to make, however, is that this inflow of the Christ spirit of love (whether it comes through a Person in bodily form or through His felt and realised Presence) will again be twofold in its effect.

This is a hard saying for the unthinking and the illogical. Both the good and the evil man will be stimulated; both material desire and spiritual aspiration will be awakened and fostered. Facts prove the truth of the saying that a heavily fertilised garden and a carefully tended and watered plot of ground will produce its crop of weeds as well as flowers. Yet in this fact you have two reactions to the same sun, the same water, the same fertilising agency and the same care. The difference exists in the seeds found in the ground upon which these factors play. The inflow of love therefore will stimulate earthly love and earthly desire and animal lust; it will foster the urge to possess in the material sense, with all the evil consequent upon this attitude, and the resulting growth of sexual reactions, and the many expressions of an ill-regulated mechanism, responding to an impersonal force. But it will also produce the growth of brotherly love and foster the development and the expression of group consciousness, of universal understanding; it will produce a new and powerful tendency to fusion, to at-one-ment and to synthesis. All this will be brought about through the medium of humanity and the Christ spirit. Steadily the love of Christ will be shed abroad in the earth, and its influence will grow stronger during the coming centuries, until at the end of the Aquarian age, and through the work of the seventh ray (bringing the pairs of opposites into closer co-operation), we can look for the "raising of Lazarus from the dead", and the emergence of humanity out of the tomb of matter. The hidden divinity will be revealed. Steadily all forms will be brought under the influence of the Christ spirit, and the consummation of love will be brought about. (EP1–279/83)

• The seventh Ray of Ceremonial Order or Organisation is felt in the house of relationships, of organisations and of mutual effort and of aspiration (either towards good or evil). The forces of this ray work out on the seventh or physical plane – the plane whereon major changes in all forms are made and on which the disciple must firmly stand as he takes initiation.

This seventh ray sweeps into organised and directed activity the world of forces upon the outer sphere of manifestation, and produces the precipitation of Karma, which, in this case leads to:

1. The working out into expression of all the subjective evil of the life of humanity, thus producing the world war.

2. The initiation of the planetary Logos and – with Him – of all who take their stand upon the side of the Forces of Light. This takes various forms as far as humanity is concerned:

    a. The initiation of the consciousness of the masses of men into the Aquarian Age, bringing them under the new influences and potencies, and enabling them to make a response of which they would not otherwise be capable.
    b. The initiation of the aspirants of the world on to the Path of Accepted Discipleship.
    c. The bringing about of certain major initiations in the case of those world disciples who are ready enough and strong enough to take them.

In spite of the vast destruction everywhere, the work of the seventh ray is being increasingly felt; the destruction of the forces of evil is going on even though at great cost to the Forces of Light; simultaneously there is a regrouping and a rearrangement of human attitudes and thought; this is brought about as a result of the tremendous demand upon the world thinkers for direction and guidance. Thus the nebulous structure and the dim outlines of the New Age civilisation can already be seen.

The underlying spirit of freedom will triumph as it is organised into revolt against slavery. To this end, the seventh ray will increasingly make contribution. (EA–540/1)

• ...It may be possible to state in broad outline the coming developments [to be looked for from the influence of the incoming seventh Ray] and to tabulate the results to be expected. Suggestions only are possible.

Development of etheric vision universally. This will be due to two causes:

First, the scientific recognition of the existence of the etheric levels, thereby freeing people from the onus of adverse public opinion, and enabling them to reveal what they have individually long realised. Etheric vision is comparatively common even now. But comment concerning it is rare, owing to the fear of criticism.

Secondly, the increased activity of the devas of the ethers, which throws the matter of the etheric levels into more active vibration, with consequent reflex action on the eye of man.

Increased mental activity and the spread of education (of the concrete mental kind) everywhere. This will result in:

Increased competition between units and between groups.

The organization of business on lines hitherto undreamt of.

The foundation of groups and aggregations of groups whose sole purpose will be to synthesise all the lines of human endeavour, and thus bring about unification of effort, and economy of force in the scientific, business, philosophic, educational, and religious worlds.

The foundation of schools of medicine along new lines, whose purpose will be to study the etheric body, its relation to the dense physical body, and its function as the receiver, storer, and transmitter of the vital fluids of the system.

The foundation of the new Church, which will be no longer along devotional and idealistic lines but which will be an outgrowth of the old idealism, demonstrating through mental forms. It will have for its basis the scientific recognition of the unseen world and its due appreciation and apprehension by means of accurate scientific ceremonial. This ceremonial of the universal church – being founded on the mental unity of all peoples – will not be ceremonial as it is now understood, as it will be the guarded, guided, scientific utilisation of sound and colour to bring about certain desired ends, such as

The aligning of the Ego,

The influencing of groups,

The making of contact with the Occult Hierarchy,

The co-operation with the devas in order to further the
constructive ends of evolution,
and many other objects which will grow out of the scientific
comprehension of the constitution of man, the nature of
vibration or radioactivity, and the demonstrated reality of the
hitherto metaphysical hypothesis and religious dogma of the
unseen world of thought and of spiritual existence.

Increased facility in approaching the Path. This will be based
on the fact that so many of the then existent humanity will
have personal knowledge of the ruling powers and forces, will
perhaps be on the Probationary Path, or will be initiates of the
first degree. Thus the present scepticism will become non-existent. The dangers then will be along other lines, – those incident
to the very influence of this ray itself: the dangers of
crystallisation into form so that the true spiritual devotee may
become rare, and the scientific aspirant will take his place. *The
true occultist is a scientist and a devotee,* and where these two
are not merged, we have the mystic and the man in danger of
black magic, being governed by the intellect and not by
selflessness; there are dangers incident also upon contact with
the deva evolution and the knowledge of the powers and forces
made available through their agency.

The coming into incarnation of numbers of old magicians and
occultists, and the rapid growth therefore of recognised psychic
powers among the people. This psychism, being tinged with
mentality and not being of a purely astral quality, will be even
more dangerous than in Atlantean days, for back of it will be
some degree of will, conscious purpose, and intellectual
apprehension, and unless this is paralleled by the growth of
spiritual realisation, and by the steady grip of the Ego upon the
lower personality, a period of real danger may ensue. Hence
the need of pointing out and of realising the menace, so that
the truth of the inner life and the need of serving the race as an
essential to advancement may be proclaimed far and wide.

Paralleling the incoming of this large band of seventh Ray
magicians (some linked to the Brotherhood and some to the
purely manasic groups) is the proposed advent of certain

members of the Hierarchy (initiates below the fourth Initiation) and of certain disciples and probationers, all on this Ray and all true psychics, who hope through their endeavours to offset the vibrations, and ward off the menace incident to the advent of the other group. The arranging of this and the preparing of the way for them in the different countries, specially in Europe and North America, is occupying the attention at this time of the Master Rakoczi and the Master Hilarion.

A group of scientists will come into incarnation on the physical plane during the next seventy-five years [published 1925] who will be the medium for the revelation of the next three truths concerning electrical phenomena. A formula of truth concerning this aspect of manifestation was prepared by initiates on the fifth Ray at the close of the last century, being part of the usual attempt of the Hierarchy to promote evolutionary development at the close of every cycle of one hundred years. Certain parts (two fifths) of that formula have worked out through the achievements of such men as Edison and those who participate in his type of endeavour, and through the work of those who have dealt with the subject of radium and radio-activity. Three more parts of the same formula have still to come, and will embody all that it is possible or safe for man to know anent the physical plane manifestation of electricity during the fifth subrace.

All that we have here considered covers the time till the coming in of the new subrace. This race will summarise and carry to a temporary conclusion the manasic effort of the fifth rootrace of mental growth, and will cause results of stupendous import. During the sixth subrace, the emphasis will not be so much on the *development* of mind, as it will be on the *utilisation* of the concrete mind, and its acquired faculty, for the development of the powers of abstract thought. Perhaps too much importance has been attached to the statement of some occult writers that the sixth subrace will be intuitive. The intuition will be awakening, and will be more prominent than now, but the outstanding characteristic will be the ability of the units of the sixth subrace to think in abstract terms, and to use

the abstract mind. Their function will be to perfect (as far as
may be in this round) the group antahkarana, or the link
between the mental and the buddhic. This bridge will be of a
usable nature during the sixth rootrace in which the intuition
will show real and general signs of existing. In this rootrace,
units only show signs here and there of real intuition, having
built the necessary bridge in their individual selves. In the sixth
rootrace small groups will be intuitive. (TCF–453/7)

• Other cosmic rays will play upon our earth as this seventh
ray activity becomes increasingly active, and the result of their
influence will be to facilitate the emergence of the new racial
types, and above all else, to destroy the veil or web which
separates the world of the seen and tangible from the world of
the unseen and the intangible, the astral world. Just as there is
a veil called "the etheric web" dividing off the various force
centres in the human body, and protecting the head centres
from the astral world, so there is a separating web between the
world of physical life and the astral world. This will be
destroyed, slowly and certainly, by the play of the cosmic rays
upon our planet. The etheric web which is found between the
centres in the spine, and which is found at the top of the head
(protecting the head centre), is destroyed in man's mechanism
by the activity of certain forces found in that mysterious fire
which we call the kundalini fire. The cosmic rays of which the
modern scientist is aware constitute aspects of the planetary
kundalini, and their effect will be the same in the body of the
planetary Logos, the Earth, as it is in the human body; the
etheric web between the physical and astral planes is in process
of destruction, and it is of this event which the sensitives of the
world and the spiritualists prophesy as an imminent happening.
(EP1–370)

• Today, as the seventh ray comes into manifestation, we shall
see the approaches between the two higher kingdoms of men
and of souls greatly facilitated, as the magical work in the
producing and bringing about of relationship begins to go
forward as desired. It is the work of the Ray of Magical Order
which will bring about sensitivity to one of the Major

Approaches which is being now attempted. Only as history is made and we learn later the amazing nature of the epoch through which the race is passing, will humanity appreciate the significance of the work of the present Hierarchy, and the magnitude and the success of its achievement since 1925, as a result of the initial impulse instituted in 1875. (EP2–273)

Inaugurating the New Age

• ...The time is near at hand wherein there will be a fuller expression of ray purpose, type or quality, and therefore a truer appearance.

This is owing to the imminent appearance, or manifestation, of certain great Lives Who will embody the energy of rays two, three, five and seven. They will thus constitute focal points for the inflow of these four types of divine energy, and this will produce a tremendous stimulation of their corresponding and responding units of life. These four Beings, Who will appear as human beings in the field of the modern world, may be looked for before the end of this [20th] century, and Their united effort will inaugurate definitely the New Age, and usher in the period which will go down in history as the time of glory for the fifth root race. Each of these four Masters, for that They will be, is also subjectively the focal point for a triple inflow of energy from the centre in the Body of God which is symbolically spoken of as "the heart of the Sun". For each ray is in its turn a triple manifesting entity, as is the solar Deity Himself. Love will be Their outstanding characteristic, and through that attractive magnetic force the new forms will come into being which will permit of purer ray types, and thus of more truly expressive appearances. A great deal of the destructive energy extant in the world today is due to the presence on the astral plane of a first ray disciple of the planetary Logos. His work it is to clear the way for the manifestation of these other four major Disciples, Who are primarily Builders; They will enter on Their work when the task of the wreckers of form has been accomplished. (EP1–73/4)

The Nations and the Rays

• Groups of people, organisations, nations and groups of nations are all the result of ray activity and magnetism. Hence an understanding of the forces which stream forth from the divine creative centre, and which we call the rays, is of value in understanding the quality, nature, and destiny of vast human masses.... Countries (viewed independently of their nationals) are likewise the result of ray activity, and thus the importance of the subject cannot be overestimated. (EP1–129)

• All of the great nations are controlled by two rays, just as is the human being.... All nations are controlled by a personality ray (if so we can call it), which is dominant and potent and the main controlling factor at this time, and by a soul ray which is sensed only by the disciples and aspirants of any nation. This soul ray must be evoked into an increased functioning activity by the New Group of World Servers, for this is one of their main objectives and tasks. This must never be lost to sight. (EP1–381/2)

• A close analysis of the following will reveal certain lines of racial understanding. There is a natural rapport indicated between the present personality rays of Germany and Great Britain, yet a relationship can be seen also between France and Great Britain through their esoteric national mottoes and also between the two symbols which are also theirs. The symbol for France is the fleur de lys, which she adopted centuries ago under divine guidance, which symbol stands for the three divine aspects in manifestation. The symbol for Great Britain, under the same divine apportioning, is the three feathers, carried as the arms of the Prince of Wales. (DN–49/51)

• India hides the light and that light, when released upon the world and revealed to humanity, will bring about harmony in the form aspect; things will then be clearly seen as they are and will be freed from glamour and illusion; this harmonising light is sorely needed in India itself and when it has been manifested it will bring about the right functioning of the first Ray of Power or Government. The will of the people will then be seen in the light. It is in this connection that Great Britain will emerge into renewed activity for her personality ray and India's soul ray are the same. Many British people are subjectively linked with India, by past incarnations and association; the quarrel between Great Britain and India is largely a family affair in the deepest sense of the term and hence its bitterness. As you know, there is a close link between the fourth and second rays and this again emerges in the relationship between England and India; a destiny is there which must be jointly worked out. (DN–52/3)

• ...Of the major nations only Brazil, Great Britain and the United States of America are definitely under the influence of the second Ray of Love-Wisdom. An interesting fact thus emerges: Great Britain is the custodian of the wisdom aspect of this second ray energy for the Aryan race; the United States will fulfil the same office for the world of the immediate future, whilst Brazil will eventually – many thousands of years hence – supersede both of them. These three races embody the attractive cohesive aspect of the second ray and will demonstrate it through wisdom and right government, based on true idealism and love. (DN–54)

• It is obvious that the governing faculty of the Ray of Will or Power is the outstanding characteristic of Great Britain. England is an exponent of the art of control and her function has been to produce the first tentative grouping of federated nations the world has seen and to demonstrate the possibility of such a grouping. The United States is doing a somewhat similar thing and is fusing the nationals of many nations into one federated state with many subsidiary states, instead of subsidiary nations. These two powers function in this way and with this wide objective in order eventually to give to the planet a system of groupings within one national border or empire, and yet with an international implication which will be symbolic of the coming new age technique of government. (DN–51/2)

• Great Britain represents that aspect of the mind which expresses itself in intelligent government, based on just and loving understanding. That is, of course, the ideal before her, but not as yet the exactly fulfilled achievement. The United States represents the intuitive faculty, expressing itself as illumination, plus the power to fuse and blend. Brazil will – at some distant date – represent a linking interpreting civilisation, based on the unfoldment of the abstract consciousness which is a blend of the intellect and the intuition and which serves to reveal the wisdom aspect of love in its beauty. (DN–54/5)

• National relationships and the major intellectual cleavages are based also upon the governing ray influences. Spain, Austria and France, being governed by the seventh, fifth and third rays, have a close inter-relation. This worked out in a most interesting manner in the Middle Ages, and the destinies of these three nations were closely related. ...The United States is likewise spiritually and intimately associated – in its form aspect – with Brazil, Russia and Italy; hence the early influx of certain types of emigrants into the country and hence also the pull of the South American countries upon the American consciousness, and the growth (rightly or wrongly) of the ideal of Pan-America. These relations are all on the form side and emerge out of the personality rays or energy of the nations concerned. (DN–56)

• ...The fourth Ray of Harmony through Conflict which before long will come into power again, is to be prominent in the destinies of India, Germany, Italy, Austria and Brazil. It is for this that there is so much preparatory turmoil in four of these countries. The sixth Ray of Idealism is potent in Russia, the United States, Italy and Spain. It is the fanatical adherence to an ideal which is responsible for the potent changes in these four countries. In Germany and Italy the harmonising of the fourth ray, working through conflict, is also to be seen. Hence we have in all these countries a process of "breaking-down" and of destruction of old forms prior to an adequate responsiveness to the influence of the incoming ray. It should be remembered that as with individuals, so with nations – the reaction to an increasing influence of the soul ray is ever accompanied by a breaking down period; this demonstration of destruction is, however, only temporary and preparatory. (DN–52)

• It is too dangerous in these days of difficulty and world turmoil to express myself more definitely as to the future lines of unfoldment. The destiny and the future functioning of the nations lie hid in their present activities. The majority of my readers are far too nationalistic in their thinking, and too deeply engrossed with the prime importance of their own nation and its supreme significance, for me to be able to do more than generalise and indicate the major lines of progress. The role of the prophet is a dangerous one, for destiny lies in the hands of the people and no one knows exactly what the people will do – once aroused and educated. The time has not yet come when the bulk of the people of any nation can see the picture whole or be permitted to know the exact part their nation must play in the history of nations. Every nation – without exception – has its peculiar virtues and vices which are dependent upon the point in evolution, the measure of control of the personality ray, the emerging control of the soul ray, and the general focus of the nation. (DN–55)

• I will give you here [see the chart overleaf] the *present* personality influences of the nations, indicated by their governing signs of the zodiac, trusting that you will give due thought to what I impart and assuring you that they are of vital significance at this time, particularly if you compare them with what I gave you anent the rays of the nations in the first volume of *A Treatise on the Seven Rays.*... I will give you two signs for each country. One will be the emerging influence which will govern the ego or the soul of the country or nation, and the other that which governs at the present moment the personality ray of the individual country, and so conditions the masses. Forget not that the soul of the people is represented by those who react to the influence of the soul ray and of the sign which is affecting it (its ascendant, one might say), whilst the masses are conditioned by the personality ray and therefore by the sun sign of the specified nation. (DN–66/8)

Country	Ruling Sign		Egoic Ray	Ruling Sign		Personality Ray
Argentina	Cancer	4th	Not given	Libra	7th	Not given
Austria	Libra	7th	Fourth	Capricorn	10th	Fifth
Belgium	Sagittarius	9th	Not given	Gemini	3rd	Not given
Brazil	Leo	5th	Fourth	Virgo	6th	Second
China	Taurus	2nd	First	Libra	7th	Third
Finland	Capricorn	10th	Not given	Aries	1st	Not given
France	Pisces	12th	Fifth	Leo	5th	Third
Germany	Aries	1st	Fourth	Pisces	12th	First
Great Britain	Gemini	3rd	Second	Taurus	2nd	First
Greece	Virgo	6th	Not given	Capricorn	10th	Not given
Holland	Aquarius	11th	Not given	Cancer	4th	Not given
India	Aries	1st	First	Capricorn	10th	Fourth
Ireland	Virgo	6th	Not given	Pisces	12th	Not given
Italy	Leo	5th	Sixth	Sagittarius	9th	Fourth
Japan	Scorpio	8th	Not given	Capricorn	10th	Not given
Poland	Taurus	2nd	Not given	Gemini	3rd	Not given
Roumania	Leo	5th	Not given	Aries	1st	Not given
Russia	Aquarius	11th	Seventh	Leo	5th	Sixth
Scandinavia (4 Nations)	Libra	7th	Not given	Cancer	4th	Not given
Spain	Sagittarius	9th	Sixth	Capricorn	10th	Seventh
Switzerland	Aries	1st	Not given	Aquarius	11th	Not given
Turkey	Cancer	4th	Not given	Scorpio	8th	Not given
U.S.A.	Aquarius	11th	Second	Gemini	3rd	Sixth

• It would, I feel, also be of value if I indicated the ruling sign of some of the capital cities of the countries dealt with.... The focus of the immediate response of the peoples of the nations is frequently to be distinguished in *the quality* (if I may so call it) of their capital city and by the decisions there made. I would like to point out that in [what was formerly] the British Empire there are several major and distinctive sections which are themselves definitely governed by certain ruling signs.... As you will have noted, Great Britain is ruled by Gemini and Taurus, and consequently the principles of multiplicity and integration are simultaneously present. Duality, triplicity (England, Scotland and Wales) and also differentiation are the conditioning aspects of the empire. Under the major control of Gemini and Taurus you have the following potencies active:

	Egoic Ruler		Personality Ruler	
Australia	Virgo	6th	Capricorn	10th
Canada	Taurus	2nd	Libra	7th
India	Aries	1st	Capricorn	10th
New Zealand	Gemini	3rd	Virgo	6th
South Africa	Aries	1st	Sagittarius	9th

...These countries are related to the mother-country through their planetary rulers, and in this statement you have a definite hint conveyed. The zodiacal signs relate, but the planets are more influential at this stage of evolution. (DN–68/9)

• An analysis of the signs ruling the different countries will make certain outstanding conditions apparent and even with the small knowledge of esoteric astrology now available will make certain definite information emerge in your minds as vitally explanatory. Capricorn, for instance, seldom appears as a sign governing the egoic expression of any nation but quite often as governing the personality manifestation, or the exoteric country. Austria, Greece, India, Japan and Spain have Capricorn as their personality rulers, indicating age, crystallisation and materialism; a little study of conditions and the present point in evolution will make this apparent. In the next great and succeeding race to this, Capricorn will appear as ruling the egoic expression, for the soul will then be in greater control and certain great groups of human beings (those who now compose the present nations) will be ready for initiation upon the mountain top of Capricorn. (DN–69)

• If students will study this information in connection with that given elsewhere…the inter-relations now emerging in world affairs will be seen as the result of the play of these forces and energies and as, therefore, to a certain extent, unavoidable. The use of the energy may be along wrong lines, producing separation and trouble; it may be along right lines, leading to eventual harmony and understanding; but the energy is there and must make its effects felt. As in the individual life, as the results of the play of soul energy upon the form aspect, one or other of the rays will dominate. If the person or the nation is spiritually oriented, the result of the energy impact will be good and will lead towards the working out of the divine plan, and thus be wholly constructive. Where personality force dominates, the effects will be destructive and may temporarily hinder divine Purpose. Nevertheless, even force which is turned to destructive ends can and does finally work towards good, for the trend of the evolutionary force is unalterable, being based on the Will-to-good of Divinity Itself. The inpouring soul energy can be slowed down or speeded on its way according to the purpose, aspiration and the orientation of the entity (human or national); it can express soul purpose or personality selfishness, but the innate urge to betterment will inevitably triumph. (DN–93/4)

• The Occident and the Orient are linked through the personality ray [fourth ray] of the Occident and the egoic ray [fourth ray] of the Orient and this indicates eventual understanding once the second ray occidental soul becomes the dominant factor. When these various relationships are somewhat grasped by the peoples of the world you will get the clue to the various happenings taking place today and will understand the goal and the method of its attainment more clearly.... What is really happening is a shift in the human consciousness from its focus on individual energies, functioning through some specific ring-pass-not (individual, national, continental or racial) to a grasp of their interrelation and effects upon each other. (EA–526/7)

The Rays and the
Planetary Kingdoms

• ...Every kingdom in nature constitutes a totality of lives. Every atom in every form in nature is a life, and these lives form the cells of a Being's body or vehicle of manifestation. There is a Being embodied in every kingdom in nature. Just as the myriads of atomic lives in the human body constitute a man's body of expression and form his appearance, so it is with the greater Life informing the fourth kingdom in nature. This appearance – as are all appearances – is qualified by some particular ray type, and is determined also by the vital principle or spirit aspect. Thus every form is composed of innumerable lives, which have in them a preponderance of some ray quality. This is an occult platitude. These qualified lives produce a phenomenal appearance, and thus constitute a unity, through the influence of the integrating principle, which is never absent. (EP1–342/3)

• A knowledge of the rays and their tendencies and energies will bring much illumination to the workers in the field of the various sciences. All the sciences find themselves on some one or other of the rays, and a science is literally the light thrown by a ray into a particular field of divine manifestation. The four kingdoms in nature are embodiments of four great Lives Who are found, each on one of the four minor rays. The Being Who is the life of the fourth or human kingdom in nature (regarding that kingdom as a distinct organism, just as man's body nature or personality is a distinct organism, separable from him as a soul) is on the fifth ray. The Being Who ensouls similarly the

138

third kingdom, the animal kingdom, vibrates to the sixth ray. The Being Who is the expression and active force of the entire vegetable kingdom is to be found upon the fourth ray. Therefore we have:

Humanity	4th Kingdom	5th Ray	Concrete Knowledge.
Animal	3rd Kingdom	6th Ray	Devotion upwards or forwards.
Vegetable	2nd Kingdom	4th Ray	Harmony and Beauty.
Mineral	1st Kingdom	7th Ray	Organisation and Ritual. (EP1–120/21)

• Certain of the rays, as might be expected, are more responsible than certain others for the qualifying of any particular kingdom. Their effect is paramount in its determination. The effect of the other rays is subsidiary, but not absent. We must never forget that, in the close interrelation of forces in our solar system, no one of the seven possible forces is without effect. All of them function, qualify and motivate, but one or other will have a more vital effect than the rest. (EP1–216)

• ...To understand the rays and their bearing on life as a whole, it is necessary that man should grasp the fact that he is only a small fraction of that whole. Man has his roots in all the three kingdoms; all have contributed to his equipment; he is the macrocosm of the lower microcosm; he is the link which unites the three lower kingdoms to the three higher. Let it ever be borne in mind that the sign of man's spiritual unfoldment lies in his ability to include in his consciousness not only the so-called spiritual values and the power to react to soul contact, but also to include the material values, and to react divinely to the potencies which lie hidden from him in the custody of the other forms of divine life, found in the three sub-human kingdoms. (EP1–230/1)

The Mineral Kingdom

Ray	Expression
Ray VII. Ceremonial Organisation	Radioactivity
Ray I. Will or Power	The basic Reservoir of Power

- ...Two basic premises can be laid down:

1. That the many mineral substances fall naturally into seven main groups, corresponding to the seven subdivisions of the influencing rays, those of organisation and power.

2. That only in those world cycles when the seventh ray is in manifestation, and therefore supremely powerful, do certain hidden changes take place in these seven groups. These are the correspondences, in the mineral evolution, to the seven initiations of man.

At these times there is an increased radiatory activity. This can be noted at this time in the discovery of radio-active substance, as the incoming ray increases its potency, decade by decade. A certain amount of radiation is basic and fundamental in any world cycle. But when the seventh ray comes in there is an intensification of that radiation, and new substances appear to come into new activity. This intensification leaves the entire mineral kingdom, as a whole, more radio-active than before, until this increased radiation becomes in its turn basic and fundamental. As the seventh ray passes cyclically out of manifestation a certain measure of inertia settles down on the kingdom, though that which is radiatory continues its activity. In this way the radiation of the mineral world steadily increases as the cycles come and go, and there is necessarily a paralleling effect upon the higher three kingdoms. People today have no idea what effect this radiation (due to the incoming ray) will have, not only upon the surrounding mineral world but on the vegetable kingdom (which has its roots in the mineral kingdom), and upon men and animals in lesser degree. The power of the incoming cosmic rays has called forth the more easily recognised radio-activity with which modern science is now concerned. It was three seventh ray disciples who "interpreted" these rays to man. I refer to the Curies and to Millikan. Being themselves on the seventh ray, they had the necessary psychic equipment and responsiveness to enable them intuitively to recognise their own ray vibration in the mineral kingdom.

The seventh ray is one of organised ritual, and in form building this quality is basic and necessary. The processes found in the mineral kingdom are profoundly geometrical. The first ray is that of dynamic will or power, and – speaking symbolically – when perfected forms and organised vehicles and dynamic power are related and unified, then we shall have a full expression, at the point of deepest and densest con-cretion, of the mind of God in form, with a radiation which will be dynamically effective. (EP1–225/6)

• The seventh ray, when manifesting on the seventh plane (as is now the case), is peculiarly potent, and its effect upon the mineral kingdom is consequently dynamically felt. If it is true that there is only one substance and one spirit, that "matter is spirit at the lowest point of its cyclic activity" and spirit is matter at its highest, then the ray of ceremonial order or ritual is but an expression of its polar opposite, – the first ray of will or power. It is the expression of the same potency under another aspect. This means therefore that:

1. The power or will of God expresses itself through the organised systematised processes of the seventh ray. The geometrical faculty of the Universal Mind finds its most material perfection on the physical or seventh plane, working through the seventh ray. So the mineral kingdom came into being as this major expression. It holds in solution all the forces and those chemicals and minerals which are needed by the forms in the other material kingdoms.

2. The mineral kingdom is therefore the most concrete expression of the dual unity of power and order. It consti-tutes the "foundation" of the ordered physical structure or the universe of our planet.

3. The rhythmic ritualistic adaptability of the seventh ray, plus the dynamic will of the power ray, are needed in conjunction for the full working out of the Plan, as it is found in the Mind of God.

This is why, in this present period of transition, the Lord of the seventh ray is taking over the control of affairs and the ordered working out of the Plan, so as eventually to restore stability to the planet and give the incoming Aquarian influences a stable and extended field in which to work....

We shall now touch upon the next two points, – condensation and its hidden secret, transmutation. From the standpoint of external matter, the mineral kingdom marks the densest expression of the life of God in substance, and its outstanding, though oft unrealised, characteristic is imprisoned or unexpressed power. Speaking in symbols, a volcano in eruption is a mild expression of this power. From the standpoint of esoteric substance, the four ethers are far more dense and "substantial".... Just as they "substand" or form the basis of the manifested world, and are regarded as the "true form", so the mineral kingdom is the fundamental kingdom in the three worlds, under the Law of Correspondences. It is, in a most peculiar sense, "precipitated etheric substance", and is a condensation or externalisation of the etheric planes. This solidification or precipitation – resulting in the production of dense objective or solid matter – is the tangible result of the interplay of the energies and qualities of the first and seventh rays. Their united will and ordered rhythm have produced this Earth and the molten content of the planet, regarding the earth as the crust.

In the turning of the great wheel, cycle after cycle, these two rays come into functioning activity, and in between their objective cycles the other rays dominate and participate in the great work. The result of this interplay of psychic potencies will manifest in the eventual transmutation of the earth substance, and its resolution back again into that of which it is the objective condensation. Again language fails to find the needed terms. They are as yet non-existent. I mention this as an indication of the difficulty of our subject. Intangible etheric substance has been condensed into the dense tangible objective world. This – under the evolutionary plan – has to be again transmuted into its original condition, plus the gain of ordered rhythm and the tendencies and qualities wrought into the consciousness of its atoms and elements through the experience of externalisation. This resolution is noted by us as radiation and the radio-active substances. We are looking on at the transmutation process. The resolving agencies are fire, intense heat and pressure. These three agencies have already succeeded in bringing about the divisions of the mineral kingdom into three parts: the baser metals, as they are called, the standard metals (such as silver and gold and platinum), and the semi-precious stones and crystals. The precious jewels are a synthesis of all three, – one of the basic syntheses of evolution. (EP1–227/9)

Radiation

• ...One of the results of the intensified new influence will be the recognition, by science, of certain effects and characteristics of the work being accomplished. This can already be seen in the work done by scientists in connection with the mineral world.... The mineral kingdom is governed by the seventh ray, and to the potency of this incoming ray can be attributed the discovery of the radio-activity of matter. The seventh ray expresses itself in the mineral kingdom through the production of radiation, and we shall find that increasingly these radiations (many of which still remain to be discovered) will be noted, their effects understood and their potencies grasped. One point remains as yet unrealised by science, and that is that these radiations are cyclic in their appearance; under the influence of the seventh ray it has been possible for man to discover and work with radium. Radium has always been present, but not always active in such a manner that we were able to detect it. It is under the influence of the incoming seventh ray that its appearance has been made possible, and it is through this same influence that we shall discover new cosmic rays. They too are always present in our universe, but they use the substance of the incoming ray energy as the path along which they can travel to our planet and thus be revealed. (EP1–369/70)

The Vegetable Kingdom

Ray	*Expression*
Ray II. Love-Wisdom	Magnetism.
Ray IV. Beauty or Harmony	Uniformity of Colour.
Ray VI. Idealistic Devotion	Upward Tendency.

• The vegetable kingdom the second ray is peculiarly active, producing among other things the magnetic attractiveness of flowers. The mystery of the second ray is found to be hidden in the significance of the perfume of flowers. (EP1–44/5)

• The influence of the three rays, blended together in the vegetable kingdom, being also the three rays of even numbers, 2. 4. 6, has produced a fourfold perfection in this kingdom which is unparalleled in any other. The rays are responsible for this result, and their effect can be seen in the following analysis:

Ray II.   The result of this influence, pouring cyclically through the kingdom, has been to produce its magnetism, its attractiveness.

Ray IV. This ray of struggle and of conflict has as its objective the production of harmony between form and life, and has brought about the synthesis and the harmony of colour in nature. As we say the words, "colour in nature", automatically we think of the vegetable kingdom and its achievement of harmony in vegetation.

Ray VI. Growth towards the light is the effect of this ray influence, plus the normal tendency of all life-forms to evolve. It has brought the latent seeds of the vegetable kingdom, inherent within the soil, to the surface. It constitutes the energy of externalisation.

The united effect of these three rays, working in unison, has been to bring forth the fourth result, the perfume of the flowers, as found in the higher units of the vegetable kingdom. This perfume can be either deadly or vitalising, and can either delight or repel. It attracts and constitutes part of the aroma of this kingdom which is sensed in the planetary aura, though unrecognised as a whole by humanity. You isolate a perfume. Yet the perfume of an entire kingdom is a well recognised phenomenon to the initiate. (EP1–242/3)

• In the vegetable kingdom, the work of the second ray of Love-Wisdom is seen, symbolically, in one of its major consummations. Attractiveness, in the sense of beauty, of colour, of form, of distribution, and of perfume, is to be seen on every hand, and had you but the eyes to vision the reality, the synthesis of life would appear to you in all its glory. But just as the last of the five senses to make its presence felt in man, the sense of smell, is as yet but little understood, and its implications are not realised, whilst its relation to the analytical and discriminative mind is not appreciated scientifically, so the "attractiveness" (esoterically speaking) of the vegetable kingdom remains uncomprehended. It is the radiant garment of the planet, and is revealed by the sun; it is the achieved expression of the informing life of this kingdom in nature, and is the effect of the manifestation of the three divine and functioning aspects of this "peculiar" son of divinity, as he works out his destiny in form and through matter. (EP1–244)

The Animal Kingdom

Ray	Expression.
Ray III. Adaptability	Instinct.
Ray VI. Devotion	Domesticity

• The third ray is...peculiarly related to the animal kingdom, producing the tendency to intelligent activity which we note in the higher domestic animals. (EP1–45)

• *Influences:* The third Ray of Active Intelligence or of Adaptability is potent in this kingdom and will express itself increasingly as time goes on, until it has produced in the animal world that reaction to life and to environment which can best be described as "animal one-pointedness". Then, at this point and cyclically, the sixth Ray of Devotion or Idealism can make its pressure felt as the urge towards a goal, and thus produce a relation to man which makes of him the desired goal. This is to be seen through the medium of the tamed, the trained and the domestic animals.

Results: In the one case we find the third ray producing the emergence of instinct, which in its turn creates and uses that marvellous response apparatus we call the nervous system, the brain, and the five senses which lie behind and which are responsible for them as a whole. It should be noted that, wide as we may regard the difference between man and the animals, it is really a much closer relation than that existing between the animal and the vegetable. In the case of the sixth ray, we have the appearance of the power to be domesticated and trained, which is, in the last analysis, the power to love, to serve and to emerge from the herd into the group. Ponder on the words of this last paradoxical statement. (EP1–251/2)

• The *animal kingdom* has the quality of growing instinctual purpose which – in its highest form – works out as the domesticity of the more evolved animals, and their devotion to man. Behind the appearance of the animals is to be found a steady orientation towards understanding, and a consequent gravitation towards the forms of life which evidence that which they desire. Hence the influence of the fifth Ray of Concrete Knowledge, which pours through the human family upon the third kingdom in nature. (EP1–198)

• The...point to be emphasized in connection with human responsibility in relation to the animals is that the animal world embodies two divine aspects, two divine principles, and two major rays are concerned with their expression or manifestation. These two aspects are found also in man, and it is along these two lines, which man shares in unison with the animals, that man's responsibility and work lie.... The same divine activity and the same divine innate intelligence are found in the form aspect of both kingdoms. They are inherent in matter itself. But this third Ray of Divine Intelligence functions more potently and influences more powerfully in the animal kingdom than in man....

The second ray is of course present in its form-building aspect, as herd instinct and as the basis of the sex relation among animal bodies. It is found performing a similar function among human beings, and along these two lines of energy will the points of contact be found and the opportunity to assume responsibility. (EP1–254/5)

• It is of course apparent that the effect of the interrelation existing between animals and men is to produce in the former that step forward which is called *individualisation*....

...[Among] the factors which determine individualisation [are]...the ray impulses which are active at any time. These are amongst others:

a. The ray of the animal itself. Elephants are upon the first ray; dogs are expressions of the second ray; the cat is a third ray life manifestation, and the horse is sixth ray.
b. The ray of the particular person or persons with whom the animal is associated.
c. The ray or rays of a particular periodic cycle. (EP1–258/260)

The Human Kingdom

Ray	Expression.
Ray IV. Harmony through Conflict	Experience. Growth.
Ray V. Concrete Knowledge	Intellect.

• *Influences:* Two rays of divine energy are peculiarly active in bringing this kingdom into manifestation. These are:

1. The fourth Ray of Harmony, beauty and unity, attained through conflict.
2. The fifth Ray of Concrete Knowledge, or the power to know.

The fourth ray is the ray *par excellence* which governs

humanity. There is a numerical relation to be noted here, for the fourth creative Hierarchy of human monads, the fourth ray, in this fourth round, on the fourth globe, the Earth, are extremely active. It is their close interrelation and interplay which is responsible for the emergence into prominence of humanity. In other rounds, humanity has not been the dominant evolution or the most important. In this round it is. In the next round, the dominant evolution will be that of souls on the astral level, and the deva kingdom. Humanity now walks in the light of day, symbolically speaking, on Earth, and these two rays were responsible for the process of initiating the human evolution in this major cycle. Our objective is the harmonising of the higher and the lower aspects, or principles, both in the individual and in the whole. This involves conflict and struggle, but produces eventually beauty, creative power in art, and synthesis. This result would not have been possible had it not been for the potent work of the fifth Ray of Concrete Knowledge which – in conjunction with the fourth ray – produced that reflection of divinity we call a *man*.

The human entity is a curious synthesis, on the subjective side of his nature, producing a fusion of life, of power, of harmonious intent and of mental activity. The following should be noted, for it is of profound psychological interest and import:

Rays I, IV and V .. predominate in the life of humanity and govern with increasing power man's mental life and determine his mental body.

Rays II and VI ... govern potently his emotional life and determine the type of his astral body.

Rays III and VII .. govern the vital physical life and the physical body. (EP1–319/21)

• *Results:* Through the active work of…[the fourth and fifth rays], we find the fourth ray producing eventually in man the appearance of the *intuition*. The fifth ray is responsible for the development in him of the *intellect*. Here again we find appearing in man his great gift of synthesis and his prerogative of unification, for – as earlier said – he blends in himself the qualities of three kingdoms in nature, including the one before and the one after his own.

1. The kingdom of souls . . . . Intuition.
2. The human kingdom . . . . Intellect.
3. The animal kingdom . . . . Instinct.

Hence his problem, and hence his glory. We might also say that through the union of the positive intuition and the negative instinct the intellect is born, for man repeats in himself the great creative process as enacted in the universe. This is the inner creative side of consciousness, just as we have the outer creative side in the creation of forms. (EP1–321/2)

• [The third] ray brings in the factor of discrimination through mental activity, and this, in its turn, balances the so-called love nature, and it is in truth the cause of our evolutionary growth. The life in forms passes through discriminative and selective activity from one experience to another in an ever widening scale of contacts. It is this Ray of Intelligent Activity which dominates man at this time. Human beings are largely centred in their personalities; they are "egocentric", in the terminology of the psychologist, which recognises the integrating principle of the ego (in many cases) but does not yet recognise the overshadowing ego or soul, except under such a vague term as "the superconscious". We have therefore a humanity engrossed by a tremendous activity and demonstrating everywhere a vital discriminating and intellectual interest in all types of phenomena. This tendency to be active will go on increasing and intensifying until the Aryan race will merge into the coming major root-race, for which we have as yet no name, though we recognise that in that race the intellect will serve the intuition. Human activity is now regarded as having reached an incredible speed and intensity of vibration, yet from the angle of the world Knowers it is only just beginning to express itself, and is relatively feeble as yet. The growth of the tendency to vital speed can be noted if history is studied, and the pace at which man now lives, and the complexity and the many dynamic interests of his life, may be compared with those of the average man two hundred years ago. The last twenty-five years of man's history have shown a tremendous speeding up as compared with conditions fifty years ago [published 1936].

The reason for this increase of intelligent activity and rapidity of response and contact is to be found in the subjective fact that humanity is with great speed integrating the three aspects of human nature into a unity, called personality. Men are steadily becoming personalities, and unifying into one expression their physical, emotional and mental aspects; hence they are more able to respond to the ray of the integrated personality of the One in Whom they live, and move, and have their being.

Speaking therefore in terms of man's life problem, we might state that it is affected potently by the two major influences which beat upon the human kingdom, the cosmic ray of the solar system, the Ray of Love-Wisdom, and the cosmic ray of the planet, which is the personality ray of the planetary Logos, the Ray of Active Intelligence or Adaptability. Man might be defined as a unit of conscious life, swept into tangible expression through the discriminating love of God. Through his life experiences he is presented with innumerable choices which gradually shift from the realm of the tangible into that of the intangible. As he attracts, or is attracted by, the life of his environment, he becomes increasingly conscious of a series of shifting values, until he reaches that point in his development when the pull or the magnetic attraction of the subjective world and the intangible mental and spiritual realities are more potent than the factors which have hitherto enticed him on. His sense of values is no longer determined by:

1. The satisfaction of his instinctual animal nature.
2. The desires of a more emotional and sentimental kind which his astral body demands.
3. The pull and pleasures of the mind nature, and of intellectual appetites.

He becomes potently attracted by his soul, and this produces a tremendous revolution in his entire life, regarding the word "revolution" in its true sense, as a complete turning around. This revolution is happening now, on such a universal scale in the lives of individuals in the world, that it is one of the main factors producing the present potency of experimental ideas in the world of modern times. The attractive power of the soul grows steadily, and the pull of the personality weakens as steadily. All this has been brought about by the process of experiment, leading to experience; by experience, leading to a wiser use of the powers of the personality; by a growing appreciation of a truer world of values and of reality, and by an effort on man's part to identify himself with the world of spiritual values and not with a world of material values. The world of meaning and of causes becomes gradually the world in which he finds happiness, and his selection of his major interests and the use to which he decides to put his time and powers are finally conditioned by the truer spiritual values. He then is on the path of illumination. I have sought to express the effects of these two major ray influences in terms of mysticism and of philosophy, but in very truth all that I have here said could be expressed scientifically and in terms of scientific formulas, if man were mentally equipped to appreciate them. But this is not yet possible. All these ray vibrations, no matter which they may be, can eventually be reduced to formulas and to symbols.

Reaction to environment, sensitive response to the ray influences which govern and express themselves through the forms which compose man's environment, a growing power to discriminate between energies and forces, a slowly developing sense of values (which sense is the one which eventually dispels illusion and glamour and reveals reality), and a shift of the discriminating interest away from the worlds of tangible experience, of emotional life and of mental interest, – all this expresses the effect of the interplay between the two rays of the solar system and of the planet. These, intermingling, pour through and affect mankind.

One of the most difficult things with which the Masters are today confronted is to prove to man that the old and recognised values and the tangible world of phenomena (emotional and physical) must be relegated to their right place in the background of man's consciousness, and that the intangible realities, and the world of ideas and causes must be, for him, in the immediate future, the main centre of attention. When man grasps this and lives by this knowledge, then the glamour which now holds the world will disappear. (EP1–338/41)

• The ray which governs the sum total of the human kingdom is the fourth Ray of Harmony through Conflict. It might be symbolically stated that the egoic ray of the Life which informs the human family is this fourth ray, and that the personality ray is the fifth ray of knowledge through discrimination, – the Ray, as it is called, of Concrete Knowledge or Science. Harmony through conflict, and the power to achieve knowledge through discriminating choice – these are the two rays or major influences which sweep through humanity as a whole, and drive it forward towards its divine destiny. They are the predisposing factors upon which a man may count and infallibly depend. They are the guarantee of attainment, but also of turmoil and temporary duality. Harmony, expressing itself in beauty and creative power, is gained through battle, through stress and strain. Knowledge, expressing itself eventually through wisdom, is attained only through the agony of successively presented choices. These, submitted to the discriminating intelligence during the process of the life experience, produce at last the sense of true values, the vision of the ideal, and the capacity to distinguish reality behind the intervening glamour. (EP1–343)

The Spiritual Hierarchy

• The seven Ashrams express each the quality of their ray, one of the seven ray types. (RI–380)

• The seven major Ashrams are each responsive to one of seven types of ray energy and are focal points in the Hierarchy of the seven rays. The central, senior and major Ashram is (at this time) the repository of second ray energy, as this ray governs this second solar system. It is the Ashram of Love-Wisdom – the Ashram in which the Buddha and the Christ received Their initiations and through which each of Them works....

The other six major Ashrams came sequentially into being as the invocation of primitive man reached such a point of intensity of expression that a response was evoked from Shamballa, via its ray Representatives, working with directed energy in the three worlds. A "point of radiatory force" was established, at first in relation to the second ray Ashram, and later to the other Ashrams. One by one, as the rays cycled into activity in the three worlds and eventually on the physical plane, the seven Ashrams were founded, developed and expanded until the time arrived – several aeons ago – when all seven Ashrams were fully organised, and through them passed a steady flow of human beings liberating themselves from the three worlds. (RI–383/4)

• There are many Ashrams upon the various rays. My Ashram, being a second ray Ashram, is naturally closely related to that of K.H., which is the central or the most important Ashram upon the second ray line of energy as it penetrates the hierarchical centre. K.H. is at this time, under the Christ, the working Representative of the second ray in the Hierarchy. The Christ is the link between the second ray as it expresses itself in the Hierarchy and Shamballa. Initiates of high degree and Masters on all the rays have Their Own Ashrams, but not all are teaching centres; this is a point to be remembered, as well as the fact that all of them are not concerned primarily with the unfoldment of the human consciousness and with the needs of the human kingdom. There are other types of consciousness of deep and real importance in the great chain of Hierarchy, stretching from below to far above the human kingdom. This is a point apt to be forgotten. (DNA2–609)

• Slowly...the Hierarchy is beginning to implement both the Shamballa energy and that of Aquarius; the Masters Themselves have to learn how to use new incoming energies in the service of the Plan, just as the individual has to learn, in any particular incarnation, to work with and use the available astrological forces which make their impact upon one or other of his bodies or upon his entire personality; such energies, as you well know, can be turned to good uses or to bad. It is not possible for the Masters to turn energy to evil ends, but They necessarily have to master new techniques and the new methods of work called for by the new conditions; these can either affect the Hierarchy itself or will produce reactions in the fourth kingdom and in the other kingdoms, producing rapidly changing orientation and attitudes.

These forces and energies – from the zodiac or from one or other of the seven rays – have poured into and through our planetary Life for countless aeons. Each time that they cyclically make their appearance, the forms and substance in the three worlds upon which they impinge and through which they pass are different in the degree of evolutionary response and of sensitive reaction to impact. The response and the reactions of the human family as a whole, or of the individual within that whole, will differ from that of the previous cycle; with these factors the Hierarchy has to contend, changing cyclically its technique and altering its modes of work in order to meet the changing need. Bear this in mind. This has never been more evident to the Masters than today. The war might be regarded as a revolt by the form side of nature against the old conditions, and against the new incoming conditioning factors on the part of the Black Lodge. Between the two forces – one sensitive, onward moving, ready for that which is new and better, and the other reactionary, static and determined to gain a strangle hold upon the life within the form – the Hierarchy stands at the midway point:

a. Throwing all its weight on the side of that which is new, spiritual and desirable.
b. Adapting itself simultaneously to new conditions and new emerging factors.
c. Standing like a wall of steel, unshatterable and immov-

able between humanity and the forces of evil.

This has been an epoch of crisis, and the great moment for which the Hierarchy has been preparing ever since it was founded upon the Earth. Slowly down the ages, men have been trained and prepared for initiation; they have been taught to develop the initiate-consciousness; they have taken then their place within the ranks of the Hierarchy and have – later – passed into the higher centre, Shamballa. (RI–235/6)

• The growth of humanity and its evolutionary status (when compared with primordial and primitive man) can be seen in the quality of the Hierarchy today, *which humanity produced* and towards which it looks for guidance and teaching. This is an interesting point which I offer for your consideration. Never forget, my brothers, that as it is humanity which has furnished the personnel of the Hierarchy – including the Christ, the first of our humanity to achieve divinity – we have, therefore, the guarantee and the assurance of humanity's ultimate success.

The three major Executives of the Hierarchy:
1. The Christ, representing the second Ray of Love-Wisdom,
2. The Manu, representing the first Ray of Will or Power,
3. The Mahachohan, representing the third Ray of Active Intelligence,

are responsible to the Lord of the World for the processing of the life and impulse which condition the evolutionary process. This statement is made without any further definition by me because the whole subject is too abstruse.... (RI–369)

The Masters and the Rays

• As the Master Morya is upon the first Ray, that of Will or Power, His work largely concerns itself with the carrying out of the plans of the present Manu. He acts as the Inspirer of the statesmen of the world, He manipulates forces, through the Mahachohan, that will bring about the conditions desired for the furthering of racial evolution. On the physical plane those great national executives who have far vision and the international ideal are influenced by Him, and with Him co-operate certain of the great devas of the mental plane, and three great groups of angels work with Him on mental levels, in connection with the lesser devas who vitalise thoughtforms, and thus keep alive the thoughtforms of the Guides of the race for the benefit of the whole of humanity. (IHS–54/5)

• The Master Koot Humi…is upon the second, or the Love-Wisdom Ray…. He has had a wide experience and education, having been originally educated at one of the British universities, and speaks English fluently…. He concerns Himself largely with the vitalising of certain of the great philosophies, and interests Himself in a number of philanthropic agencies. To Him is given the work very largely of stimulating the love manifestation which is latent in the hearts of all men, and of awakening in the consciousness of the race the perception of the great fundamental fact of brotherhood.

At this particular time the Master M., the Master K.H. and the Master Jesus are interesting Themselves closely with the work of unifying, as far as may be, eastern and western thought, so that the great religions of the East, with the later development of the Christian faith in all its many branches, may mutually benefit each other. Thus eventually it is hoped one great universal Church may come into being. (IHS–55/6)

• The Master Djwhal Khul…is another adept on the second Ray of Love-Wisdom…. He works with those who heal, and co-operates unknown and unseen with the seekers after truth in the world's great laboratories, with all who definitely aim at the healing and solacing of the world, and with the great philanthropic world movements such as the Red Cross. He occupies Himself with various pupils of different Masters who can profit by His instruction, and within the last ten years has relieved both the Master M. and the Master K.H. of a good deal of Their teaching work, taking over from Them for certain stated times some of Their pupils and disciples. He works largely, too, with certain groups of the devas of the ethers, who are the healing devas, and who thus collaborate with Him in the work of healing some of the physical ills of humanity. He it was

Who dictated a large part of that momentous book *The Secret Doctrine,* and Who showed to H.P.Blavatsky many of the pictures, and gave her much of the data that is to be found in that book. (IHS–57/8)

• Now we come to the work which I (D.K.), a second ray Master, am attempting to do. With what energies am I working? What is the goal towards which I am striving under the direction of the three great Lords of the Hierarchy? I am working with the energy of right human relations; this is a definite and integral part of the energy of the second ray. It is a magnetic type of energy and draws men together for betterment and for right understanding. It is also related in a peculiar way to the energy of the first Ray of Will or Power. Perhaps this will be clearer to you if I point out that the will-to-good is an aspect of the Ray of Will, but that goodwill is an attribute of the second Ray of Love-Wisdom, thus relating that ray to the first ray....

In this particular though relatively short cycle, my Ashram is in a key position. It is closely linked to the first ray Ashram of the Master Morya, through the work of Men of Goodwill and through all goodwill movements in the world at this time. Goodwill is essentially an expression of the second Ray of Love Wisdom, and is therefore an aspect of all the Ashrams in that great second ray Ashram, the Hierarchy. But all goodwill work is today being galvanised also into violent activity through the dynamic energy of the first ray, expressing the will-to-good.

You have, therefore, this dynamic type of energy channelled through the Ashram for which I am responsible. This Ashram works also in close co-operation with that of the Master R. because the *intelligent* activity of the energy of goodwill is our objective, and its expression through intelligence, applied with wisdom and with skill in action, is the task demanded of all men and women of goodwill throughout the world. When the Labour Movement is swept by the energy of goodwill, basic changes in world affairs will take place. I would ask all workers for goodwill to attempt to reach labour in all countries with these ideas, correctly presented. (EXH–669/70)

• The energy of right human relations…is a subsidiary expression of the energy of Love-Wisdom – the first of the great
outpouring energies. It emanates, therefore, from the subsidiary
Ashram for which I [D.K.] am responsible. I have written and
taught much about it, and with some success. "Right human
relations" is not simply goodwill, as people seem to think; it is
a product or result of goodwill and the instigator of constructive changes between individuals, communities and nations.
About it I need not write, for you have enough teaching from
me to guide you. Your daily actions will be those of goodwill,
directed towards the establishing of right human relations *if* you
are rightly oriented *within* the race of men and *towards* the
spiritual Hierarchy. (EXH–647)

• …The Master Serapis…is the Master upon the fourth ray,
and the great art movements of the world, the evolution of
music, and that of painting and drama, receive from Him an
energising impulse. At present He is giving most of His time
and attention to the work of the deva, or angel evolution, until
their agency helps to make possible the great revelation in the
world of music and painting which lies immediately ahead.
(IHS–60)

• On the fifth Ray of Concrete Knowledge or Science, we find
the Master Hilarion, who in an earlier incarnation was Paul of
Tarsus.… He it was Who gave out to the world that occult
treatise *"Light on the Path"*, and His work is particularly
interesting to the general public at this crisis, for He works
with those who are developing the intuition, and controls and
transmutes the great movements that tend to strip the veil from
the unseen. His is the energy which, through His disciples, is
stimulating the Psychical Research groups everywhere, and He
it was Who initiated, through various pupils of His, the Spiritualistic movement. He has under observation all those who are
psychics of the higher order, and assists in developing their
powers for the good of the group, and in connection with
certain of the devas of the astral plane He works to open up to

the seekers after truth that subjective world which lies behind the grossly material. (IHS–59)

• The Master Jesus, Who is the focal point of the energy that flows through the various Christian churches…works specially with masses more than with individuals, though He has gathered around Him quite a numerous body of pupils. He is upon the sixth Ray of Devotion, or Abstract Idealism, and His pupils are frequently distinguished by that fanaticism and devotion which manifested in earlier Christian times amongst the martyrs…. To Him is given the problem of steering the thought of the occident out of its present state of unrest into the peaceful waters of certitude and knowledge, and of preparing the way in Europe and America for the eventual coming of the World Teacher. (IHS–56)

• The Master Rakoczi is upon the seventh Ray, that of Ceremonial Magic or Order, and He works largely through esoteric ritual and ceremonial, being vitally interested in the effects, hitherto unrecognised, of the ceremonial of the Freemasons, of the various fraternities, and of the Churches everywhere. (IHS–58/9)

• The Hierarchy is working primarily during the next few years [published 1942] through three groups of Masters who are on the first, second and third rays. Those on the first ray are dealing with the important figures today in world government, for all of them are subject to impression from their souls and all are fulfilling their individual destiny, and influencing their respective nations along the lines of national destiny. The period of intensive and seemingly destructive readjustment has been drastic and needed. This must not be forgotten. Mistakes in techniques have necessarily been made, and oft the law of love has been infringed. Sometimes, however, the love of the form aspect of consciousness has been interpreted as synchronous and similar to the law of love by critics of the methods employed. This is understandable. But the time of the great national readjustments must soon end, and the necessary processes of realignment be completed. This should then inaugurate a period of renewed relationships on a wide scale throughout the world; it should see the beginning of the establishment of friendships and the commencement of a new era of right and constructive world contacts. Hitherto this has never been possible on a large scale, owing to the fact that humanity had not suffered enough and therefore was not adequately sensitive to others. It had no inner integration such as is now possible through our developed means of communication, and the growth of telepathic sensitivity. The abuses of the law of living had not been generally recognised and known for what they are by a sufficient number of people. The work of the great first ray influences is rapidly and materially changing all this, and out of the lessons learnt, the structure of the new civilisation can become possible.

The work of the second ray Masters is now intensifying, and the builders of the new civilisation – working, through the religious organisations, the educational systems of every country and the great army of thinking men and women everywhere – can definitely begin to make their presence felt. It is in this department primarily that the work of the New Group of World Servers can be noted and can be developed....

The third ray Masters are working strenuously in the world of business and of finance through the agency of those who are animated by a spirit of selfless service – and there are many such. It is a new field for spiritual endeavour. It is not possible to enlarge within a brief space upon the methods and the plans of the Hierarchy at this time of crisis and emergency in connection with the field of money and its significance and right use. The general method employed is one of inspiration and of *the presentation of moments of crisis.* These moments offer opportunity for the activity of some disciple, and thus the learning of a needed lesson by the groups or nations implicated becomes possible. The technique employed by these third ray Masters is to develop the minds of aspirants and thinkers in the specific field of business so that they can think in larger terms than those of their own selfish business interests. Moments of contact are also arranged between members of the New Group of World Servers and these prominent people, working in the field of economic enterprise, and thus opportunities are provided for certain recognitions and certain definite co-operation. (EP2–729/31)

Seventh Ray Influence on the Kingdoms in Nature

• At this time [the seventh ray's] major expression will come through the relationships and adjustments required between capital and labour, and labour will be primarily involved. This energy is being assimilated in the Ashram of the Master... [who] was responsible for the formation of the labour move-ment – a movement bringing into relation the workers of the world. It is interesting to have in mind that today labour functions internationally; it is a group which learns with rapidity and has in it the seeds of vast good; it is probably the group which will place goodwill in the forefront of human thinking-upon a pinnacle of thought. This Master to Whom I refer belongs to the Ashram of the Master R. He relieves Him of the work to be done. (EXH–646/7)

• One of the inevitable effects of seventh ray energy will be to relate and weld into a closer synthesis the four kingdoms in nature. This must be done as preparatory to the long fore-ordained work of humanity which is to be the distributing agency for spiritual energy to the three subhuman kingdoms. This is the major task of service which the fourth kingdom, through its incarnating souls, has undertaken. The radiation from the fourth kingdom will some day be so potent and far-reaching that its effects will permeate down into the very depths of the created phenomenal world, even into the mineral kingdom. Then we shall see the results to which the great initiate, Paul, refers when he speaks of the whole creation waiting for the manifestation of the Sons of God. That manifes-tation is that of radiating glory and power and love.

Incidentally I might point out here that the seventh ray influence will have three definite effects upon the fourth and third kingdoms in nature. These are as follows:

1. All animal bodies will be steadily refined and in the case
    of humanity consciously refined, and so brought to a
    higher and more specialised state of development. This is
    today proceeding with rapidity. Diet and athletics, open air
    and sunshine are doing much for the race and in the next
    two generations fine bodies and sensitive natures will make
    their appearance and the soul will have far better instru-
    ments through which to work.

2. The relation between the human and the animal kingdoms
    will become increasingly close. The service of the animal
    to man is well recognised and of ceaseless expression. The
    service of man to the animals is not yet understood though
    some steps in the right direction are being taken. There
    must eventually be a close synthesis and sympathetic
    coordination between them and when this is the case some
    very extraordinary occurrences of animal mediumship
    under human inspiration will take place. By means of this,
    the intelligent factor in the animal (of which instinct is the
    embryonic manifestation) will be rapidly developed and
    this is one of the outstanding results of the intended
    human-animal relationship.

3. There will be, as a consequence of this quickened evol-
    ution, the rapid destruction of certain types of animal
    bodies. Very low grade human bodies will disappear,
    causing a general shift in the racial types towards a higher
    standard. Many species of animals will also die out and are
    today disappearing, and hence the increasing emphasis
    upon the preservation of animals and the establishing of
    game preserves. (DN–124/5)

• The effect upon the animal kingdom of the force of this
[seventh] ray will be far less than upon the human, for it is not
yet ready to respond to the vibration of this planetary Logos,
and will not be until the sixth round when His influence will
bring about great events. Nevertheless, certain effects might

here be noticed.

Owing to the increased activity of the deva evolution, and specially of the devas of the ethers, the lesser builders will be stimulated to build, with greater facility, bodies of a more responsive nature, and the etheric bodies of both men and animals and also their responsiveness to force or prana will be more adequate. During the sixth subrace, disease as we know it in both kingdoms will be materially lessened owing to the pranic response of the etheric bodies. This will likewise bring about changes in the dense physical body and the bodies of both men and animals will be smaller, more refined, more finely attuned to vibration, and consequently more fitted to express essential purpose.

Owing to the recognition by man of the value of mantrams, and his gradual comprehension of the true ceremonial of evolution, coupled with the use of sound and colour, the animal kingdom will be better understood, and better trained, considered and utilised. Indications of this already can be seen; for instance, in all our current magazines at this time, stories which deal with the psychology of animals, and with their mental attitude to man, are constantly appearing, and by the means of these and through the force of the incoming Ray, man may (if he cares to do so) come to a much wider sympathy with his brothers of less degree. Thus by the turning by man of his thought force upon the animals, stimulation of their latent mentality will ensue, leading in due course of time to the crisis in the next round. More attention should be paid by occult students to the effect of the consciousness of one group upon another group, and the advancement of the lesser, by the means of the stimulating power of the greater, should be studied....

Growth and development in one part of the body logoic produces a corresponding advance in the whole. No man, for instance, can make definite and specialised progress without his brother benefiting, – this benefiting taking the form of:

The increase of the total consciousness of the group.
The stimulation of units in the group.
The group magnetism producing increased healing or

blending effects upon allied groups.

In this thought lies, for the servant of the Master, incentive to effort; no man who strives for mastery, who struggles to attain, and who aims at expansion of consciousness but is having some effect – in ever widening spirals – upon all whom he contacts, devas, men, and animals. That he knows it not, and that he may be totally unaware of the subtle stimulating emanation which proceeds from him may be true, but nevertheless the law works.

The third effect of the coming in of this [seventh] ray is one that may at first repel – it will cause a great destruction in the animal kingdom. During the next few hundred years many of the old animal forms will die out and become extinct. To supply the wants of man, through disease, and through causes latent in the animal kingdom itself, much destruction will be brought about. It must ever be borne in mind that a building force is likewise a destroying one, and new forms for the animal evolution are, at this time, one of the recognized needs. The immense slaughter in America is part of the working out of the plan. The inner life or fire which animates the animal groups, and which is the life expression of an Entity, will, under this seventh influence, blaze up and burn out the old, and permit the escape of the life, to newer and better forms. (TCF–462/5)

The Rays and
Human Development

Esoteric Psychology

• The many psychologies have made their contribution to the whole subject, and all of them have value, for all have embodied an aspect of truth. Through them we have arrived at an amazing knowledge of man, of his instincts and animal mechanisms, of his reactions to his environment and of his sensitive apparatus; we have learnt much about the subconscious, through which ancient racial sins and knowledges, suppressed complexes and latent desires, as well as highly organised psychic reactions, well up into the conscious mind so disastrously. We know much anent the man as a whole functioning unity, and of the interactions existing between the nervous system, the glandular system, the muscles, and their expression, in forms of quality, character, personality, and the environment. We have learnt much, therefore, about that composite being called Man, and man, as a psychic entity, is an established fact in nature, as is man, the animal. But man, the soul, remains still a speculation, a hope, a belief. The fact of the soul is not yet substantiated; and in helping the truth into the light I seek to bring the subject of the seven rays to the notice of the thinkers of modern times, so that the light of this esoteric knowledge may be thrown upon the science of psychology. Thus may the work of revelation be aided.

If there is one thing that has emerged into the minds of investigators, as they have studied man, it is the fact that he is essentially dual. Psychology has shown that in the consciousness of every human being is a sense of duality, that man is in some mysterious sense two beings, and that it is the warfare between these two which has led to all the neuroses and complexes which tax the ingenuity of trained psychologists to solve. The initiate Paul referred to this when he spoke of the eternal warfare going on between the carnal mind and the heavenly nature, and all aspirants who are occupied with an intelligent struggle towards liberation bear witness to the same. Paul points out that victory is won through Christ, and I give a clue to the importance of this study of the rays when I state that, esoterically, these seven rays are the sevenfold expressions of the Cosmic Christ, the second Person of the Trinity. Bewildered men and women go in their thousands to the clinics of the psychologists, carrying with them the burden of their dual natures; and psychologists in their thousands recognise this duality and seek to unify the dissociated aspects. When the true nature of the seven rays is grasped, and when their effect on humanity in expressing the seven types of men is also understood, we shall then approach the subject of man's duality with greater intelligence. We shall comprehend better the nature of the forces which constitute one or another of these dualities. This is the true esoteric science. The science of the seven qualities or rays, and their effect upon the myriad forms which they mould and energise, is the coming new approach to the correct method of training and developing the human family. Modern exoteric science knows much about the outer form, or matter aspect, and its electrical nature. Esoteric science knows much about the nature of the subjective energies and the qualities which colour and condition the form. When these two knowledges are brought intelligently together, we shall evolve a truer and more accurate psychology and a new science of human culture. Then the work of unifying man – man, the psychic entity, and man, the conditioning soul – will go rapidly forward. (EP1–118/20)

• It is of course to the human interest that a study of the rays makes its main appeal. It is this study that will vivify and awaken psychologists to the true understanding of man. Every human being finds himself upon one of the seven rays. His personality is found, in every life, upon one of them, in varying rotation, according to the ray of the ego or soul. After the third initiation he locates his soul (if one may use such an inappropriate word) on one of the three major rays, though until that time it may be found in one of the seven ray groups. From that exalted attitude he strives towards the essential unity of the Monad. The fact of there being seven ray types carries great implications, and the intricacy of the subject is baffling to the neophyte.

A ray confers, through its energy, peculiar physical conditions, and determines the quality of the astral-emotional nature; it colours the mind body; it controls the distribution of energy, for the rays are of differing rates of vibration, and govern a particular centre in the body (differing with each ray) through which that distribution is made. Each ray works through one centre primarily, and through the remaining six in a specific order. The ray predisposes a man to certain strengths and weaknesses, and constitutes his principle of limitation, as well as endowing him with capacity. It governs the method of his relations to other human types and is responsible for his reactions in form to other forms. It gives him his colouring and quality, his general tone on the three planes of the personality, and it moulds his physical appearance. Certain attitudes of mind are easy for one ray type and difficult for another, and hence the changing personality shifts from ray to ray, from life to life, until all the qualities are developed and expressed. Certain souls, by their ray destiny, are found in certain fields of activity, and a particular field of endeavour remains relatively the same for many life expressions. A governor or statesman has learnt facility in his craft through much experience in that field. A world Teacher has been teaching for age-long cycles. A world Saviour has been, for many lives, at the task of salvaging. When a man is two-thirds of the way along the evolutionary path his soul ray type begins to dominate the personality ray type and will therefore govern the trend of his expression on earth, not in the spiritual sense (so-called) but in the sense of pre-disposing the personality towards certain activities.

A knowledge therefore of the rays and their qualities and activities is, from the standpoint of psychology, of profound importance.... (EP1–128/9)

• ...In this solar system, the triumph of the soul and its final dominance and control is a foregone conclusion, no matter how great the glamour or how fierce the strife. Thus, the ascertaining (by the aspirant) of his ray influence is one of the first steps towards understanding the nature of his problem and the method of release. The psychology of the future will direct attention to the discovery of the two rays which govern the soul and personality. Having done this through a study of the physical type, emotional reactions and mental tendencies, attention will then be directed to the discovery of the rays governing the specialised vehicles [the mental, astral and physical bodies]. (GWP–118)

• The impact of ray force upon people embodying differing aspects of ray energy will be one of the coming developments in the field of esoteric psychology.... (DNA1–295)

• ...The rays affecting humanity...are so many and so diverse that the complexity of the subject is very great. There are numerous influences which tend to make man what he is, and of many of them little is as yet known. In the early stages of his development, it is well-nigh impossible for any one (except an initiate) to deal with the various phases or even to recognise the indications of humanity's reactions to these rays. But as mankind evolves, and as the form aspect becomes increasingly a better and finer response apparatus and a more plastic sensitive reflector of the inner man, definition and analysis become easier. Types emerge with greater clarity in their delineations, and the ray qualities begin to dominate. The impress of the controlling rays can be more clearly noted and the point in evolution can be more accurately realised. (EP1–347)

• At the stage of *Individualisation,* the rays governing the physical and emotional bodies are dominant. The soul ray is scarcely felt and only flickers with a dim light at the heart of each lotus.

At the stage of *Intellection,* the ray of the mental body comes into activity. This second process is itself divided into two stages:

1.   That in which the lower concrete mind is developing.
2.   That in which the man becomes an integrated, coordinated person.

At each of these latter two stages, the rays of the lower nature become increasingly powerful. Self-consciousness is developed, and then the personality becomes clearer and clearer, and the three elementals of the lower nature, the force of the so-called "three lunar Lords" (the triple energies of the integrated personality) come steadily under the control of the ray of the personality. At this stage, therefore, four rays are active in the man, four streams of energy make him what he is and the ray of the soul is beginning, though very faintly, to make its presence felt, producing the conflict which all *thinkers* recognise.

At the stage of *Discipleship,* the soul ray comes into increased conflict with the personality ray and the great battle of the pairs of opposites begins. The soul ray or energy slowly dominates the personality ray, as it in its turn has dominated the rays of the three lower bodies.

At the stage of *Initiation,* the domination continues and at the third initiation the highest kind of energy which a man can express in this solar system – that of the monad, begins to control.

At the stage of individualisation, a man comes into being; he begins to exist. At the stage of intellection, the personality emerges with clarity and becomes naturally expressive. At the stage of discipleship, he becomes magnetic. At the stage of initiation, he becomes dynamic. (EP2–307/8)

• Whilst [the] process of soul control is being perfected (and the time consumed is, from the angle of the limiting personality consciousness, of vast duration), the ray types of the vehicles steadily emerge, the ray of the personality begins to control the life, and finally the soul ray begins to dominate the personality ray and subdue its activity.

Eventually, the monadic ray takes control, absorbing into itself the rays of the personality and of the soul (at the third and fifth initiations) and thus duality is finally and definitely overcome and "only the *One Who Is* remains". (EP2–341)

• In all that has been said anent the Rays it will be apparent that from the present standpoint two are paramountly concerned with the evolution of Man: the *fourth Ray of Harmony,* which is the dominant ray of the greater cycle which includes the fourth round and globe, and the *seventh Ray of Ceremonial Magic,* which is one of the foremost influences concerned in all objective manifestations. These two Rays, or the force of these two planetary Logoi, are largely instrumental in bringing about coherency in our chain, the fourth of the fourth scheme, and on our physical globe, the Earth. The fourth and the seventh interact, one acting temporarily as a negative force and the other as a positive. (TCF–441)

• …Use as the basis of all your work that which I have written upon the seven rays and accept this teaching as a proven hypothesis; be not deterred from this acceptance by any academic word-phrasing. You belong to the new school which is entrusted with the task of producing the new, esoteric psychology, based upon the five rays which are manifesting through every human being – the soul ray, the personality ray, and the rays of the three bodies of the personality. It is all energy and force and this the modern psychologist does not remember. If you accept and determine this occult hypothesis as your basic premise and apply all you may learn to the touchstone of the occult and spiritual teaching, you may achieve much. But, my brother, let two things take first place: The study of the rays and, secondly, their application to human life. Then will follow the practice and active work with individuals. You will learn much more through personal contacts and service than you will from lectures and books, though these, in reason, have their place.

Your work for the rest of your life must be based upon right perspective (free from false values) and an organised active service. Discipline for yourself...and service for your fellow-men, will release in you the knowledge which you gained in earlier lives.... (DNA1–644)

• The ray of the personality in a previous life leaves definite habits of thought and of activity; it has built into the life rhythm certain unalterable tendencies for which much gratitude can sometimes be felt. This is so in your own life. In a previous incarnation, your personality was on the second ray, thus leaving you with a deeply loving and understanding nature and a power *to include,* which is a major asset; it serves to offset the first ray tendencies which are so dominant in this particular life. It is hard for the disciple who sees not the picture whole, and who only knows the quality of the present life and its natural tendencies (due to ray influence) to think truly about himself. (DNA1–315)

Techniques of Integration

• The progress of humanity is from one *realised* integration to another; man's basic integrity is, however, in the realm of consciousness....

All these various integrations work out into some definite form of activity. First, there is the service of the personality, selfish and separative, wherein man sacrifices much in the interests of his own desire. Then comes the stage of service of humanity, and, finally, the service of the Plan. However, the integration with which we shall primarily deal as we study the seven *Techniques of Integration* is that of the personality as it integrates into the whole of which it is a part, through service to the race and to the Plan. Bear in mind that these ray techniques are *imposed by the soul upon the personality after it has been somewhat integrated into a functioning unity* and is, therefore, becoming slightly responsive to the soul, the directing Intelligence.

Ray One

"The love of power must dominate. There must also be repudiation of those forms which wield no power.

The word goes forth from soul to form: 'Stand up. Press outward into life. Achieve a goal. For you, there must be not a circle, but a line.

Prepare *the form*. Let the eyes look forward, not on either side. Let the ears be closed to all the outer voices, and the hands clenched, the body braced, and mind alert. Emotion is not used in furthering of the Plan. Love takes its place.'

The symbol of a moving point of light appears above the brow. The keynote of the life though uttered not, yet still is clearly heard: 'I move to power. I am the One. We are a Unity in power. And all is for the power and glory of the *One*' ".

Such is the pattern of the thought and the process of the life of the man upon the first ray who is seeking first of all to control his personality, and then to dominate his environment. His progress is that of "achieved control; that of being controlled, and then again controlling". At first, his motive is that of selfish, separative achievement, and then comes failure to be satisfied. A higher achievement then takes place as a result of the service of the Plan, until the time eventually comes when the first ray man can be trusted to be God's Destroying Angel – the Angel who brings life through the destruction of the form. Such integrated personalities are frequently ruthless at first, selfish, ambitious, self-centred, cruel, one-pointed, implacable, undeviating, aware of implications, of significances, and of the results of action but, at the same time, unalterable and undeviating, moving forward to their purposes. They destroy and tear down in order to rise to greater heights upon the ruin they have wrought. They do thus rise. They trample on other men and upon the destinies of the little person. They integrate their surroundings into an instrument for their will and move relentlessly forward upon their own occasions. This type of man will be found expressing these qualities in all walks of life and spheres of action, and is a destroying force in his home, business or in the nation.

All this is made possible because the first ray has at this stage integrated the personality vehicles and has achieved their simultaneous control. The man functions as a *whole*.

This process and method of work brings him eventually to a *point of crisis*, – a crisis based upon the unalterable fact of his essentially divine nature or being, which cannot remain satisfied with the gaining of power in a personality sense and in a material world. Power selfishly used exhausts its user and evokes a display of power antagonistic to him; he is thereby destroyed, because he has destroyed. He is separated off from his fellow men because he has been isolated and separative in his nature. He walks alone because he has cried forth to the world: "I will brook no companion; I am the one alone."

This crisis of evocation brings him to an inner point of change which involves an alteration in his direction, a change of method, and a different attitude. These three changes are described in the *Old Commentary* (in which these techniques are to be found) in the following terms:

> "The one who travels on a line returns upon his way. Back to the centre of his life he goes, and there he waits. He reaches out his arms and cries: I cannot stand and walk alone. And standing thus, a cross is formed and on that cross he takes his place – with others."

The change of direction takes him back to the centre of his being, the heart; a change of method takes place, for, instead of moving straight forward, he waits in patience and seeks to feel. A change of attitude can be noted, for he reaches out his arms to his fellow men – to the greater whole – and thus becomes inclusive.

Standing thus in quietness at the centre, and searching within himself for responsiveness to his environment, he thus loses sight of self and the light breaks in. It is as if a curtain were raised. In that light, the first thing which is revealed to him is the devastating sight of that which he has destroyed. He is subjected to what has esoterically been called "the light which shocks". Slowly and laboriously, using every power of his aligned personality and, in his realised desperation, calling in the power of his soul, he proceeds one-pointedly to rebuild that which he has destroyed. In rebuilding, he lifts the entire structure on to a higher level than any he has hitherto touched. This is the task of the destroyers and of those who work with civilisations and who can be trusted to act as agents of destruction under the Plan.

It is interesting to note that when this stage is reached (the stage of rebuilding as the first ray man understands it), he will usually pass through four incarnations in which he is first of all "the man at the centre", a focal point of immobile power. He is conscious of his power, gained whilst functioning as a selfish destroyer, but he is also conscious of frustration and futility. Next he passes through a life in which he begins to reorganise himself for a different type of activity, and it will be found that in these cases he will have a third or a seventh ray personality. In the third incarnation he definitely begins rebuilding and works through a second ray personality until, in the fourth life, he can function safely through a first ray personality without losing his spiritual balance, if we might use such a phrase. Through this type of personality, his first ray soul can demonstrate, because the disciple has "recovered feeling, gained divine emotion, and filled his waiting heart with love". In such cases as this, the astral body is usually on the second ray, the mental body upon the fourth ray, and the physical body upon the sixth ray. This naturally tends to balance or offset the intensity of the first ray vibrations of the personality and soul. It is in the third life of reorientation that he gains the reward for the arresting of his selfish efforts, and aspects of the Plan are then revealed to him. (EP2–350/4)

Ray Two

• " 'Again I stand; a point within a circle and yet myself.'

The love of love must dominate, not love of being loved. The power to draw unto oneself must dominate, but into the worlds of form that power must some day fail to penetrate. This is the first step towards a deeper search.

The word goes forth from soul to form: 'Release thyself from all that stands around, for it has naught for thee, so look to me. I am the One who builds, sustains and draws thee on and up. Look unto me with eyes of love, and seek the path which leads from the outer circle to the point.

I, at the point, sustain. I, at the point, attract. I, at the point, direct and choose and dominate. I, at the point, love all, drawing them to the centre and moving forward with the travelling points towards that great Centre where the One Point stands. What mean you by that *Word?*"

In reference to this second ray, it is advisable to recollect that all the rays are but the subrays of the second Ray of Love-Wisdom. The One in the centre, Who is the "point within the circle" of manifestation, has three major qualities: life or activity in form, love and the power of abstraction. It is these last two qualities of Deity with which we are concerned in these formulas and (in connection with the second ray) the dualities of attraction and abstraction emerge, both latent and both capable of perfected activity in their own field.

There comes ever the moment in the life of the aspirant when he begins to consider with wonder the significance of that familiar reaction of finding no satisfaction in the familiar things; the old life of desire for well known forms of existence and expression ceases to attract his interest. The pull or attractive power of the *One* at the centre (Who is his true self) also fails. It is not yet a familiar "call". The aspirant is left, unsatisfied and with a deepening sense of futility and empti-ness, "pendent upon the periphery" of the divine "ring-pass-not" which he has himself established. It is at this point and in this situation that he must reflect upon and use this formula.

The question might here be interjected: What should now be the procedure and right use? Upon this it is not possible here to enlarge, beyond pointing out that all the meditation processes connected with the Raja-Yoga system are intended to bring the aspirant to a point of such intense inner focusing and alert mental detachment that he will be in a position to use these formulas with understanding, according to his ray type, and to use them with efficacy and power. His meditation has produced the needed *alignment.* There is therefore a direct way or line (speaking symbolically) between the thinking, meditative, reflective man upon the periphery of the soul's influence and the soul itself, the One Who is at the centre. The crisis of evocation succeeds, once this line of contact, this antahkarana, has been established and recognised, and a crisis of intense activity ensues, wherein the man occultly "detaches himself from the furthest point upon the outer rim of life, and sweeps with purpose towards the central Point". Thus speaks the *Old*

Commentary, which is so oft quoted in these pages.

It is not possible to do more than put these ideas into symbolic form, leaving these mysteries of the soul to be grasped by those whose soul's influence reaches to that periphery, and is there *recognised for what it is.* This crisis usually persists for a long time, a far longer one than is the case with the aspirant upon the first ray line of activity. However, when the second ray aspirant has understood and has availed himself of the opportunity and can see ahead the line between himself and the centre, then the "light breaks in"....

Light reveals, and the *stage of revelation* now follows. This light upon the way produces vision and the vision shows itself as:

1. A vision, first of all, of defects. The light reveals the man to himself, as he is, or as the soul sees the personality.
2. A vision of the next step ahead, which, when taken, indicates the procedure next to be followed.
3. A vision of those who are travelling the same way.
4. A glimpse of the "Guardian Angel", who is the dim reflection of the Angel of the Presence, the Solar Angel, which walks with each human being from the moment of birth until death, embodying as much of the available light as the man – at any given moment upon the path of evolution – can use and express.
5. A fleeting glimpse (at high and rare moments) of the Angel of the Presence itself.
6. At certain times and when deemed necessary, a glimpse of the Master of a man's ray group. This falls usually into two categories of experience and causes:

    a. In the early stages and whilst under illusion and glamour, that which is contacted is a vision of the astral, illusory form upon the planes of glamour and illusion. This is not, therefore, a glimpse of the Master Himself, but of His astral symbol, or of the form built by His devoted disciples and followers.
    b. The Master Himself is contacted. This can take place

when the disciple has effected the needed integrations
of the threefold lower nature.

It is at this moment of "integration as the result of revelation" that there comes the fusion of the personality ray with
the egoic ray. (EP2–355/8)

Ray Three

- " 'Pulling the threads of Life, I stand, enmeshed within my self-
created glamour. Surrounded am I by the fabric I have woven. I see
naught else.

  '*The love of truth* must dominate, not love of my own thoughts, or
love of my ideas or forms; love of the ordered process must control,
not love of my own wild activity.'

  The word goes forth from soul to form: 'Be still. Learn to stand
silent, quiet and unafraid. I, at the centre, *Am*. Look up along the line
and not along the many lines which, in the space of aeons, you have
woven. These hold thee prisoner. Be still. Rush not from point to
point, nor be deluded by the outer forms and that which disappears.
Behind the forms, the Weaver stands and silently he weaves.' "

It is this *enforced* quiet which brings about the true alignment. This is the quiet not of meditation but of living. The
aspirant upon the third ray is apt to waste much energy in
perpetuating the glamorous forms with which he persistently
surrounds himself. How can he achieve his goal when he is
ceaselessly running hither and thither – weaving, manipulating,
planning and arranging? He manages to get nowhere. Ever he
is occupied with the distant objective, with that which may
materialise in some dim and distant future, and he fails ever to
achieve the immediate objective. He is often the expression and
example of waste energy. He weaves for the future, forgetting
that his tiny bit of weaving is an intrinsic part of a great Whole
and that time may enter in and frustrate – by change of circumstance – his carefully laid plans, and the dreams of earlier
years. Therefore futility is the result.

To offset this, he must stand quiet at the centre and (for a
time at any rate) cease from weaving; he must no longer make
opportunities for himself but – meeting the opportunities which

come his way (a very different thing) – apply himself to the need to be met. This is a very different matter and swings into activity a very different psychology. When he can do this and be willing to achieve divine idleness (from the angle of a glamoured third ray attitude), he will discover that he has suddenly achieved *alignment*. This alignment naturally produces *a crisis* which is characterised by two qualities:

a. The quality of deep distress. This is a period of difficulty and of real concern because it dawns upon his consciousness how useless, relatively, are his weaving and his manipulations, and how much of a problem he presents to the other Weavers.

b. The quality which might be expressed as the determination to stand in spiritual being and to comprehend the significance of the ancient aphorism, given frequently to third ray aspirants:

"Cease from thy doing. Walk not on the Path until thou hast learnt the art of standing still.

Study the spider, brother, entangled not in its own web, as thou art today entangled in thine own."

This crisis evokes understanding, which is, as many will recognise, an aspect of *light*. The aspirant slowly begins to work with the Plan as it is, and not as he thinks it is. As he works, *revelation* comes, and he sees clearly what he has to do. Usually this entails first of all a disentangling and a release from his own ideas. This process takes much time, being commensurate with the time wasted in building up the agelong glamour. The third ray aspirant is always slower to learn than the second ray, just as the first ray aspirant learns more rapidly than the second ray. When, however, he has learnt to be quiet and still, he can achieve his goal with greater rapidity. The second ray aspirant has to achieve the quiet which is ever present at the heart of a storm or the centre of a whirlpool. The third ray aspirant has to achieve the quiet which is like to that of a quiet mill pond, which he much dislikes to do.

Having, however, learned to do it, integration then takes

place. The man stands ready to play his part. (EP2–360/2)

Ray Four

- " 'Midway I stand between the forces which oppose each other. Longing am I for harmony and peace, and for the beauty which results from unity. I see the two. I see naught else but forces ranged opposing, and I, the one, who stands within the circle at the centre. Peace I demand. My mind is bent upon it. Oneness with all I seek, yet form divides. War upon every side I find, and separation. Alone I stand and am. I know too much.'

  The love of unity must dominate, and love of peace and harmony. Yet not that love, based on a longing for relief, for peace to self, for unity because it carries with it that which is pleasantness.

  The word goes forth from soul to form. 'Both sides are one. There is no war, no difference and no isolation. The warring forces seem to war from the point at which you stand. Move on a pace. See truly with the opened eye of inner vision and you will find, not two but one; not war but peace; not isolation but a heart which rests upon the centre. Thus shall the beauty of the Lord shine forth. The hour is now.' "

It is well to remember that this fourth ray is preeminently the ray of the fourth Creative Hierarchy, the human kingdom, and therefore has a peculiar relation to the functions, relationships and the service of man, as an intermediate group, a bridging group, upon our planet. The *function* of this intermediate group is to embody a type of energy, which is that of at-one-ment. This is essentially a healing force which brings all forms to an ultimate perfection through the power of the indwelling life, with which it becomes perfectly at-oned. This is brought about by the soul or consciousness aspect, qualified by the ray in question. The *relation* of the human family to the divine scheme, as it exists, is that of bringing into close rapport the three higher kingdoms upon our planet and the three lower kingdoms of nature, thus acting as a clearing house for divine energy. The *service* humanity is to render is that of producing unity, harmony, and beauty in nature, through blending into one functioning, related unity the soul in all forms. This is achieved individually at first, then it takes place in group formation, and finally it demonstrates through an entire kingdom in nature. When this takes place, the fourth Creative Hierarchy will be controlled predominantly by the fourth ray (by which I mean that the majority of its egos will have fourth ray personalities, thus facilitating the task of fusion), and the consciousness of its advanced units will function normally upon the fourth plane of buddhic energy or intuitional awareness.

It is this realisation which will provide adequate incentive for alignment. This alignment or sense of oneness is not in any way a mystical realisation, or that of the mystic who puts himself *en rapport* with divinity. The mystic still has a sense of duality. Nor is it the sense of identification which can characterise the occultist; with that there is still an awareness of individuality, though it is that of an individual who can merge at will with the whole. It is an almost indefinable consciousness of *group* fusion with a greater whole, and not so much individual fusion with the whole. Until this is experienced, it is well nigh impossible to comprehend, through the medium of words, its significance and meaning. It is the *reflection*, if I might so express it, of the Nirvanic consciousness; the reflection I would point out, but not that consciousness itself.

When this fourth ray alignment is produced and the disciple becomes aware of it, *a crisis* is evoked. The phrase "the disciple becomes aware of it", is significant, for it indicates that states of consciousness can exist and the disciple remain unaware of them. However, until they are brought down into the area of the brain and are recognised by the disciple in waking, physical consciousness, they remain subjective and are not usable. They are of no practical benefit to the man upon the physical plane. The crisis thus precipitated leads to fresh illumination when it is properly handled. These crises are produced by the bringing together (oft the clashing together) of the higher forces of the personality and soul energy. They cannot therefore be produced at a low stage of evolutionary development, in which low grade energies are active and the personality is neither integrated nor of a high grade and character. (Is such a phrase as "low grade energies" permissible? When all are divine? It conveys the idea, and that is what is desired.) The forces which are involved in such a crisis are the forces of integration at work in a personality of a very high order, and they are themselves necessarily of a relatively high potency. It is the integrated personality force, brought into relation with soul energy, which ever produces the type of crisis which is here discussed. These constitute, consequently, a very difficult moment or moments in the life of the disciple.

This fourth ray crisis, evoked by a right understanding and a right use of the fourth ray formula, produces the following sequential results:

1. *A sense of isolation.* Putting this into more modern language, a complex is produced of the same nature as that which temporarily overcame Elijah. He was overwhelmed with a sense of his clarity of vision in relation to the problem with which he was faced, of his unique response to it, and also with a sense of aloneness which devastated him.

2. *A sense of despairing futility.* The forces arraigned against the disciple seem so great and his equipment so inadequate and feeble!

3. *A determination to stand* in the midst and, if not victorious, at least to refuse to admit defeat, taking with determination the position which St. Paul expressed in the words: "Having done all, to stand."

4. *A sudden recognition* of the Warrior within, Who is invisible and omnipotent but Who can only now begin His real work when the personality is aligned, the crisis recognised, and the will-to-victory is present. We would do well to ponder on this.

When, therefore, this state of mind is achieved, and the disciple and inner Master, the soldier and the Warrior are known to be at-one, then there takes place what has been called in some of the ancient books "the breaking forth of the light of victory" – a victory which does not inflict defeat upon those who are at war, but which results in that triple victory of the two sides and of the One Who is at the centre. All three move forward to perfection. This is typical of a fourth ray consummation, and if this thought is applied with due reflection to the problem of the fourth kingdom in nature, the fourth Creative Hierarchy, humanity itself, the beauty of the phrasing and the truth of the statement must inevitably appear.

With this blazing forth of light comes the revelation expressed for us so adequately in the closing words of the fourth ray formula. Man sees and grasps the final purpose for the race and the objective ahead of this fourth kingdom in the great sweep of the divine manifestation. It is valuable also to remember that this revelation comes to the race in three stages:

1. *Individually,* when the disciple "relinquishes the fight in order to stand, thereby discovering victory ahead, achieving oneness with the enemy, the Warrior and the *One*".

2. *In group formation*. This approach to the revelation is today going on in the world, and is producing a moment of extreme crisis in connection with the work of the New Group of World Servers. Their moment of crisis lies immediately ahead [published 1942].

3. *In the human family as a whole*. This revelation will come to the race at the end of the age and with it we need not for the moment, therefore, concern ourselves. It is essentially the revelation of the *Plan* as a whole, embodying the various aspects of the Plan as – from cycle to cycle – the race has grasped the smaller aspects and revelations and succeeded eventually in bringing them into concrete manifestation. It is a revelation of the purposes of Deity – past, present and future purposes – as grasped by those who have developed the divine aspects and are, consequently, in a position to understand.

This series of spiritual happenings or unfoldments of consciousness in the life of the individual and the group produces a definite integration upon the three levels of personality work (mental, emotional and physical). It also lays the ground for those processes of fusion which will blend the rays of the personality and of the soul. If you will carry this concept of integration (achieved upon the three levels of the three worlds of human endeavour) into the activities and relationships of groups, you will find much of interest and of informative value anent the work of the New Group of World Servers. This group is, if I might so express it, an effort at an externalisation of the group personality of the disciples, connected with the Hierarchy. If we ponder on this, the function and relation will be apparent.

Let us now add to the three words expressing the three ray formulas already given, the word for this ray: *Steadfastness*. Therefore we have:

Ray One	. . . .	Inclusion.
Ray Two	. . . .	Centralisation.
Ray Three	. . . .	Stillness.
Ray Four	. . . .	Steadfastness.

As we brood on these words and on the remaining three which are indicated hereafter, we shall bring clearly into our consciousness the keynote for the disciples of the world at this time, who are in a position to discover that their personalities or their souls are on some one or other of these rays. The use of these words by those who are not pledged disciples in connection with their personality rays and personality expression might be definitely undesirable. The third ray personality, emphasising *stillness*, for instance, might find himself descending into the sloughs of lethargy; the first ray personality, seeking to develop *inclusiveness* might go to extremes, deeming himself a centre of inclusiveness. These are Words of Power, when used by a disciple, and must be employed in the light of the soul or may have a striking harmful effect. (EP2–363/8)

Ray Five

● " 'Towards me I draw the garment of my God. I see and know His form. I take that garment, piece by piece. I know its shape and colour, its form and type, its parts component and its purposes and use. I stand amazed, I see naught else. I penetrate the mysteries of form, but not the *Mystery.* I see the garment of my God. I see naught else.'

Love of the form is good but only as the form is known for what it is – the veiling vase of life. Love of the form must never hide the Life which has its place behind, the *One* who brought the form into the light of day, and preserves it for His use, – The *One* Who lives, and loves and serves the form, the One Who *Is*.

The Word goes forth from soul to form: 'Behind that form, I am. Know Me. Cherish and know and understand the nature of the veils of life, but know as well the One Who lives. Know Me. Let not the forms of nature, their processes and powers prevent thy searching for the Mystery which brought the mysteries to thee. Know well the form, but leave it joyously and search for Me.

'Detach thy thought from form and find Me waiting underneath the veils, the many-sided shapes, the glamours and the thoughtforms which hide my real Self. Be not deceived. Find Me. Know Me. Then use the forms which then will neither veil nor hide the Self, but will permit the nature of that Self to penetrate the veils of life, revealing all the radiance of God, His power and magnetism; revealing all there is of form, of life, of beauty and usefulness. The mind reveals the *One*. The mind can blend and fuse the form and life. Thou art the One. Thou art the form. Thou art the mind. Know this.' "

This fifth ray formula is of exceeding potency at this time and should be used often, but with care, by those upon this line of divine energy. It has most powerful integrating properties, but the person who employs it must be mindful to visualise and hold in his mind's eye the even, balanced, equilibrised distribution of the divine energy set in motion by the use of this fifth ray formula so that the three aspects of the spiritual entity concerned – the mind, the One Who uses it (the Self) and the form nature – may be equally stimulated. This statement means, for instance, that if all the emphasis of the soul energy available is poured into the lower nature, the natural man, it might result in the shattering of the form and the consequent uselessness of the man in service. If all of it, on the other hand, is poured into the receiving chalice of the astral nature, it might only serve to intensify the glamour and to produce fanaticism.

1. The lower psychic man – physical and astral – must receive a balanced quota of force.

2. The mind must receive its share of illuminating energy.
3. A third part of that energy must be retained within the periphery of the soul nature to balance thus the other two.

This is a replica of the experience of the Monad when coming into manifestation, for the monad retains a measure of energy within itself, it sends energy forth which is anchored in that centre of energy which we call a soul. Still more energy pours forth also, via the soul, for the production of a human being – an expression of the soul upon the physical plane, just as the soul is an expression of the monad upon the mental plane, and both are expressions also of that one monad.

The use of this formula, which produces eventually a definite relation between the soul and the various aspects of the form, brings about a needed alignment, and again (as in the other cases considered previously) produces also, and evokes, *a crisis*. This crisis must be regarded as producing two lesser crises in the consciousness of the personality:

1. That in which there comes the achieving of equilibrium and what might be called a "balanced point of view". This balanced vision causes much difficulty and leads to what might be called the "ending of the joy-life and of desire". This is not a pleasant experience to the disciple; it leads to much aridness in the life-experience and to a sense of loss; it often takes much wise handling, and frequently time elapses before the disciple emerges on the other side of the experience.
2. This balanced condition in which the not-Self and the Self, the life-aspect and the form-aspect, are seen as they essentially are (through the aid and the use of the discriminating faculty of the mind), leads eventually to a crisis of choice, and to the major task of the disciple's life. This is the detaching of himself from the grip of form experience, and consciously, rapidly, definitely and with intention preparing himself for the great expansions of initiation.

When this dual crisis is over and that which it has evoked has been rightly handled, then the light streams forth, leading to the revelation of the relationships of form to soul. These two are then seen as one in a sense never before realised and are then regarded as possessing a relation quite different to the theoretical relationships posited in ordinary occult and religious work. It will be apparent, therefore, how a new relationship and a new type of integration then becomes possible and how the mind quality of the fifth ray (critical, analytical, separative and over-discriminating) can become, what in the middle ages it used to be called, the "common sense".

When this takes place, form and life are indeed one unity and the disciple uses the form at will as the instrument of the soul for the working out of the plans of God. These plans are at-one with the intention of the Hierarchy. We now have five words for disciples upon the five rays to study:

> Ray One . . . . Inclusion.
> Ray Two . . . . Centralisation.
> Ray Three . . . . Stillness.
> Ray Four . . . . Steadfastness.
> Ray Five . . . . Detachment. (EP2–368/71)

Ray Six

• " 'I see a vision. It satisfies desire; it feeds and stimulates its growth. I lay my life upon the altar of desire – the seen, the sensed, that which appeals to me, the satisfaction of my need – a need for that which is material, for that which feeds emotion, that satisfies the mind, that answers my demand for truth, for service, and my vision of the goal. It is the vision which I see, the dream I dream, the truth I hold, the active form which meets my need, that which I grasp and understand. *My* truth, *my* peace, *my* satisfied desire, *my* dream, *my* vision of reality, *my* limited ideal, *my* finite thought of God; – for these I struggle, fight and die.'

Love of the truth must always be. Desire and aspiration, reaching out for that which is material or soaring upward towards the vision of reality must ever find their satisfaction. For this men work, driving themselves and irking others. They love the truth as they interpret it; they love the vision and the dream, forgetting that the truth is limited by mind – narrow and set, one-pointed, not inclusive; forgetting that the vision touches but the outer fringe of mystery, and veils and hides reality.

The word goes out from soul to form: 'Run not so straight. The path that you are on leads to the outer circle of the life of God; the line goes forward to the outer rim. Stand at the centre. Look on every side. Die not for outer forms. Forget not God, Who dwells behind the vision. Love more your fellow men.' "

It will be apparent, therefore, that the sixth ray disciple has first of all to achieve the arduous task of dissociating himself from his vision, from his adored truth, from his loved ideals, from his painted picture of himself as the devoted follower and disciple, following his Master unto death, if need be; forcing himself (from very love of form) and forcing all his fellowmen to dedicate themselves to that which he sees.

It must be recognised that he lacks the wide love of the second ray disciple which is a reflection of the love of God. He is all the time occupied with *himself*, with *his* work, *his* sacrifice, *his* task, *his* ideas, and *his* activities. He, the devotee, is lost in his devotion. He, the idealist, is driven by his idea. He, the follower, runs blindly after his Master, his chosen ideal and loses himself in the chaos of his uncontrolled aspirations and the glamour of his own thoughts....

The problem, therefore, of the sixth ray aspirant is to divorce himself from the thralldom of form (though not from form) and to stand quietly at the centre, just as the third ray disciple has to learn to do. There he learns breadth of vision and a right sense of proportion. These two qualities he always lacks until the time comes when he can take his stand and there align himself with all visions, all forms of truth, all dreams of reality, and find behind them all – God and his fellow men. Then and only then can he be trusted to work with the Plan.

The alignment evoked by this "peaceful standing still" naturally produces *a crisis* and it is, as usual, a most difficult one for the aspirant to handle. It is a crisis which seems to leave him destitute of incentive, of motive, of sensation, of appreciation by others and of life purpose. The idea of "my truth, my master, my idea, my way" leaves him and as yet he has nothing to take its place. Being sixth ray, and therefore linked with the world of astral psychic life, the sixth plane, he is peculiarly sensitive to his own reactions and to the ideas of others where he and his truths are concerned. He feels a fool and considers that others are thinking him so. The crisis therefore is severe, for it has to produce a complete readjust-ment of the Self to the self. His fanaticism, his devotion, his furious driving of himself and others, his wasted efforts, and his lack of understanding of the point of view of others have all gone, but as yet nothing has taken their place. He is swept by futility and his world rocks under him. Let him stand still at the centre, fixing his eyes on the soul and ceasing activity for a brief period of time until the light breaks in....

But by facing futility and himself and by surrendering himself to the life at the centre and there holding himself poised and still, yet alert, the light will break in and reveal to the disciple that which he needs to know. He learns to express that inclusive love which is his major requirement and to let go the narrow, one-pointed attitude which he has hitherto regarded as love. He welcomes then all visions, if they serve to lift and comfort his brothers; he welcomes all truths, if they are the agents of revelation to other minds; he welcomes all dreams if they can act as incentives to his fellow men. He shares in them all, yet retains his poised position at the centre.

Thus we can see that the essential integration of this unit into his group can now take place.

The problem of the disciple upon this ray is greatly increased by the fact that the sixth ray has been the dominant ray for so many centuries and is only now passing out. Therefore the idealistic, fanatical thoughtforms, built up by the devotees upon this ray, are powerful and persistent. The world today is fanatically idealistic, and this is one of the causes of the present world situation. It is hard for the man who is the one-pointed devotee to free himself from the prevailing influence, for the energy thus generated feeds that which he seeks to leave behind. If he can, however, grasp the fact that devotion, ex-pressing itself through a personality, engenders fanaticism and that fanaticism is separative, frequently cruel, often motivated by good ideals, but that it usually overlooks the immediate reality by rushing off after a self-engendered vision of truth, he will go far along the way to solving his problem. If he can then realise that devotion, expressing itself through the soul, is love and inclusiveness plus understanding, then he will learn eventually to free himself from the idealism of others and of himself and will identify himself with that of the Hierarchy, which is the loving working out of God's Plan. It is free from hatred, from intense emphasis upon an aspect or a part, and is not limited by the sense of time. (EP2–371/5)

Ray Seven

• " 'I seek to bring the two together. The plan is in my hands. How shall I work? Where lay the emphasis? In the far distance stands the One Who *Is*. Here at my hand is form, activity, substance, and desire. Can I relate these and fashion thus a form for God? Where shall I send my thought, my power the word that I can speak?

'I, at the centre, stand, the worker in the field of magic. I know some rules, some magical controls, some Words of Power, some forces which I can direct. What shall I do? Danger there is. The task that I have undertaken is not easy of accomplishment, yet I love power. I love to see the forms emerge, created by my mind, and do their work, fulfil the plan and disappear. I can create. The rituals of the Temple of the Lord are known to me. How shall I work?

'*Love not the work.* Let love of God's eternal Plan control your life, your mind, your hand, your eye. Work towards the unity of plan and purpose which must find its lasting place on earth. Work with the Plan; focus upon your share in that great work.'

The word goes forth from soul to form: 'Stand in the centre of the pentagram, drawn upon that high place in the East within the light which ever shines. From that illumined centre work. Leave not the pentagram. Stand steady in the midst. Then draw a line from that which is without to that which is within and see the Plan take form.' "

It is not possible to be more explicit than this. This great and powerful ray is now coming into manifestation and it brings new energies to man of so potent a nature that the disciples of today must move and work with care. They are literally handling fire. It is the children who are now coming into incarnation who will eventually work more safely and more correctly with these new potencies. There is much, however, to be done in the meantime, and the disciples upon this seventh ray can ponder on this formula and seek their own interpretation of it, endeavouring first of all to stand in the East, within the protection of the pentagram. As he realises the task to be carried out and the nature of the work to be done by the seventh ray worker, and appreciates the fact that it is the magical work of producing those forms on earth which will embody the spirit of God (and in our particular time, this necessitates the building of new forms), each seventh ray disciple will see himself as a relating agent, as the one who stands in the midst of the building processes, attending to his portion of the task. This, if really grasped and deeply considered will have the effect of producing alignment. The moment that this alignment is achieved, then let the disciple remember that it will mean a tremendous inflow of power, of energy from both the aligned points, from both directions, converging upon him, as he stands in the midway place. Ponder deeply upon this truth, for it is this fact which always evokes a seventh ray crisis. It will be obvious what this crisis is. If the man concerned is materially minded, selfishly ambitious and unloving, the inpouring energy will stimulate the personality nature and he will immediately be warring furiously with all that we mean by the instinctual, psychic, intellectual nature. When all these three are stimulated, the disciple is often for a time swung off the centre into a maelstrom of magical work of the lower kind – sex magic and many forms of black magic. He is glamoured by the beauty of his motive, and deceived by the acquired potency of his personality.

If, however, he is warned of the danger and aware of the possibility, he will stand steady at the centre within the mystical pentagram, and there *suffer* until the light in the East rises upon his darkness, discovering him still at the midway point. Then comes the revelation of the Plan, for this has ever to be the motivating power of the seventh ray disciple. He works on earth, upon the outer plane of manifestation, with the construction of those forms through which the divine will can express itself. In the field of religion, he works in collaboration with the second and sixth ray disciples. In the field of government he labours, building those forms which will enable the first ray activity to be expressed. In the field of business, he co-operates with third ray energies and the executives of the Plan. In the field of science, he aids and assists the fifth ray workers. He is the expression of the builder, and the creator, bringing into outer manifestation God's Plan. He begins, however, with himself, and seeks to bring into expression the plan of his soul in his own setting and worldly situation. Until he can do this, he is unable to stand in the East within the pentagram.

It is occultly said that "the pentagram is open and a place of danger when the disciple knows not order within his own life, and when the ritual of the soul is not imposed and its rhythm not obeyed. The pentagram is closed when order is restored and the ritual of the Master is imposed". The writing goes on to say that "if the disciple enters through the open pentagram, he dies. If he passes over into the closed pentagram, he lives. If he transmutes the pentagram into a ring of fire, he serves the Plan". (EP2–375/8)

The Rays and the Etheric Body

• Here is a basic statement – one that is so basic that it governs and controls all thinking anent the etheric body:

> *The etheric body is primarily composed of the dominant energy or energies to which the man, the group, the nation, or the world reacts in any particular time cycle or world period.*

If you are to understand clearly, it is essential that I lay down certain propositions anent the etheric body which should govern all the student's thinking; if they do not, he will be approaching the truth from the wrong angle; this, modern science does not do. The limitation of modern science is its lack of vision; the hope of modern science is that it does recognise truth when proven. Truth in all circumstances is essential and in this matter science gives a desirable lead, even though it ignores and despises occultism. Occult scientists handicap themselves either because of their presentation of the truth or because of a false humility. Both are equally bad.

There are six major propositions which govern all consideration of the etheric body, and I would like to present them to students as a first step:

1. There is nothing in the manifested universe – solar, planetary or the various kingdoms in nature – which does not possess an energy form, subtle and intangible yet substantial, which controls, governs and conditions the outer physical body. This is the etheric body.

2. This energy form – underlying the solar system, the planets and all forms within their specific rings-pass-not – is itself conditioned and governed by the dominant solar or planetary energy which ceaselessly and without break in time, creates it, changes and qualifies it. The etheric body is subject to ceaseless change. This, being true of the Macrocosm, is equally true of man, the microcosm, and – through the agency of humanity – will eventually and mysteriously prove true of all the subhuman kingdoms in nature. Of this, the animal kingdom and the vegetable kingdom are already evidences.

3. The etheric body is composed of interlocking and circulating lines of force emanating from one or other, or from one or many, of the seven planes or areas of consciousness of our planetary Life.

4. These lines of energy and this closely interlocking system of streams of force are related to seven focal points or centres to be found within the etheric body. These centres are related, each of them, to certain types of incoming energy. When the energy reaching the etheric body is not related to a particular centre, then that centre remains quiescent and unawakened; when it is related and the centre is sensitive to its impact, then that centre becomes vibrant and receptive and develops as a controlling factor in the life of the man on the physical plane.

5. The dense physical body, composed of atoms – each with

its own individual life, light and activity – is held together by and is expressive of the energies which compose the etheric body. These, as will be apparent, are of two natures:

a.   The energies which form (through interlocked "lines of forceful energy") the underlying etheric body, as a whole and in relation to all physical forms. This form is qualified then by the *general* life and vitality of the plane on which the Dweller in the body functions, and therefore where his consciousness is normally focused.

b.   The particularised or specialised energies by which the individual (at this particular point in evolution, through the circumstances of his daily life and his heredity) *chooses* to govern his daily activities.

6.   The etheric body has many centres of force, responsive to the manifold energies of our planetary Life, but we shall consider only the seven major centres which respond to the inflowing energies of the seven rays. All lesser centres are conditioned by the seven major centres; this is a point which students are apt to forget. It is here that knowledge of the egoic and of the personality rays is of prime usefulness.

It can be seen, therefore, how exceedingly important this subject of energy becomes, because it controls and makes the man what he is at any given moment, and likewise indicates the plane on which he should function, and the method whereby he should govern his environment, circumstances and relationships. If this is grasped by him, it will enable him to realise that he will have to shift his whole attention from the physical or the astral planes on to the etheric levels of awareness; his objective will then be to determine what energy should control his daily expression (or energies, if he is an advanced disciple). He will realise also that as his attitude, attainment and comprehension shift to ever higher levels, his etheric body will be constantly changing and responding to the newer energies. These energies he will be *will-fully* bringing in; this is the right use of the word "will-full". (TEV–141/4)

• *...The effect of the impact of energy is dependent upon the nature of the vehicle of response.* According to his equipment and the nature of his bodies, so will man react to the inflowing energies. This is a fundamental statement. It is a law and should be most carefully considered.... Each man brings to the impact of [a] vibration a type of physical body, an astral or emotional nature, and a mind which are in each case different from all the others. The use each makes of the stimulating energy will be different; the focus of his consciousness is very different; his type of mind is quite different; his centres, their activity and their internal organisation are different. And it is the same for groups, organisations and nations. (EXH–85)

• The etheric body of the individual is, as you know, a part of the etheric body of humanity and this, in its turn, is an aspect of the etheric body of the planet, which is likewise an intrinsic part of the etheric body of the solar system. Incidentally, in this far-reaching factual relationship, you have the basis of all astrological influences. Man moves, therefore, in a whirlpool of forces of all types and qualities. He is composed of energies in every part of his manifested and unmanifested expression; he is, therefore, related to all other energies. His task is one of supreme difficulty and needs the great length of the evolutionary cycle. With the mass of world energies and systemic forces we cannot here deal, but we will confine ourselves to the consideration of the individual problem, advising the student to endeavour to extend his understanding of the microcosmic situation to the macrocosmic.

[The aspirant] knows that if that intermediate aspect of himself, the etheric body, can be controlled and rightly directed, then vision and expression will and must finally coincide. He is also aware that the dense physical body (the outer tangible appearance) is only an automaton, obedient to whatever forces and energies are the controlling factors in the subjective, conditioning the man. Is that physical body to be controlled by emotional force, pouring through the sacral centre and producing desire for the satisfaction of the physical appetites, or through the solar plexus leading to emotional satisfaction of some kind? Is it to be responsive to the mind and work largely under the impulse of projected thought? Is it perhaps to be directed by an energy greater than any of these but hitherto apparently impotent, the energy of the soul as an expression of pure Being? Is it to be swept into action under the impulse of sentient reactions, ideas and thoughts, emanating from other human beings or is it to be motivated and spurred into activity under the direction of the spiritual Hierarchy? Such are some of the questions to which answers must be found. The stage of aspiring, dreaming and of wishful thinking must now be superseded by direct action and by the carefully planned use of the available forces, swept into activity by the breath, under the direction of the inner eye and controlled by the spiritual man. Which energies can and must be thus used? What forces must be brought under direction? In what manner can they be controlled? Should they be ignored and so rendered futile by that ignoring, or are they forces which are needed in the great creative work?

It will be apparent to you that the first step the spiritual investigator has to take is to ascertain – truly and in the light of his soul – where exactly is his focus of identification. By that I mean: Is his major use of energy to be found upon the mental plane? Is he predominantly emotional and utilising force from the astral plane the greater part of the time? Can he contact the soul and bring in soul energy in such a manner that it negates or offsets his personality force? Can he thus live like a soul upon the physical plane, via the etheric body? If he earnestly studies this problem, he will in time discover which forces are dominant in the etheric body and will become aware *consciously* of the times and experience which call for the expenditure of soul energy. This, my brother, will take time and will be the result of prolonged observation and a close analysis of acts and sentient reactions, of words and thoughts. We are here concerned, as you can see, with an intensely practical problem which is at the same time an intrinsic part of our study and which will be evocative of basic changes in the life of the disciple.

He will add to this observation and analysis of the strength of the force or the forces engaged, the conditions which will swing them into action, the frequency of their appearance, indicating to him novelty or habit, and likewise the nature of their expression. In this way, he will arrive at a new understanding of the conditioning factors which work through his vital body and make him – upon the physical plane – what he essentially is. This will prove to him of deep spiritual and significant help.

This period of observation is, however, confined to mental and intelligent observation. It forms the background of the work to be done, giving assurance and knowledge but leaving the situation as it was. His next step is to become aware of the quality of the forces applied; in ascertaining this, he will find it necessary to discover not only his soul ray and his personality ray but to know also the rays of his mental apparatus, and his emotional nature. This will lead necessarily to another period of investigation and careful observation, if he is not already aware of them. When I tell you that to this information he must add a close consideration of the potencies of the forces and energies reaching him astrologically, you will see what a stern task he has set himself. Not only has he to isolate his five ray energies, but he has to allow for the energy of his sun sign as it conditions his personality, and of his rising sign as it seeks to stimulate that personality into soul responsiveness, thus working out soul purpose through personality co-operation.

There are, therefore, seven factors which condition the quality of the forces which seek expression through the etheric body:

1. The ray of the soul.
2. The ray of the personality.
3. The ray of the mind.
4. The ray of the emotional nature.
5. The ray of the physical vehicle.
6. The energy of the sun sign.
7. The influence of the rising sign.

Once, however, these are ascertained and there is some assurance as to their factual truth, the entire problem begins to clarify and the disciple can work with knowledge and understanding. He becomes a scientific worker in the field of hidden forces. He knows then what he is doing, with what energies he must work, and he begins to *feel* these energies as they find their way into the etheric vehicle.

Now comes the stage wherein he is in a position to find out the reality and the work of the seven centres which provide inlet and outlet for the moving forces and energies with which he is immediately concerned in this particular incarnation. He enters upon a prolonged period of observation, of experiment and experience and institutes a trial and error, a success and failure, campaign which will call for all the strength, courage and endurance of which he is capable. (GWP–246/50)

• In all I have said anent the etheric body of men, anent the planet, anent the spirit of the earth, the crux of the whole situation lies in the fact that the five rays at this time have the seventh ray as their predominating ray. The seventh ray is the ray that controls the etheric and the devas of the ethers. It controls the seventh sub-plane of all planes but it dominates at this time the seventh sub-plane of the physical plane. Being in the fourth round also, when a ray comes into definite incarnation, it not only controls on planes of the same number but has a special influence on the fourth sub-plane. Note how this works at this time in the three worlds:

1.   The fourth ether, the lowest of the ethers, is to be the next physical plane of consciousness. Etheric matter is even now becoming visible to some, and will be entirely visible at the end of this century to many.
2.   The fourth sub-plane of the astral holds the majority of men when they pass over and consequently much work on the greatest number can therefore be accomplished.
3.   The fourth mental sub-plane is the plane of devachan. (TWM–373/4)

• It has become a truism with students of the occult that the etheric body conditions, controls and determines the life expression of the incarnated individual. It is a secondary truism that this etheric body is the conveyor of the forces of the personality, through the medium of the centres, and thereby galvanises the physical body into activity. These forces, routed through the centres, are those of the integrated personality as a whole, or are simply the forces of the astral or emotional body and the mind body; they also transmit the force of the personality ray or the energy of the soul ray, according to the point in evolution reached by the man. The physical body, therefore, is not a principle. *It is conditioned and does not condition* – a point oft forgotten. It is a victim of personality life or the triumphant expression of soul energy. (EH–190)

The Centres as Transmitters of Ray Energy

• [The] Ray influences work through their focal points in all cases (macrocosmic and microcosmic) and these are the etheric centres. The centres, in the case of all Beings, are ever seven in number, and are composed of deva and human units in group activity, or of force vortices which contain in latency, and hold in ordered activity, cells with the potentiality of human manifestation. Forget not the occult truism that all forms of existence pass at one stage of their career through the human kingdom. (TCF–437)

• The seven centres with which man is concerned are themselves found to exist in two groups: a lower four, which are related to the four Rays of Attributes, or the four minor rays, and are, therefore, closely connected with the quaternary, both microcosmic and macrocosmic, and a higher three which are transmitters for the three rays of aspect.

These energy centres are transmitters of energy from many and varied sources which might be briefly enumerated as follows:

a. From the seven Rays, via the seven subrays of any specific monadic ray.

b. From the triple aspects of the planetary Logos as He manifests through a scheme.

c. From what are called "the sevenfold divisions of the logoic Heart", or the sun in its sevenfold essential nature, as it is seen lying esoterically behind the outer physical solar form.

d. From the seven Rishis of the Great Bear; this pours in via the Monad and is transmitted downward, merging on the higher levels of the mental plane with seven streams of energy from the Pleiades which come in as the psychical force demonstrating through the solar Angel.

All these various streams of energy are passed through certain groups or centres, becoming more active and demonstrating with a freer flow as the course of evolution is pursued. As far as man is concerned at present, this energy all converges, and seeks to energise his physical body, and direct his action via the seven etheric centres. These centres receive the force in a threefold manner:

a. Force from the Heavenly Man and, therefore, from the seven Rishis of the Great Bear via the Monad.

b. Force from the Pleiades, via the solar Angel or Ego.

c. Force from the planes, from the Raja Devas of a plane, or fohatic energy, via the spirillae of a permanent atom.

It is this fact which accounts for the gradual growth and development of a man. At first it is the force of the plane substance, which directs him, causing him to identify himself with the grosser substance and to consider himself a man, a member of the fourth Kingdom, and to be convinced, therefore, that he is the Not-Self. Later as force from the Ego pours in, his psychical evolution proceeds (I use the word "psychical" here in its higher connotation) and he begins to consider himself as the Ego, the Thinker, the One who uses the form. Finally, energy from the Monad begins to be responded to and he knows himself to be neither the man nor the angel, but a divine essence or Spirit. These three types of energy demonstrate during manifestation as Spirit, Soul, and Body, and through them the three aspects of the Godhead meet and converge in man, and lie latent in every atom. (TCF–1156/8)

• ...One aspect of the *Science of Impression*...is the place of the centres as focal points, as transmitters or as agencies for the seven ray energies. It is known to esotericists that each of the seven centres comes under the influence or is the recipient of some ray energy, and there is a general acceptance of the fact that the head centre is the agent of the first Ray of Will or Power, the heart centre is the custodian of second Ray energy of Love-Wisdom, whilst the third Ray of active creative Intelligence passes through and energises the throat centre. These Rays of Aspect do find expression through the three centres above the diaphragm, and – on the larger scale – through Shamballa, the Hierarchy and Humanity. It is, however, equally true that Shamballa is primarily second ray as it is expressed, because that is the ray of the present solar system of which Shamballa is a part; and that the first ray, or its dynamic life aspect, is focused in the heart, for the heart is the centre of life. The great centre which we call Humanity is predominantly governed by the third Ray of Active Intelligence. This ray energy arrives at the throat centre via the head and the heart centres. I am pointing this out for two reasons which must form part of your thinking as you study this science:

1. All the centres come under the influence of all the rays, and this must surely be obvious in relation to average and undeveloped human beings. Were this not so, such human beings would be unable to respond to first ray, second ray and third ray energy, for the centres above the diaphragm are, in their case, inactive.
2. In time and space and during the evolutionary process, it is not possible to say which centre is expressing the energy of any particular ray, for there is a constant movement and activity. The centre at the base of the spine is frequently the expression of first ray energies. This is apt to be confusing. The human mind seeks to make everything precise, stable, to bracket certain relations or to assign certain centres to

certain ray energies. This cannot be done. (TEV–135/6)

• ...The incoming seventh ray plays through the planetary sacral centre, and then through the sacral centre of every human being. Because of this, we can look for the anticipated developments in that human function which we designate the sex function. We shall see consequent changes in the attitude of man towards this most difficult problem. (EP1–268)

• ...The evolution of the centres is a slow and gradual thing, and proceeds in ordered cycles varying according to the ray of man's Monad.

The life of the Pilgrim can be, for purposes of discussion, divided into three main periods:

1. That period wherein he is under the influence of the Personality Ray.
2. That wherein he comes under the Ray of the Ego.
3. That wherein the Monadic Ray holds sway.

The first period is by far the longest, and covers the vast progression of the centuries wherein the activity aspect of the threefold self is being developed. Life after life slips away during which the aspect of manas or mind is being slowly wrought out, and the human being comes more and more under the control of his intellect, operating through his physical brain.... Centuries go by and the man becomes ever more actively intelligent, and the field of his life more suitable for the coming in of this second aspect.... The Love-Wisdom aspect is latent in the Self, and is part of the monadic content, but the.... Activity-Intelligence aspect precedes its manifestation in time. The Tabernacle in the Wilderness preceded the building of the Temple of Solomon; the kernel of wheat has to lie in the darkness of mother Earth before the golden perfected ear can be seen, and the Lotus has to cast its roots down into the mud before the beauty of the blossom can be produced.

The second period, wherein the egoic ray holds sway, is not so long comparatively; it...marks the lives wherein the man throws his forces on the side of evolution, disciplines his life, steps upon the Probationary Path, and continues up to the third Initiation. Under the régime of the Personality Ray, the man proceeds upon the five Rays to work consciously with Mind, the sixth sense, passing first upon the four minor Rays and eventually upon the third. He works upon the third Ray, or that of active Intelligence, and from thence proceeds to one of the subrays of the two other major Rays, if the third is not his egoic Ray.

Enquiry might naturally arise as to whether the egoic ray is necessarily one of the three major rays, and if Initiates and Masters are not to be found upon some of the rays of mind, the minor four.

The answer lies here: The egoic ray can always be one of the seven, but we need to remember that, in this astral-buddhic solar system, wherein love and wisdom are being brought into objectivity, the bulk of the monads are on the love-wisdom ray. The fact, therefore, of its being the synthetic ray has a vast significance. This is the system of the SON, whose name is Love. This is the divine incarnation of Vishnu. The Dragon of Wisdom is in manifestation, and He brings into incarnation those cosmic Entities who are in essence identical with Himself. After the third Initiation all human beings find themselves on their monadic ray, on one of the three major rays, and the fact that Masters and Initiates are found on all the rays is due to the following two factors:

First. Each major Ray has its subrays, which correspond to all the seven.

Second. Many of the guides of the race transfer from one ray to another as They are needed, and as the work may require. When one of the Masters or Initiates is transferred it causes a complete re-adjustment.

When a Master likewise leaves the hierarchy of our Planet to take up work elsewhere, it frequently necessitates a complete re-organisation, and a fresh admission of members into the great White Lodge. These facts have been but little realised. We might here also take the opportunity to point out that we are not dealing with earth conditions when we consider the

Rays, nor are we only concerned with the evolution of the Monads upon this planet, but are equally concerned with the solar system in which our earth holds a necessary but not supreme place. The earth is an organism within a greater one, and this fact needs wider recognition. The sons of men upon this planet so often view the whole system as if the earth were in the position of the sun, the centre of the solar organism....

The third period, wherein the monadic ray makes itself felt on the physical plane, is by far the shortest.... It marks the period of achievement, of liberation, and therefore, although it is the shortest period when viewed from below upward, it is the period of comparative permanence when viewed from the plane of the Monad. (TCF–173/8)

Factors Determining
Individual Differences

• The nature of our septenary universe must be considered, and the relation of the threefold human being to the divine Trinity must be noted. A general idea of the entire symbolic picture is of value. Each student, as he takes up the study of the rays, must steadily bear in mind that he himself – as a human unit – finds his place on one or other of these rays. The problem thus produced is a very real one. The physical body may be responsive to one type of ray force, whilst the personality as a whole may vibrate in unison with another. The ego or soul may find itself upon still a third type of ray, thus responding to another type of ray energy. The question of the monadic ray brings in still another factor in many cases, but this can only be implied and not really elucidated. As I have oft told you, it is only the initiate of the third initiation who can come in touch with his monadic ray, or his highest life aspect, and the humble aspirant cannot as yet ascertain whether he is a monad of Power, of Love or of Intelligent Activity. (EP1–xxiv)

• One point I feel the need definitely to re-emphasise and that is the necessity, when considering the human being and his expression and existence, to remember that we are really considering *energy*, and the relation or non-relation of forces. As long as this is carefully borne in mind, we shall not go astray as we deal with our subject. We are considering related units of energy, functioning in a field of energy; remembering this always, we shall (at least symbolically) be enabled to get a fairly clear idea of our theme. As long as we regard our problem as consisting of the inter-relation of many energies, their fusion and their balancing, plus the final synthesis of two major energies, their fusion and their balancing, we shall arrive at some measure of understanding and subsequent solution. The field of energy which we call the soul (the major energy with which man is concerned) absorbs, dominates or utilises the lesser energy which we call the personality. This it is necessary for us to realise; and to remember, at the same time, that this personality is itself composed of four types of energy. (EP2–424/5)

• ...Every human being is swept into manifestation on the impulse of some ray, and is coloured by that particular ray quality, which determines the form aspect, indicates the way he should go, and enables him (by the time the third initiation is reached) to have sensed and then to have co-operated with his ray purpose. After the third initiation he begins to sense the synthetic purpose towards which all the seven rays are working... (EP1–61)

• In the human being you have...two major energies anchored; one unrealised, to which we give the name of the PRESENCE, the other realised, to which we give the name of the Angel of the PRESENCE. These are the soul (the solar angel) and the monad. One embodies the monadic ray and the other the soul ray, and both of these energies actively or subtly condition the personality.

The other five energies which are present are the ray of the mind or the conditioning force of the mental body; the ray of the emotional nature, and the ray of the physical body, plus a fourth ray which is that of the personality. The ray of the physical body esoterically "ascends upward towards juncture, whereas the others all move down", to quote an ancient writing. The ray of the personality is a consequence or result of the vast cycle of incarnations. You have therefore:

1. The monadic ray.
2. The soul ray.
   3. Ray of the Mind.
   4. Ray of the emotions.
   5. Ray of the physical body.
6. Ray of the personality.
   7. The planetary ray.

The planetary ray is always the third Ray of Active Intelligence because it conditions our Earth and is of great potency, enabling the human being to "transact his business in the world of planetary physical life".

I have made only casual reference to these rays elsewhere and have said little anent the planetary ray; I have laid the emphasis upon another analysis of the conditioning rays, and in this analysis recognised only five rays for practical usefulness to the man. These are:

1. The soul ray.
2. The personality ray.
   3. The mental ray.
   4. The astral ray.
   5. The ray of the physical body.

However, with the creation and development of the antahkarana, the ray of the monad must also be brought into line, and then that which is its polar opposite, the planetary "livingness", the third ray, will have to be recognised. I have here imparted a point of much importance to you. All these energies play an active part in the life cycle of every man and cannot be totally ignored by the healer, even though the information may be relatively useless at this time. (EH–590/1)

• Every human being is, in reality, like a miniature whirlpool in that great ocean of Being in which he lives and moves – ceaselessly in motion until such time as the soul "breathes upon the waters" (or forces) and the Angel of the Presence descends into the whirlpool. Then all becomes still. The waters stirred by the rhythm of life, and later stirred violently by the descent of the Angel, respond to the Angel's healing power and are changed "into a quiet pool into which the little ones can enter and find the healing which they need". So says the *Old Commentary*. (EH–140)

• One of the first things we need to grasp, as we study man and the rays, is the large number of these ray influences which play upon him, and which form him, and "enliven" him, and make him the complexity he is.... It might therefore be noted that the following rays and influences must be considered in the case of every individual man, for they make him what he is and determine his problem:

1.   The ray of the solar system itself.
2.   The ray of the planetary Logos of our planet.
3.   The ray of the human kingdom itself.
4.   Our particular racial ray, the ray that determines the Aryan race.
5.   The rays that govern any particular cycle.
6.   The national ray, or that ray influence which is peculiarly influencing a particular nation.
7.   The ray of the soul, or ego.
8.   The ray of the personality.
9.   The rays governing:
     a. The mental body.
     b. The emotional or astral body.
     c. The physical body.

There are other rays, but the above are the most powerful and have the greater conditioning power. (EP1–333/4)

• Students of human nature (and this all aspirants should be) would do well to bear in mind that there are temporary differences. People differ in:

a.   Ray (which affects predominantly the magnetism of the life).
b.   Approach to truth, either the occult or the mystic path having the stronger drawing power.

c. Polarisation, deciding the emotional, mental or physical intent of a life.

d. Status in evolution, leading to the diversities seen among men.

e. Astrological sign, determining the trend of any particular life.

f. Race, bringing the personality under the peculiar racial thought form.

The sub-ray on which a man is found, that minor ray which varies from incarnation to incarnation, largely gives him his colouring for this life. It is his secondary hue. Forget not, the primary ray of the Monad continues through the aeon. It changes not. It is one of the three primary rays that eventually synthesise the sons of men. The ray of the ego varies from round to round, and, in more evolved souls, from race to race, and comprises one of the five rays of our present evolution. It is the predominating ray to which a man's causal body vibrates. It may correspond to the ray of the monad, or it may be one of the complementary colours to the primary. The ray of the personality varies from life to life, till the gamut of the seven sub-rays of the Monadic ray has been passed through.

Therefore, in dealing with people whose monads are on a similar or complementary ray it will be found that they approach each other sympathetically. We must remember however that evolution must be far advanced for the ray of the monad to influence extensively. So the majority of cases come not under this category.

With average advanced men, who are struggling to approximate themselves to the ideal, similarity of the egoic ray will produce mutual comprehension, and friendship follows. It is easy for two people on the same egoic ray to comprehend each other's point of view, and they become great friends, with unshaken faith in each other, for each recognizes the other acting as he himself would act.

But when (added to the egoic similarity of ray) you have the same ray of personality, then you have one of those rare things a perfect friendship, a successful marriage, an unbreakable link between two. This is rare indeed.

When you have two people on the same personality ray but with the egoic ray dissimilar, you may have those brief and sudden friendships and affinities, that are as ephemeral as a butterfly. These things need bearing in mind and with their recognition comes the ability to be adaptable. Clarity of vision results in a circumspect attitude.

Another cause of difference can be due to the polarization of the bodies. Unless this too meets with recognition in dealing with people lack of comprehension ensues. When you use the term: "a man polarized in his astral body" – you really mean a man whose ego works principally through that vehicle. Polarity indicates the clarity of the channel....

When you speak of the ego taking more or less control of a man you really mean that he has built into his bodies matter of the higher sub-planes.

The ego takes control with interest only when the man has almost entirely eliminated matter of the seventh, sixth, and fifth sub-planes from his vehicles. When he has built in a certain proportion of matter of the fourth sub-plane the ego extends his control; when there is a certain proportion of the third sub-plane, then the man is on the Path; when second sub-plane matter predominates then he takes initiation, and when he has matter only of atomic substance, he becomes a Master. Therefore, the sub-plane a man is on is of importance, and the recognition of his polarization elucidates life.

The third thing you need to remember is that even when these two points are admitted, the age of the soul's experience frequently causes lack of comprehension. The above two points do not carry us very far, for the capacity to sense a man's ray is not for this race as yet. Approximate supposition and the use of the intuition is all that is now possible. The little evolved cannot comprehend completely the much evolved, and in a lesser degree, the advanced ego comprehends not an initiate. The greater can apprehend the lesser but the reverse is not the case. (TWM–111/3)

● ...In every rootrace you have a continuous mingling and intermingling of the rays with what might be called the "constant" or dominating ray, which appears and re-appears with greater frequency and potency than do the other rays. There is therefore a close correspondence between certain rays and certain races, with their subraces, and these are coloured by these predominant ray influences. (EP1–317)

• ...A recognition of those ray problems and liabilities which exist in your own life and in the lives of those around you involves no criticism on my part or any on yours. The facts of nature exist; the wise man faces them, knowing them for what they are and he then endeavours to transcend them.... (DNA1–627)

• ...Until there is a more adequate knowledge of ray qualities, and until a man's soul ray is determined and the effect of that ray upon the personality ray is charted and known, the true nature of his temperament and the real subjective cause of his varied reactions, his complexes and inhibitions will remain a problem most difficult to handle. When, for instance, psychologists realise that it is the play of soul quality and energy which determines whether a man in any particular life will function as an introvert or an extrovert, then they will work to produce that balancing of the ray forces which will make the man able to express himself in such a way that the path to the outer world is left open, and that to the inner world is also cleared of obstacles.

What is the real nature of a true mystic or introvert? He is one whose soul force, ray or quality is too strong for the personality to handle. The man then finds that the path to the inner worlds of desire-emotion, of mind and of spiritual vision are, for him, the line of least resistance, and the physical plane integration and expression suffer as a consequence. The "pull" of the soul offsets the outer "pull", and the man becomes a visionary mystic. I refer not to the practical mystic who is on the way to becoming a white occultist. The reverse condition can also be true, and then you have the pure extrovert. The personality ray focuses itself upon the physical plane, and the inner lure of the soul is temporarily offset, sometimes for several lives. (EP1–160/1)

The Spiritual Path
and the Rays

• Ray one governs the Path of Initiation, producing detachment from form, the destruction of all that hinders, and fostering that dynamic will in the initiate which will enable him to take the needed steps towards the Initiator. (EP1–351)

• Ray two governs the Path of Discipleship and transmutes knowledge into wisdom, feeding likewise the Christ life in each disciple. (EP1–351)

• ...Ray six governs the Path of Probation and nourishes the fires of idealism in the aspirant. (EP1–351)

• Our present task is that of treading the Path of Probation or of Discipleship and of learning discipline, dispassion, and the other two necessities on the Way, – discrimination and decentralisation. It is possible, nevertheless, to indicate the goal and point out the potency of the forces to which we shall be increasingly subjected as we pass – as some of us can so pass – on to the Path of Accepted Discipleship. This we will do in the form of seven stanzas[1] which will give a hint (if one is an aspirant) of the technique to which one will be exposed; if one has passed further on the Way, they will give one a command which, as a disciple with spiritual insight one will obey, because one is awakened; if

---

[1] These seven stanzas comprise the Law of Repulse. The effect of this law...as it works out in the world of discipleship and destroys that which hinders, sends the pilgrim hurrying back consciously along one of the seven rays that lead to the centre.

one is an initiate, they will evoke the comment: "This I know."

The Direction of Ray 1

"The garden stands revealed. In ordered beauty live its flowers and trees. The murmur of the bees and insects on their winged flight is heard on every side. The air is rich with perfume. The colours riot to the blue of heaven....

The wind of God, His breath divine, sweeps through the garden.... Low lie the flowers. Bending, the trees are devastated by the wind. Destruction of all beauty is followed by the rain. The sky is black. Ruin is seen. Then death....

Later, another garden! but the time seems far away. Call for a gardener. The gardener, the soul, responds. Call for the rain, the wind, the scorching sun. Call for the gardener. Then let the work go on. Ever destruction goes before the rule of beauty. Ruin precedes the real. The garden and the gardener must awake! The work proceeds."

The Direction of Ray 2

"The Scholar knows the truth. All is revealed to him. Surrounded by his books, and sheltered in the world of thought, he burrows like a mole, and finds his way into the darkness; he arrives at knowledge of the world of natural things. His eye is closed. His eyes are opened wide. He dwells within his world in deep content.

Detail on detail enter into the content of his world of thought. He stores the nuggets of the knowledge of the world, as a squirrel stores its nuts. The storehouse now is adequately full.... Sudden a spade descends, for the thinker tends the garden of his thought, and thus destroys the passages of mind. Ruin arrives, destroying fast the storehouse of the mind, the safe security, the darkness and the warmth of a satisfied enquiry. All is removed. The light of summer enters in and the darkened crannies of the mind see light.... Naught is left but light, and that cannot be used. The eyes are blinded and the one eye seeth not as yet....

Slowly the eye of wisdom must be opened. Slowly the love of that which is the true, the beautiful and good must enter the dark passages of worldly thought. Slowly the torch of light, the fire of right must burn the garnered treasures of the past, yet show their basic usefulness....

The seven ways of light must wean away the attention of the Scholar from all that has been found and stored and used. This he repulses and finds his way into that Hall of Wisdom which is built upon a hill, and not deep under ground. Only the opened eye can find this way."

The Direction of Ray 3

"Surrounded by a multitude of threads, buried in folds and folds of woven goods, the Weaver sits. No Light can enter where he sits. By the light of a tiny candle, carried upon the summit of his head, he dimly sees. He gathers handful after handful of the threads and seeks to weave the carpet of his thoughts and dreams, his desires and his aims. His feet move steadily; his hands work swiftly; his voice, without cessation, chants the words: 'I weave the pattern which I seek and like. The warp and woof is planned by my desire. I gather here a thread and here a colour. I gather there another. I blend the colours and I mix and blend the threads. As yet I cannot see the pattern, but it will surely measure up to my desire.'

Loud voices, and a movement from outside the darkened chamber where the Weaver sits; they grow in volume and in power. A window breaks and, though the Weaver cries aloud, blinded by the sudden light, the sun shines in upon his woven carpet. Its ugliness is thus revealed....

A voice proclaims: 'Look from out thy window, Weaver, and see the pattern in the skies, the model of the plan, the colour and the beauty of the whole. Destroy the carpet which you have for ages wrought. It does not meet your need.... Then weave again, Weaver. Weave in the light of day. Weave, as you see the plan.' "

The Direction of Ray 4

" 'I take and mix and blend. I bring together that which I desire. I harmonise the whole.'

Thus spoke the Mixer, as he stood within his darkened chamber. 'I realise the unseen beauty of the world. Colour I know and sound I know. I hear the music of the spheres, and note on note and chord on chord, they speak their thought to me. The voices which I hear intrigue and draw me, and with the sources of these sounds I seek to work. I seek to paint and blend the pigments needed. I must create the music which will draw to me those who like the pictures which I make, the colours which I blend, the music which I can evoke. Me, they will therefore like, and me, they will adore....'

But crashing came a note of music, a chord of sound which drove the Mixer of sweet sounds to quiet. His sounds died out within the Sound and only the great chord of God was heard.

A flood of light poured in. His colours faded out. Around him naught but darkness could be seen, yet in the distance loomed the light of God. He stood between his nether darkness and the blinding light. His world in ruins lay around. His friends were gone. Instead of harmony, there was dissonance. Instead of beauty, there was found the darkness of the grave....

The voice then chanted forth these words: 'Create again, my child, and build and paint and blend the tones of beauty, but this time for the world and not thyself.' The Mixer started then his work anew and worked again."

The Direction of Ray 5

"Deep in a pyramid, on all sides built around by stone, in the deep dark of that stupendous place, a mind and brain (embodied in a man) were working. Outside the pyramid, the world of God established itself. The sky was blue; the winds blew free; the trees and flowers opened themselves unto the sun. But in the pyramid, down in its dim laboratory, a Worker stood, toiling at work. His test tubes and his frail appliances he used with skill. In rows and rows, the retorts for fusing, and for blending, for crystallising and for that which sought division, stood with their flaming fires. The heat was great. The toil severe....

Dim passages, in steady progress, led upward to the summit. There a wide window stood, open unto the blue of heaven, and carrying one clear ray down to the worker in the depths.... He worked and toiled. He struggled onwards toward his dream, the vision of an ultimate discovery. He sometimes found the thing he sought, and sometimes failed; but never found that which could give to him the key to all the rest.... In deep despair, he cried aloud unto the God he had forgot: 'Give me the key. I alone can do no more good. Give me the key.' Then silence reigned....

Through the opening on the summit of the pyramid, dropped from the blue of heaven, a key came down. It landed at the feet of the discouraged worker. The key was of pure gold; the shaft of light; upon the key a label, and writ in blue, these words: 'Destroy that which thou has built and build anew. But only build when thou has climbed the upward way, traversed the gallery of tribulation and entered into light within the chamber of the king. Build from the heights, and thus shew forth the value of the depths.'

The Worker then destroyed the objects of his previous toil, sparing three treasures which he knew were good, and upon which the light could shine. He struggled towards the chamber of the king. And still he struggles."

The Direction of Ray 6

" 'I love and live and love again,' the frenzied Follower cried aloud, blinded by his desire for the teacher and the truth, but seeing naught but that which lay before his eyes. He wore on either side the blinding aids of every fanatic divine adventure. Only the long and narrow tunnel was his home and place of high endeavour. He had no vision except of that which was the space before his eyes. He had no scope for sight, – no height, no depth, no wide extension. He had but room to go one way. He went that way alone, or dragging those who asked the way of him. He saw a vision, shifting as he moved, and taking varying form; each vision was to him the symbol of his highest dreams, the height of his desire.

He rushed along the tunnel, seeking that which lay ahead. He saw not much and only one thing at a time, – a person or a truth, a bible or his picture of his God, an appetite, a dream, but only one! Sometimes he gathered in his arms the vision that he saw, and found it naught. Sometimes, he reached the person whom he loved and found, instead of visioned beauty, a person like himself. And thus he tried. He wearied of his search; he whipped himself to effort new.

The opening dimmed its light. A shutter seemed to close. The vision he had seen no longer shone. The Follower stumbled in the dark. Life ended and the world of thought was lost.... Pendent he seemed. He hung with naught below, before, behind, above. To him, naught was.

From deep within the temple of his heart, he heard a Word. It spoke with clarity and power: 'Look, deep within, around on every hand. The light is everywhere, within thy heart, in Me, in all that breathes, in all that is. Destroy thy tunnel, which thou has for ages long constructed. Stand free, in custody of all the world.' The Follower answered: 'How shall I break my tunnel down? How can I find a way?' No answer came....

Another pilgrim in the dark came up, and groping, found the Follower. 'Lead me and others to the Light,' he cried. The Follower found no words, no indicated Leader, no formulas of truth, no forms or ceremonies. He found himself a leader, and drew others to the light, – the light that shone on every hand. He worked and struggled forward. His hand held others, and for their sake, he hid his shame, his fear, his hopelessness and his despair. He uttered words of surety and faith in life, and light and God, in love and understanding....

His tunnel disappeared. He noticed not its loss. Upon the play-ground of the world he stood with many fellow-players, wide to the light of day. In the far distance stood a mountain blue, and from its summit issued forth a voice which said: 'Come forward to the mountain top and on its summit learn the invocation of a Saviour.' To this great task the Follower, now a leader, bent his energies. He still pursues this way...."

The Direction of Ray 7

"Under an arch between two rooms, the seventh Magician stood. One room was full of light and life and power, of stillness which was purpose and a beauty which was space. The other room was full of movement, a sound of great activity, a chaos without form, of work which had no true objective. The eyes of the Magician were fixed on chaos. He liked it not. His back was towards the room of vital stillness. He knew it not. The arch was tottering overhead....

He murmured in despair: 'For ages I have stood and sought to solve the problem of this room; to rearrange the chaos so that beauty might shine forth, and the goal of my desire. I sought to weave these colours into a dream of beauty, and to harmonise the many sounds. Achievement lacks. Naught but my failure can be seen. And yet I know there is a difference between that which I can see before my eyes and that which I begin to sense behind my back. What shall I do?'

Above the head of the Magician, and just behind his back, and yet within the room of ordered beauty, a magnet vast began to oscillate.... It caused the revolution of the man, within the arch, which tottered to a future fall. The magnet turned him round until he faced the scene and room, unseen before....

Then through the centre of his heart the magnet poured its force attractive. The magnet poured its force repulsive. It reduced the chaos until its forms no longer could be seen. Some aspects of a beauty, unrevealed before, emerged. And from the room a light shone forth and, by its powers and life, forced the Magician to move forward into light, and leave the arch of peril."

Such are some thoughts, translated from an ancient metrical arrangement, which may throw some light upon the duality of personality and the work to be done by the beings found upon the septenate of rays. Know we where we stand? Do we realise what we have to do? As we strive to enter into light, let us count no price too great to pay for that revelation. (EP2–166/72)

Meditation

• Meditation is a technique of the mind which eventually produces correct, unimpeded relationship; this is another name for alignment. It is therefore the establishment of a direct channel, not only between the one source, the monad, and its expression, the purified and controlled personality, but also between the seven centres in the human etheric vehicle. This is – perhaps astonishingly to you – putting the results of meditation on the basis of physical, or rather of etheric, effects, and may be regarded by you as indicating the very lowest phase of such results. This is due to the fact that you lay the emphasis upon your mental reaction to the produced alignment, on the satisfaction you acquire from such an alignment, in which you register a new world or worlds of phenomena, and on the new concepts and ideas which consequently impinge upon your mind. But the true results (as divine and as esoterically desirable) are correct alignment, right relationship, and clear channels for the seven energies in the microcosmic system, thereby bringing about eventually a full expression of divinity. (EH–620/1)

Ray Forms in Meditation

• This is a profoundly interesting and vast subject, and may only be indicated in general terms. Certain forms, built up on the numerical aspect of the various rays, are the special property of those rays and embody their geometrical significance, demonstrating their place in the system. Some of these forms being on the concrete rays or building rays are the line of least resistance for the occultist, while other forms on the abstract or attributive rays are more easily followed by the mystic.

These forms are for three objects:–

a. They put the pupil in direct contact with his own ray, either the egoic or personality ray.

b. They link him up with his group on the inner planes, either the group of servers, the group of invisible helpers, or later with his egoic group.

c. They tend to merge the occult and the mystic paths in the life of the pupil. Should he be on the mystic path he will work at the forms upon the Rays of Aspect, and so develop knowledge of the concrete side of Nature – that side which works under law. You can reverse the case for the man of occult tendency, till the time comes when the paths merge and all forms are alike to the Initiate.

You have to remember that at this point of merging a man works ever primarily on his own ray when he has transcended the personality and found the egoic note. Then he manipulates matter of his own ray, and works through his own ray-forms with their six representative sub-ray forms until he is adept, and knows the secret of synthesis. These forms are taught by the Teacher to the pupil.

You will find that though I have imparted but little on this subject, yet, if you brood over what I have given, it contains much. It may give those who wisely assimilate it the key they seek for their next step on. (LOM–157/8)

• These forces, or virtues, or influences (I reiterate synonymous terms because of the need of clear thinking on your part) are gradually received into the bodies of the personality with ever greater facility and fuller expression. As the bodies are refined they provide better mediums for incoming forces, and the quality of any particular force, – or, to reverse it, the force of any particular quality – becomes more perfectly expressed. Here comes in the work of the student in meditation. Early in evolution these forces played through and on the bodies of a man with little understanding on his part, and small ability to profit thereby. But as time proceeds, he comprehends more and more the value of all that eventuates, and seeks to profit by the sum of the qualities of his life. Herein comes opportunity. In the intelligent apprehension of quality, in the striving after virtue, and in the building-in of God-like attribute, comes response to those forces and a facilitating of their action. The student of meditation ponders on those forces or qualities, he seeks to extract their essence, and to comprehend their spiritual significance; he broods on his own lack of response, he realises the deficiencies in his vehicle as a medium for those forces; he studies the rate of his rhythmic vibration, and he strenuously endeavours to bend every opportunity to meet the need. He concentrates on the virtue, and (if he is so situated that he is aware of the incoming ray or of the ray in dominance at that time), he avails himself of the hour of opportunity and co-operates with the force extant. All this he does through the ordered forms of the true and occult meditation.

As time progresses – yes, again I prophesy – occult students will be given certain facts anent the dominating rays which will enable them to avail themselves of the opportunity any particular ray affords. (LOM–235/6)

Ray Mantrams in Meditation

• Each ray has its own formulas and sounds which have a vital effect upon the units gathered on those rays. The effect of sounding it by the student of meditation is threefold:

1. It links him and aligns him with his Higher Self or Ego.
2. It puts him in contact with his Master, and through that Master with one of the Great Lords, – dependent upon the ray.
3. It links him with his egoic group and binds all into one composite whole, vibrating to one note.

These mantrams are one of the secrets of the last three initiations and may not be sounded by the pupil before that time without permission, though he may participate at times in the chanting of the mantram under the Master's direction....

When the race has reached a certain point of development, and when the higher mind holds greater sway, these occult mantrams – rightly imparted and rightly enunciated – will be part of the ordinary curriculum of the student. He will start his meditation by the use of his ray mantram, thereby adjusting his position in the scheme; he will follow this with the mantram that calls his Master, and which puts him en rapport with the Hierarchy. Then he will begin to meditate with his bodies adjusted, and with the vacuum formed that may then be used as a medium of communication. (LOM–165/6)

Meditation as Determined by the Egoic Ray

• The ray on which a man's causal body is found, the egoic ray, should determine the type of meditation. Each ray necessitates a different method of approach, for the aim of all meditation is union with the divine. At this stage, it is union with the spiritual Triad, that has its lowest reflection on the mental plane. Let me illustrate briefly:

When the egoic ray is what is termed the [first or] *Power Ray,* the method of approach has to be by the application of the will in a dynamic form to the lower vehicles; it is largely what we term achievement by an intense focusing, a terrific one-pointedness, that inhibits all hindrances and literally forces a channel, thus driving itself into the Triad.

When the egoic ray is the *second or the Love-Wisdom Ray,* the path of least resistance lies along the line of expansion, of a gradual inclusion. It is not so much a driving forward as it is a gradual expanding from an inner centre to include the entourage, the environment, the allied souls, and the affiliated groups of pupils under some one Master, until all are included in the consciousness. Carried to the point of achievement, this expansion results in the final shattering of the causal body at the fourth Initiation. In the first instance – achievement via the Power Ray – the driving forward and the forcing upward had a like result; the opened channel admitted the downflow of force or fire from the Spirit and the causal body in time is equally destroyed.

When the egoic ray is the *third or Activity-adaptability Ray,* the method is somewhat different. Not so much the driving forward, not so much the gradual expansion as the systematic adaptation of all knowledge and of all means to the end in view. It is in fact the process of the utilisation of the many for the use of the one; it is more the accumulation of needed material and quality for the helping of the world, and the amassing of information through love and discrimination that eventually causes the shattering of the causal body. In these "Rays of Aspect" or of divine expression, if so I may call them, the shattering is brought about by the widening of the channel, due to the driving power of will in the first case; by the expansion of the lower auric egg, the causal body, in the second case, due to the inclusiveness of the synthetic Ray of Love and Wisdom; and by the breaking of the periphery of the causal body in the third case, due to the accumulative faculty and systematic absorption of the Adaptability Ray.

All these three different methods have the same result, and are fundamentally all forms of the one great method employed in the evolution of love or wisdom, – the goal of endeavour in this present solar system.

You have *the will* driving a man on to perfection, through realisation of the Higher, and resulting in the service of power through love in activity.

You have *the wisdom or love* aspect driving a man on to perfection through the realisation of his oneness with all that breathes, resulting in the service of love through love in activity.

You have the *activity* aspect driving a man on to perfection through the utilisation of all in the service of man; first by the utilisation of all for himself, then by the graded steps of the utilisation of all for the family, of all for those he personally loves, of all for his environing associates, and thus on and up till all is utilised in the service of humanity.

When the egoic ray is the attributive *Ray of Harmony,* the fourth ray, the method will be along the line of the inner realisation of beauty and harmony; it causes the shattering of the causal body by the knowledge of Sound and Colour and the shattering effect of Sound. It is the process that leads to the realisation of the notes and tones of the solar system, the note and tone of individuals, and the endeavour to harmonise the egoic note with that of others. When the egoic note is sounded in harmony with other egos, the result is the shattering of the causal body, dissociation from the lower and the attainment of perfection. Its exponents develop along the line of music, rhythm and painting. They withdraw within in order to comprehend the life side of the form. The outer manifestation of that life side in the world is through that which we call art. The great painters and the superlative musicians are in many cases reaching their goal that way.

When the fifth ray, the *Ray of Concrete Science or Knowledge* is a man's ray, the method is very interesting. It takes the form of the intense application of the concrete mind to some problem for the helping of the race; it is the bending of every mental quality and the controlling of the lower nature so that one supreme endeavour is made to pierce through that which hinders the downflow of the higher knowledge. It involves also the will element (as might be expected) and results in the wresting of the desired information from the source of all knowledge.

As the process is continued, the piercing of the periphery of the causal body becomes so frequent that in the end disintegration is produced and a man is set free. It is mentality driving a man on to perfection and forcing him to utilise all knowledge in the loving service of his race.

The *Ray of Devotion* [the sixth] is pre-eminently the ray of sacrifice. When it is the egoic ray the method of approach through meditation takes the form of one-pointed application, through love of some individual or ideal. A man learns to *include* through love of person or ideal; he bends every faculty and every effort to the contemplation of what is required, and in sacrifice for that person or ideal lays even his causal body on the flames of the altar. It is the method of divine fanaticism that counts all lost apart from the vision, and that eventually sacrifices joyously the entire personality. The causal body is destroyed through fire, and the liberated life streams upward to the Spirit in divine beatification.

When the egoic ray is the seventh or *Ray of Ceremonial Law or Magic,* the method is that of the glorification and comprehension of form in approach. As said earlier, the goal of all the meditation practices is approach to the divine within each one, and, through that, approach to the Deity Himself.

The method, therefore, is the bringing under law, order and rule, of every act of the life in all the three bodies, and the building within the causal body of an expanding form that results in the shattering of that body. It is the building of the Shrine under certain rules into a dwelling place for the Shekinah, and when the spiritual light flames forth, the Temple of Solomon rocks, reels and disintegrates. It is the study of the law and the consequent comprehension by the man of how that law is wielded and why; it is then the definite application of that law to the body of causes so as to render it needless and thus effect its shattering. Emancipation is the result, and the man frees himself from the three worlds. Many occultists are coming in on this ray at this time to continue the liberating process. It is the method that leads a man to liberation through the understanding and the intelligent application of the law to his own life, and to the ameliorating of conditions in the body of humanity, thus making the man a server of his race. (LOM–15/19)

Meditation as Determined by the Personality Ray

• As you know, the personality ray is ever a sub-ray of the spiritual ray, and varies with greater frequency than the egoic ray. With evolved egos such as may be contacted among the thinkers of the race and among the prominent workers in all departments of world work everywhere, the personality ray may vary from life to life, each life being based on a different note and demonstrating a different colour. In this way the causal body is more rapidly equipped. When the reincarnating unit has reached a point where he can consciously choose his mode of expression, he will first review his past lives, and from the knowledge gained thereby, he will guide his choice for the next. Prior to incarnation he will sound his egoic note and will note the lack of fullness or the discord it may contain; he will then decide upon which note he will base his coming personality vibration.

The whole life, therefore, may be given over to the sounding of a particular note and to the stabilising of one particular vibration. This note must be sounded and this vibration stabilised in diversity of circumstances. Hence the necessity in the life of the aspirant or disciple for frequent change, and the explanation of the obvious condition of variety and apparent chaos in which these lives are spent.

When the discord has been corrected and when the vibration becomes steady and is not subject to change, then the needed work is done. The Ego can call in again his forces, prior to continuing the work of perfecting the causal body and carrying to perfect accuracy and clarity of tone the desired chord. See then the necessity of adapting the method of meditation to the need of the personality, and of synchronising it at the same time with the first factor, involving the ray of the Ego. (LOM–19/20)

Building The Antahkarana

• Students would do well to consider the building of the antahkarana *as an extension in consciousness*. This extension is the first definite effort made upon the Path to bring in the monadic influence with full awareness, and finally directly. (RI–471)

• The bridge to be built is called frequently the "rainbow bridge" because it is constituted of all the colours of the seven rays. Speaking specifically and from the angle of the disciple, the bridge which he builds between the personality and the Spiritual Triad is composed of seven strands of energy, or seven streams of force; he uses all the seven rays, having gained facility in so doing because again and again his personality has (in the long cycle of incarnations) been on all the seven rays many times. But his soul ray dominates eventually, and in the rainbow bridge the "colours of his rays are heard vibrating; the note of his ray is seen". The bridge built by humanity as a whole is one bridge composed of the multiplicity of individual bridges, built by the many disciples. It is therefore formed eventually of seven strands or streams of energy coming from the seven egoic groups (one group of each ray type). To this bridge the creative work of all human beings who reach the stage of soul contact contributes. Their dominant strands of light fuse into one whole and their lesser strands are lost to sight in the radiant light of the sevenfold bridge which *humanity* will eventually complete.

Even in this finally completed bridge – at the end of the world cycle – one ray light and colour will predominate, the second ray, with the fourth ray as the subsidiary ray. (RI–505)

• I would like to...make a few remarks anent this relatively new process of building the antahkarana. It has been known and followed by those who were training for affiliation with the Hierarchy, but it has not been given out before to the general public. There are two things which it is essential that the student should note: One is that unless it is borne in mind that we are concerned with *energy*, and with energy which must be scientifically used, this whole teaching will prove futile. Secondly, it must be remembered that we are dealing with a technique and process which are dependent upon the use of *the creative imagination*. When these two factors are brought together (consciously and deliberately) – the factor of energy substance and the factor of planned impulse – you have started a creative process which will be productive of major results. (RI–482)

Ray Words of Power

• With this vision...let us now ascertain the seven [ray] techniques to be employed at the projection stage of the building process.

Ray One – Will or Power

To understand the first ray technique, the basic quality of the ray must be grasped. It is *dynamic*. The point at the centre is the First Ray of Power, and its technique is never to move from the centre but from that point to work dynamically. Perhaps the word that would best express its mode of work is *Inspiration*. The Father inspires response from the material aspect, or from the Mother if you like that symbolism, but it accomplishes this by remaining immovably itself. From the point where he is, the Builder (human or divine) works, not by the Law of Attraction, as does the second ray, but by the Law of Synthesis, by a fiat of the will, based on a clearly formulated purpose and programme. (RI–508)

• The first ray disciple has, therefore, to meet the requirements to the best of his ability. ...Personality and soul fusion has to be consciously attempted and to some measure achieved, and then these blended factors are held steady in the triadal light. Another point of focused intention is now brought about, resulting in a new and still more dynamic tension. In the completed silence which results, the act of projecting the antahkarana is performed, and it is then carried forward on the impetus of a Word of Power....

The meaning of the Word of Power to be used at this point of accomplished projection might be summed up in the words: "I ASSERT THE FACT." (RI–514/5)

Ray Two – Love-Wisdom

• Again the first two stages of Intention and Visualisation have been carefully followed and the four stages of the Projection have been carried through to their highest point. The vivid light of the second ray soul (the most vivid in this second ray solar system) dominates the light of form and radiates out to the triadal light. Then comes a moment of intense concentration and the...Word of Power of the second ray is enunciated. ...This word...takes form in the mind of the disciple and signifies the assertion: "I SEE THE GREATEST LIGHT." (RI–516)

Ray Three – Active Intelligence

• The processes of Intention and Visualisation have been followed, and again the four stages of the Projection technique have been concluded. At the point of highest tension, the disciple utters the Word of Power for the third ray. It is not easy for the disciple on this ray to achieve the necessary focal point of silence; his intense fluidity leads to many words or to great mental activity, frequently carried forward under the impulse of glamour. This lessens the potency of what he seeks to do. But when he has succeeded in achieving "mental silence" and is simply a point of intelligent concentration, then he can use the Word of Power with great effectiveness. The difficulty is that he has to overcome the tendency to use it with the idea of physical plane results in his consciousness. Always he works from the angle of that divine quality which characterises matter; just as the second ray disciple works always from the angle of quality and the first ray disciple from the positivity of spirit. But once he intuitively comprehends and factually grasps the concept that spirit-matter are one reality, and once he has achieved within himself the sublimation of matter, then he can divorce himself from all that the human being understands in relation to form. He can then utter the Word of Power which will make possible his complete identification with spirit, via the antahkarana. This word is "PURPOSE ITSELF AM I".

As regards the other and remaining Words of Power connected with the four Rays of Attribute, I shall simply list them, as there is little that I can say about them. They can be comprehended in the light of what I have said anent the three Words of Power used upon the Rays of Aspect.

Ray Four – Harmony through Conflict
"TWO MERGE WITH ONE"

Ray Five – Concrete Knowledge or Science
"THREE MINDS UNITE"

(This asserts the fact that the Universal Mind, the higher mind and the lower concrete mind are blended through the projected antahkarana.)

Ray Six – Devotion or Idealism
"THE HIGHEST LIGHT CONTROLS"

Ray Seven – Ceremonial Law or Order
"THE HIGHEST AND THE LOWEST MEET"

(RI–517/8)

Seventh Ray Influence on Esoteric Development

• The seventh ray influence is that which will produce in a peculiar and unexpected sense the Western School of Occultism just as the sixth ray impulse has produced the Eastern School of Occultism – the latter bringing the light down on to the astral plane and the new incoming influence carrying it down on to the physical. The Eastern teaching affected Christianity and indicated and determined the lines of its development and Christianity is definitely a bridging religion. The roles will eventually be reversed and the shift of the "light in the East" will be over Europe and America. This will inevitably bring about the needed and desired synthesis of the mystical way and the occult path. It will lead later to the formulation of the *higher way*; of this it is useless to speak at this time for you would not comprehend. None of the foundational and ancient *Rules of the Road* will ever be abrogated or discarded. Just as men used to travel on the ancient highways on foot, conforming to the requirement of their time and age, and today travel by rail or automobile (arriving at the same destination) so the same road will be followed, the same goal achieved but there may be different procedures, varying safeguards, and changed protective measures. The rules may vary from time to time in order to provide easier indication and adequate protection. The training of the disciple in the future will differ in detail from that of the past but the basic rules remain authoritative....

The keynote of the seventh ray disciple is "Radiatory Activity". Hence the emergence in world thought of certain new ideas – mental radiation or telepathy, the radiatory use of heat, the discovery of radium. All this connotes seventh ray activity.

The divine principle with which the seventh ray humanity will be mainly concerned is that of life as it expresses itself through the medium of the etheric body. It is for this reason that we find a growing interest in the nature of vitality; the function of the glands is being studied and before long their major function as vitality generators will be noted. (DN–132/3)

• The need today is for sound teaching as to the laws of thought, and the rules which govern the building of those thoughtforms which must embody the ideas sent forth from the universal divine Mind. Men must begin on the subjective planes of life to work out the needed order. When this is realised, we shall have every important group of men engaged in world affairs, or in the work of government in all its branches, aided on the mental plane by trained thinkers, so that there may be right application and correct adjustment to the Plan. This time is as yet far away, and hence the distortions and misrepresentations on earth of the Plan as it exists in heaven, to use the Christian phraseology.

It was the realisation of the present world need for illumined thinkers and subjective workers which prompted Those Who guide so to direct the incoming spiritual energies that the formation of the esoteric groups everywhere came about; it led also to the publication.of the mass of mystical and Oriental literature on meditation and allied topics which has flooded the world today. Hence also the effort that I, a worker on the inner side of life, am making to teach the newer psychology in this treatise, and so show to man what is his equipment and how well suited he is to the work for which he has been created, and which he has as yet failed to comprehend. The force and the effect of the seventh ray influence will, however, reveal to him the magical work, and the next twenty-five hundred years will bring about so much change and make possible the working of so many so-called "miracles" that even the outer appearance of the world will be profoundly altered; the vegetation and the animal life will be modified and developed, and much that is latent in the forms of both kingdoms will be brought into expression through the freer flow and the more intelligent manipulation of the energies which create and constitute all forms. The world has been changed beyond belief during the past five hundred years, and during the next two hundred years the changes will be still more rapid and deep-seated, for the growth of the intellectual powers of man is gathering momentum, and Man, the Creator, is coming into possession of His powers. (EP1–82/3)

• [There is] a wide intention (during the coming cycle) to open the door wide into the temple of the hidden mystery to man. One by one we shall undergo the esoteric and spiritual counterpart of the psychological factor which is called "a mental test". That test will demonstrate a man's usefulness in mental work and power, it will show his capacity to build thoughtforms and to vitalise them. This I dealt with in *A Treatise on White Magic*, and the relation of that treatise to the magical work of the seventh ray and its cycle of activity will become increasingly apparent. *A Treatise on White Magic* is an attempt to lay down the rules for training and for work which will make it possible for the candidate to the mysteries to enter the temple and to take his place as a creative worker and thus aid in the magical work of the Lord of the Temple. (EP1–84/5)

The Soul or Egoic Ray

• In [the] study of the ray of the Ego or Soul, certain major premises might be briefly stated and incorporated into a series of propositions, fourteen in number. They are as follows:

1.   The egos of all human beings are to be found upon one or

another of the seven rays.

2. All egos found upon the fourth, the fifth, the sixth and the seventh rays must eventually, after the third initiation, blend with the three major rays, or monadic rays.

3. The monadic ray of every ego is one of the three rays of aspect, and the sons of men are either monads of power, monads of love, or monads of intelligence.

4. For our specific purposes, we shall confine our attention to the seven groups of souls found upon one or other of the seven rays or streams of divine energy.

5. For the major part of our racial and life experience we are governed sequentially, and later simultaneously by:

    a. The physical body, which is dominated by the ray governing the sum total of the atoms of that body.

    b. The emotional desire nature, which is to be found influenced and controlled by the ray which colours the totality of astral atoms.

    c. The mind body or mental nature, and the calibre and quality of the ray determining its atomic value.

    d. Later, on the physical plane, the soul ray begins to work in and with the sum total of the three bodies, which constitute – when aligned and functioning in unison – the personality. The effect of that general integration is actively to produce an incarnation and incarnations wherein the personality ray emerges clearly, and the three bodies or selves constitute the three aspects or rays of the lower personal self.

6. When the personality ray becomes pronounced and dominant, and the three body rays are subordinated to it, then the great fight takes place between the egoic ray or soul and the personality ray. The differentiation becomes clearly marked, and the sense of duality becomes more definitely established....

7. Eventually, the soul ray or influence becomes the dominating factor, and the rays of the lower bodies become the sub-rays of this controlling ray. This last sentence is of basic importance, for it indicates the true relation of the personality to the ego or soul. The disciple who under-

stands this relation and conforms to it is ready to tread the path of initiation.

8. Each of the seven groups of souls is responsive to one of the seven types of force, and all of them are responsive to the ray of the planetary Logos of our planet, which is the third Ray of Active Intelligence. All are therefore upon a sub-ray of this ray, but it must never be forgotten that the planetary Logos is also upon a ray, which is a sub-ray of the second Ray of Love-Wisdom. Therefore we have:

The Ray of the Planetary Logos

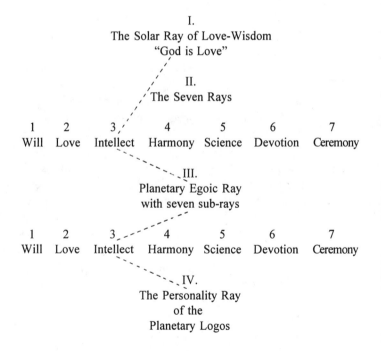

I.
The Solar Ray of Love-Wisdom
"God is Love"

II.
The Seven Rays

1	2	3	4	5	6	7
Will	Love	Intellect	Harmony	Science	Devotion	Ceremony

III.
Planetary Egoic Ray
with seven sub-rays

1	2	3	4	5	6	7
Will	Love	Intellect	Harmony	Science	Devotion	Ceremony

IV.
The Personality Ray
of the
Planetary Logos

It should be remembered that our planetary Logos functioning through the planet Earth is not considered as producing one of the seven sacred planets.

9. The work of each individual aspirant is therefore to arrive at an understanding of:

a. His egoic ray.
b. His personality ray.
c. The ray governing his mind.
d. That governing his astral body.
e. The ray influencing his physical body. When he has achieved this fivefold knowledge, he has fulfilled the Delphic injunction: "Know thyself", and can consequently take Initiation.

10. Every human being is also governed by certain group rays:
    a. Those of the fourth kingdom in nature. This will have different effects, according to the ray of the personality or soul. The fourth kingdom has:
       1). The fourth ray as its egoic ray.
       2). The fifth ray as its personality ray.
    b. The racial rays, at this time, are the third and fifth, for our Aryan race, and this powerfully affects every human being.
    c. The cyclic ray.
    d. The national ray.
    All of these control the personality life of each man. The egoic ray of the individual, plus the egoic ray of the fourth kingdom, gradually negate the rays governing the personality as the man nears the path of probation and discipleship.

11. Man therefore is an aggregate of forces which dominate him serially and together; these colour his nature, produce his quality, and determine his "appearance", using this word in its occult sense of *exteriorisation*. For ages he is wielded by one or other of these forces, and is simply what they make him. As he arrives at a clearer understanding, and can begin to discriminate, he definitely chooses which of them shall dominate, until he eventually becomes controlled by the Soul ray, with all the other rays subordinated to that ray and used by him at will.

12. In studying the egoic ray of man we have to grasp:
    a. The process followed . . . . externalisation.

b. The secret to be found . . . . manifestation.

c. The purpose to be known . . . . realisation.

We have also to understand the dominant ray influences of the kingdom of souls, the fifth kingdom. These are:

   1). Ray five . . . . . . working through the personality.

   2). Ray two . . . . working through the intuition.

13.   The *Personality ray* finds its major field of activity and expression in the physical body. It determines its life trend and purpose, its appearance and occupation. It is selective of quality, when influenced by the egoic ray.

The *Egoic ray* has direct and specific action upon the astral body. Hence the battlefield of the life is ever on the plane of illusion; as the soul seeks to dispel the ancient glamour, the aspirant is enabled to walk in the light.

The *Monadic ray* influences the mental body, after integration of the personality has been brought about. It causes the mind nature to achieve that clear vision which finds its consummation at the fourth initiation, and releases the man from the limitations of form. There is an analogy to this triplicity and an interesting symbolic relation in the three Initiators.

a. The first Initiator . . . . the soul of man. This controls gradually the personality.

b. The second Initiator . . . . the Christ. Releasing the love nature.

c. The final Initiator . . . . the Planetary Logos. Illumining the mind.

14.   The egoic or soul ray begins to make its presence actively felt, via the astral body, as soon as alignment has been achieved. The process is as follows:

a. It plays on the astral body externally.

b. It stimulates it internally to greater size, colour and quality.

c. It brings it and all parts of the physical life into activity and under control.

All the above propositions could be summed up in the statement that the personality ray induces a *separative* attitude and causes a detachment from the group of souls of which the personality is an externalisation, and a consequent attachment to the form side of manifestation. The egoic ray induces *group consciousness* and detachment from external forms, causing attachment to the life side of manifestation and to the subjective whole. The monadic ray has an effect which can be understood only after man has taken the third initiation. (EP1–401/7)

• At the third initiation there is revealed to the initiate the purpose of the subray of the ray to which he belongs, that upon which his Ego finds itself. All egoic units are upon some subray of the monadic ray. This knowledge is conferred upon the initiate so as to enable him eventually to find for himself (along the line of least resistance) the ray of his Monad. This subray bears upon its stream of energy many groups of Egos, and the initiate is therefore made aware not only of his egoic group and its intelligent purpose, but of many other groups, similarly composed. Their united energy is working towards a clearly defined goal. (IHS–121)

• The soul ray or energy is all this time steadily increasing its rhythmic potency, and seeking to impose its purpose and will upon the personality. It is the united relation and the interplay between these two which – when a point of balance has been achieved – sweeps the man on to the Probationary Path, on to the Path of Discipleship, and right up to the gate of initiation. (GWP–117)

• You have also been sorely tested in the emotional nature; surely…you know by this time that when a definite transition is being made by the soul…from one ray to another, that abnormal testing is automatically inevitable? This will be particularly the case when a disciple is moving on to the second ray… (DNA2–522)

The Tibetan's Group of Disciples

The two volumes of "Discipleship in the New Age" include sequences of letters written by the Tibetan to individual disciples in which he often comments on their ray make up and the specific problems and opportunities that these were presenting to his disciples. The following section contains extracts mainly from these letters.

The Five Determining Rays of the Disciple

• ...I find it useful to indicate to all in my group of pledged disciples their five determining or conditioning rays so that they can work with intelligence at the fusion of

    a. The various personality rays.
    b. The personality ray with the soul ray. (DNA1–218/9)

• As you study your rays, the reason for the close relation between you and some of your fellow disciples will emerge into your consciousness more clearly. It is a relation not only of age-long mutual service and of understanding but also of analogous energies and forces and similarity in use. (DNA1–275)

• It should always be borne in mind that when I speak of the rays of the various bodies, I am referring to the dominant force which conditions them in any particular life, to the possible effect that the impact of that force – regulated or unregulated – may have upon surrounding people, and to the responsive, sensitive or impressionable substance with which the soul has

234

perforce to work. I refer to what constitutes the material expression. (DNA1–446)

• It is the effect of your mental body upon others that I would seek to have you most definitely consider. Upon the probationary path, the forces of man's lower nature and their interior interplay is of paramount importance; he must learn to know himself. On the path of discipleship, these same forces must be studied in relation to those with whom destiny, karma and vocational choice has thrown the disciple. On the path of initiation, these same forces are used in conscious co-operation with the Plan, and with adequate skill in action, due to the lessons learnt on the earlier stages of the path. (DNA1–447)

• Until there is sufficient *pronounced* development to allow of a true diagnosis, it is not possible to say definitely what is the ray of the personality. The defining of the egoic ray comes later still and can only be surmised at first from the nature of the conflict of which the personality is aware, based as it will be on a growing sense of duality. It will also be capable of expert diagnosis from certain physical and psychical characteristics which indicate the quality of the higher nature of the person concerned, and also through a study of the type of a man's group affiliations as they begin to appear upon the physical plane. A man who – being, through personality predilection, a creative artist – suddenly takes a deep and profound interest in mathematics, might be inferred to be coming under the influence of a second ray soul; or a man, whose whole personality was definitely upon the sixth ray of fanatical idealism or devotion to an object of his idealism, and who had functioned during life as a religious devotee, and who then switched the centre of his life interest into scientific investigation, might be, therefore, responding to a fifth ray soul impression. (EP2–334/5)

Understanding Ray Types

• …Your major life problem [is]: To stand free whilst surrounded; to work in the subjective world whilst active in the exterior world of affairs; to achieve true detachment whilst rendering to all that which is due. An understanding of your ray types may greatly aid in this process of release, of relinquishment, and of final renunciation. (DNA1–314)

• It would be a profitable thing if students would gather together all the information they can anent their two major rays, with the view to practical work with themselves…. You can [thus] aid [the group] in gaining the needed group poise for the work to be done. (DNA1–317)

• It is no easy task which you and all disciples have set themselves these days. It means facing up to the issue which each has for himself created and this involves facing one's life with truth as well as one's environment, one's characteristics and one's responsibilities. It is an arduous undertaking to deal clear-sightedly with the lower self, to see life and the self truly and to guard the precious jewel of the vision untouched. (DNA1–329)

• A knowledge of the ray influences, techniques, mechanics and objectives will be ascertained by disciples in whom these rays are pronouncedly manifesting.

It is not possible for anyone under the degree of accepted disciple to find out much. The type must be definitely pronounced and the investigator advanced enough to have reached the stage of a detached observer…. The second ray disciple has to learn detachment while at the same time he remains "attached and inclusive" esoterically, and this must be consciously achieved and the attitude preserved. The first ray disciple has to remain detached and at the same time to learn attachment and to admit entry into his aura of the entire world in a series of progressive attachments. This makes for difficulty for it involves that training in paradoxes which is the secret of occultism. (DNA2–574/5)

Ray Charts

• …[Ray] charts could be drawn up and studied, and many such hypothetical cases could present the basis for occult investigation, for diagram, and for the study of the Law of Correspondences. Students would find it of interest to study themselves in this way, and, in the light of the information given in [the] *Treatise on the Seven Rays*, they could formulate their own charts, study what they think may be their own rays and the consequent ray effect in their lives, and thus draw up most interesting charts of their own nature, qualities and characteristics.

It might be of interest to mention the fact that the moment a man becomes an accepted disciple, some such chart *is* prepared and placed in the hands of his Master. In fact, four such charts are available, for the rays of the personality vary from one cycle of expression to another and necessitate the keeping of the personality chart up to date. The four basic charts are:

1. The chart of a man's expression at the time of his individualisation. This is of course a very ancient chart. In it, the rays of the mental body and of the emotional body are most difficult to ascertain as there is so little mental expression or emotional experience. Only the ray of the soul and of the physical body are clearly defined. The other rays are regarded as only suggestive.

    This is the chart of the *man who is asleep.*

2. The chart of a man's expression when the personality reaches its highest independent point of development; – that is, before the soul has taken over *conscious* control and is functioning at all dominantly.

    This is the chart of *the man who dreams.*

3. The chart of a man's expression at that peculiar moment of determining crisis when the soul and personality are at war, when the battle for reorientation is at its highest and the aspirant knows it. He knows that upon the issue of that battle much depends. He is Arjuna upon the field of Kurukshetra.

    This is the chart of *the man awakening.*

4. The chart of a man's expression during the life wherein

the orientation has been altered, the emphasis of the life forces changed, and the man becomes an accepted disciple.

These four charts, depicted or drawn in colour according to ray, form the *dossier* of a disciple, for the Master only deals with general tendencies and never with detail. General trends and predispositions and emphasised characteristics concern Him, and the obvious life patterns. (EP2–298/9)

The Rays of the Soul

The First Ray as the Soul Ray

• In dealing with first ray egos...or with those souls who are working through first ray personalities, I am faced always with the initial difficulty of their "isolated independence". It is not easy for such first ray types to co-operate, to fall into line with group suggestion, with group rhythm or group discipline, or with united synchronised activity which is the announced goal of all groups of disciples. Frequently the inner attitude *is* at one with the main purpose and ideals but the outer expression, the physical man, remains unadaptable and basically unwilling to conform. Were it not for your second ray personality, you would find it hard to work in my Ashram, but it is this second ray quality of yours – strongly marked and the product of a long series of incarnations in a second ray vehicle – which can make you, if you so desire, one of the focal points for the work which I plan to have this band of disciples do. (DNA1–136)

• Comradeship, you are learning and it is not an easy lesson at any time for first ray souls to master and express. The littleness of the personalities and the pettiness of individual points of view are irksome to the server of the Plan who stands, serene and detached, upon a first ray pinnacle of vision and resultant comprehension. (DNA1–169)

• Handle with care the force which flows through you as you shift increasingly into the consciousness of your first ray soul.... See to it that your second ray personality can rightly deal with that force, blending it with love and tempering its power with understanding. The first ray force must deal with circumstance and must *not* make its impact upon personalities. It is needed *to force issues and determine results* (note that phrase) but not to shatter and to hurt. True impersonality must be borne in mind and your personality must note its effect upon other personalities and offset its innate and oft most useful destructive work. (DNA1–169/70)

• Fight not the glamour which seeks to impose itself upon you with your first ray indifference – a potent attitude easily assumed by you as by all first ray types. Fight it by non-recognition and by complete absorption in the immediate task; I refer to a wise absorption which neglects no due physical care nor due time for relaxation. (DNA1–170)

• Your *soul ray* is the first Ray of Will or Power, as is also the ray of your *physical body*. Hence, if you so choose, comes the facility and ease with which your soul can impress your brain. This tends also to make you very intuitive, though not at all psychic. It gives you – again if you so choose – organising power, and the use of a dynamic, spiritual will which can carry you through and over all obstacles. (DNA1–204)

• In an earlier teaching, I endeavoured to awaken you to the risk of constantly assuming the position of the "one in the centre". That attitude…is also distinctive of a first ray soul and the presence of these two attitudes (of the one in the centre and the one who stands alone) are indicative of the fact that your first ray soul is beginning to assume some control over your personality.… You might rightly ask me how and in what manner you can offset these tendencies. I can but reply to you with simple and ordinary truths – so simple and so ordinary that their scientific value is easily overlooked. I say to you: Lose interest in your personality life, in its contacts and affairs by substituting a dynamic interest in world work. Do not arrive at this detachment through an intensification of your sixth ray personality attitudes; we do not desire to have fanatics in association with us. Arrive at it through a deepening of your love nature as it includes others and excludes your own lower nature. I say to you: Work with detachment and, because you are demanding nothing for the separated self, all things will, therefore, come to you. You will not then stand alone but will function as an attractive magnetic unit in group service. Here, therefore, lies your immediate problem. You have to learn to be decentralised and to step out of the centre of your own picture. You have to learn to be magnetic and to build and not destroy. Ponder on these suggestions and work simply, quietly and happily at your problem. (DNA1–244/5)

• Leave people free and seek not to influence them or to impose your ideas upon them. Your interpretation of them and of their need (no matter how close they may be to you) is not necessarily correct. Leave people free in all respects – with the freedom that you demand and expect for yourself. (DNA1–245)

• I am impelled to give you just two words of practical import. They are *gracious loving-kindness*. These qualities of gracious-ness and of loving-kindness mark the superficial (occultly understood) outer expression of the soul and for a first ray person they are ever difficult; their need is oft not recognised nor are they deemed necessary. The first ray person frequently does not know he lacks them. The inner, dynamic and realised goodness of a first ray disciple can be marred by a haste and an outer quickness of speech and attitude. So sure is a first ray person of his essential kindness and love (and he is rightly sure) that he judges other people as himself. The inner rectitude of attitude and the inner love matter more to him than the outer expression. But lesser people and those upon the other rays are apt to misunderstand. The potency of your work is so real and the opportunities opening before you are so great that if you add to that potency a gracious outer attitude of loving-kindness, you can be much used. Ponder on this.... (DNA1–325)

• The power of your first ray soul can galvanise the personality into continued action and aspiration, into continued mental control; for you, therefore, there need be no cessation of activity and no settling back into inertia until the final activity of transition engrosses the dual attention of your soul and your personality, and the final detachment takes place. (DNA1–388)

• Your aim must be to avoid all static conditions. Many first ray people become static or crystallised, as that is the method whereby the first ray destroyers work.... (DNA1–621)

• The first ray person is conscious of ordered life, the majesty of ordered forces; the glory of the intelligent "arrangement" of the powers which lie behind the manifested world is his rightful field of service. But to this must be added the power to intuit the Plan as it exists in the heart of love, for only love reveals the Plan and the part to be played in it by souls at any given time and place. (DNA1–625)

• The first ray disciple loves isolation. It is for him the line of least resistance. He is, as you know, normally the one who stands alone. This is his strength and it is also his weakness. He glories in detachment....

It is not easy for the first ray disciple to learn *attachment* (of the right and spiritual description).... The problem of attachment and of detachment is one. It is the problem of right values. The first ray type loves himself, his power and his isolation too much.... The first ray type errs in not giving enough thought to the reaction of others to what he says and does; he prides himself on his detached attitude and on his immunity from attachment; he likes to have his strength and isolation appreciated. [He suffers] from pride....

It is this inner "isolation", deeply loved by you...which militates against your being telepathically sensitive to other people. Instead of so much "will to love", why not just love more simply?... In you the head dominates, and you sit on the summit of your tower, whilst all the time the call of the heart sounds throughout your being and in your ears. Yet you fear to descend and walk among your fellow-men in loving identification with them. It is only through walking the dusty street of life with our brothers that we find ourselves passing eventually through the portal of initiation. (DNA1–625/6)

• You have much wisdom and also the first ray capacity to take a stand upon principle.... Before you speak the words of power and of wisdom (which you speak with such facility and truth from the storehouse of a long experience), you must pour out the love of your heart upon those who turn to you for light and strength. Men today have need of love. (DNA1–630)

• Your replies to the questions which I set you…were so like you – earnest, sincere, mental, logical and with the impersonality of the first ray type. (DNA1–631)

• With first ray disciples, I can ever speak with clarity and frankness, knowing that they will take my words in the right spirit. (DNA1–635)

• Loneliness, isolation, a sense of being deserted and a separativeness (based on sensitivity in most cases) distinguish the first ray disciple, until he learns to preserve his divine sense of "unified identity" whilst merging, at the same time, with others.…

…The work which you do is planned by us and…your task is to render yourself sensitive to our "impression". This developed sensitivity is ever a difficult task for the first ray person. They prefer to stand alone and to generate within themselves the plans which they consider fitted for the type of service which they seek to render. But today disciples are learning that a fused and organised and blended plan or scheme of world-wide service is required, and that a master Plan of the Hierarchy must be carried out, and that into this Plan all disciples…must endeavour to fit. (DNA2–497/8)

• [You need to learn] to gather people together and work through them. This…is very difficult for a first ray disciple to master, particularly when the soul ray and the ray of the astral or emotional nature are both first ray. It is easy for the first ray disciple to withdraw into his soul consciousness, far easier than for any other ray types, and your problem…is to give the second ray personality fuller sway, and thus balance the first ray ability to demonstrate detachment by the functioning of the opposite quality of attachment – so distinctive of the second ray nature. Ponder on this.

…A "detached attachment" (paradoxical as it sounds) is the

goal of the first ray working disciple. (DNA2–504/5)

• ...You are and can increasingly be a channel, for the simplicity of the first ray type of person is a terrific potency. Use it,
my brother, free from isolation. It is ever easier for a first ray
worker to proceed alone upon the way of his decision, but I
would suggest that you work in closer co-operation with your
fellow disciples. (DNA2–592)

• You have certain difficulties to overcome in the use of first
ray energy, and any mistakes you may have made in harsh
judgments and in its physical expression in speech are simply
incidental to the learning of the right use of soul energy....
    Every time that first ray energy pours through you it leads to
a trifling or a true crisis in your relationships with others. You
need to acquire a more general and genuine liking (as a means
to understanding) of your fellowmen, particularly of those who
are your co-workers in my work.... Be not ruthless or dis-
satisfied with their efforts to make good....
    You need, my brother, to be more appreciative of effort and
less critical of accomplishment. With true failures you are ever
kind and understanding and have demonstrated this often, but
you are apt to despise (behind a kind manner) those who
appear satisfied with what they have done. You need also to
learn with wisdom to choose your workers when it is your task
to do so. It is not easy for you or for any first ray disciple to
get close enough, or want to get close enough, to a person to
really know him.... It lies in the natural isolation of the first
ray type. Have this in mind.
    ...First ray workers provide the substance with which the
second ray workers build and the other ray workers qualify and
modify. You inspire substance with the energy and purpose and
with the life necessary to render it responsive to the plan – the
Plan of goodwill which the Masters are at present implementing
and for which They seek workers. (DNA2–594/5)

• ...There are no pure first ray types on the planet. All so-
called first ray egos are on the first subray of the second ray,
which is in incarnation. A pure first ray ego in incarnation at

this time would be a disaster. There is not sufficient intelligence and love in the world to balance the dynamic will of an ego on the ray of the destroyer. (EP1–26/7)

The Second Ray as the Soul Ray

• You have the problem...of a heart attached to many and hence unduly strained and taxed by others. There are many demands upon your sympathies. (DNA1–138)

• You have...the vices of your second ray virtues. You suffer from attachment and from a too rapid identification with other people. This can be handled if you stand steadfast as a soul and do not focus as a personality in dealing with people – both in your home circle and in your world service. You need to bear in mind that your relation is with souls and not with temporary forms and so you must live detached from personalities, serving them but living ever in the consciousness of the soul – the true sannyasin. (DNA1–139)

• Relinquish that close attention to the lives of those around you which is the easy way of working for all who are second ray disciples. Their sense of responsibility is so great and their desire to shelter and to guard so strong that they unduly cherish those who are linked to them by karmic obligation and whose lives touch theirs in the life of every day. Go your own way with strength and silence, and do that which your soul demands. Let not the lesser voices of the loved and near deflect you from your progress upon the path of service. You belong now to the world, and not to a handful of your fellowmen. (DNA1–140/1)

• It is the use of the will aspect that second ray disciples have to acquire.... (DNA1–141)

• When the heart is full of love and the head is full of wisdom, nothing then is ever done that can cause distress to others in the long run. By this, I refer not to action but to the fruits of action. A decision can be made and a line of conduct followed (and the decision can be right) but the eventuating conditions may not be harmoniously adjusted unless there is a subjective freedom from fear, a heart full of love and that loving understanding which is the truest wisdom. The man who is fearless, wise and loving can do anything and the effects will be harmless and good producing. (DNA1–143/4)

• Very seldom is the second ray disciple a good executive, unless the secondary ray makes him so. (DNA1–144)

• ...The path of the World Saviours is a hard one, owing primarily to the power to suffer which the second ray type embodies. (DNA1–149)

• Always has your problem been that of the true second ray disciple. This involves the ability to identify yourself with others, their ideas and reactions and you thereby limit and hinder your own activity from the indecision which arises from too much understanding and too great a sympathy with the personality problems and the form side of expression. When you can stand with greater firmness in spiritual being and when you can work more definitely and consciously with the soul aspect and less engrossingly with the personality, your life will simplify and certain of your unique personality problems will disappear. Then and only then will your soul call to you those who can be your true co-operators. (DNA1–153/4)

• ...This [second] ray is pre-eminently the teaching ray, the ray that is sometimes called that of "light-giving influence" or the "ray of the illuminator". (DNA1–177)

• In the six members who are at present working together in [this group] there are five second ray egos. This is interesting in that it indicates a predominant capacity in the group to heal and to teach, and these are, in the last analysis, your two major objectives. (DNA1–344)

• ...It is [not] easy for the second ray disciple to learn detachment.... The problem of attachment and of detachment is one. It is the problem of right values.... The second ray type errs through deep attachment to others and through a too fluid inclusiveness which is expressed before the disciple understands the true nature of inclusiveness. The second ray type errs through fear of not being understood or not adequately loved, and cares too much what others may think of him and say of him.... [He] suffers from fear. (DNA1–626)

• ...The healing ray, above all others, is the second ray. There are two major healing rays among the seven. They are the second and the seventh. (DNA1–641)

• ...The Way of Joy has been for you a hard way to go. Yet it is one of the needed characteristics of discipleship, leading – as it does – to soul strength; it is an essential quality for all those second ray people who are oriented particularly to treading, at some future date and after initiation, the difficult way of all world saviours. (DNA1–668)

• ...Your second ray emphasis is that of wisdom and not of love. Therefore the love quality is not so potent, and this presents difficulties to you of which you are curiously unaware. It is your task – at any cost – to develop the love quality. The wisdom attitude makes you hard, and you have not yet balanced it – in intensity – by the love quality. This hardness you *must* transmute on a large and general scale. You can transmute for individuals you love or for whom you feel a sense of responsibility. It is this quality of love which you must develop before you see the Christ – not simply as an initiate taking an initiation, but as a disciple warranting His attention.... Today, few disciples realise that the Christ has two relationships to them: that of initiation, and another – far rarer – that of One Whom they may consult in connection with their work. This permission to approach is only accorded when love and wisdom are balanced and equal. (DNA2–673)

• ...Your soul ray is the Ray of Love-Wisdom...therefore, through the right alignment and the discipline of the personality, will that love nature of yours (in all its fullness and richness) be poured through you to others. (DNA1–533)

The Third Ray as the Soul Ray
• ...Your [third ray] egoic or soul ray focuses itself in and through your fifth ray mental body. This...has given you your defined mental focus, your critical attitude and your isolation,

relatively speaking.

...What you need to do is to focus the energy of your soul in your sixth ray astral body instead of in your mind, so that intelligent love may be your outstanding characteristic. (DNA1–125/6)

The Sixth Ray as the Soul Ray

• I told you that you were shifting egoically from the sixth Ray of Devotion on to the second Ray of Love-Wisdom – the ray whereon I myself am found.... Your sixth ray soul-polarisation has served to enhance the dynamic one-pointedness of your first ray force. Now that condition is beginning to change and during this transition period you suffer much. (DNA1–215/6)

The Seventh Ray as the Soul Ray

• Your *soul ray* is the seventh, which would enable you to work with facility in the new world which is emerging into manifestation with such rapidity. It will aid you also in producing order and rhythm in your environment; in these days of turmoil and difficulty, every rhythmic centre is of value to us. (DNA1–646)

• I would remind you as you seek decision that your soul is on the seventh ray and that you are working through a first ray personality. Hence my brother, your problem. A mystic of wide consciousness with a powerful personality ray and with a soul vibration in line with the New Age, seeking to impose upon the personality the rhythm of a "ceremonial order and organisation". (DNA1–290)

The Rays of the Personality

• The personality is always predominantly allied with or focused in one of its three aspects. (DNA1–257)

• It is of value to students to study what rays are *not* represented in the personality equipment. (DNA1–351)

• It will be of service to you if I indicate...the rays which govern your threefold personality. You will then be in a position to handle yourselves with greater wisdom, to trace more easily the causes of difficulty and to study more intelligently the effect you may have upon each other and upon those you contact in daily life.

...The rays govern the three bodies in the following order:

1. Rays governing the mental body . . . . . Rays 1.4.5.
2. Rays governing the astral body . . . . . . Rays 2.6.
3. Rays governing the physical body . . . . Rays 3.7.

Thus you will note that all the rays play their part in the mechanism of man, making all circumstances the vehicles of opportunity and all conditions the medium of development. This statement as to the governing rays is a statement of an infallible rule, except in the case of accepted disciples. (GWP–92)

• ...Another influence...is the planetary ray under which each human being is born. It must of course be understood that the so-called influence of a planet is really the influence of the Hierarchy ruling over that planet. This personal ray is an important factor in the character of a man during the one life-time of its operation. I say one lifetime, but it may of course be one or more, if the karmic conditions demand it, for the moment of birth for every individual is fixed in accordance with karmic necessities, and probably all of us – whatever our primary or individual rays – have passed lifetimes again and again under the personal influence of all the seven rays. (EP1–169)

The First Ray as the Personality Ray

• You are on the first ray where your personality is concerned, and broad general schemes and the wider plans are for you easy to grasp. (DNA1–214)

• Your first ray personality gives you power with men and this power you know you possess, and you have endeavoured to use it wisely. (DNA1–215)

• This capacity to be impersonal has been greatly developed in you by your first ray lower nature which renders you easily impersonal – if you so choose. But for you the lesson of all disciples must be learned which is to be impersonally personal. That is not easy of attainment. An attached detachment is for you the goal. (DNA1–216)

• You are learning to leave others free – a hard lesson for a first ray personality.... (DNA1–219)

• Your personality ray, your mind ray, and the ray of your physical body are all governed by your first ray energy and this presents a very real problem because it predisposes you to the following conditions:

1. A loneliness which is based on a sense of isolation. This is due also to the sense of isolation which the first ray always gives. It is essentially the ray of detachment....

2. Owing to the fact that first ray energy in your case is focused in your personality and in two of its mediums of expression, you wield – owing to the unbalance – an undue power or effect upon all you meet and seek to help. Fortunately for you, and also owing to the quality of your soul ray and to an achieved measure of control, your effect upon those you seek to serve is good. You are, however, definitely aware...of the powerful influence you can call into play and thus affect other people's lives. You know also the powerful reaction you can evoke from them. This is the effect of first ray force when focused upon the physical plane.

...Your first ray personality makes it easily possible for you to dominate those you meet. (DNA1–221/2)

• A first ray personality can cause the soul much difficulty when not subordinated in all humility to group service. When the personality is guided by the intuition and by clear thinking and the life on the physical plane is given to the freely imposed rhythm of organised service, then power can be conferred, and definite usefulness be the result. (DNA1–280/1)

• In a previous life your personality ray was the first Ray of Power, and hence the evidence of power which seizes you at times. (DNA1–293)

• Much of your present difficulty is based on the fact that your personality ray is, as you know, that of the first Ray of Will or Power. This gives you a sense of centralisation, of uniqueness and aloneness. It makes the man who is conditioned by it "isolated". It makes his attitude to his work one of an unconscious separativeness. It is the line of least resistance for you to be separated off from your co-workers or – when urged to identification by your second ray soul – the response is one of going out to them with the inner distinction ever clearly held. I am not here referring to any pride, brother of mine, but to the absorbing, assimilating, isolating characteristics of the first ray nature. It is the great first ray Lord (to use an illuminating simile) Who, at the end of the age, absorbs all things into Himself and thereby brings about the final and needed destruction of the form nature. This is a right and good use of His first ray qualities. But first ray personalities can also do this type of work, that of absorbing, but this time with destructive results; in their case the task is unnecessary and wrong. (DNA1–377/8)

• You...are afraid of your equals. You want to be the one alone as your first ray powerful personality (focused naturally in your first ray astral body) would normally incline you. It is not easy for you to be one among the many – all equal, all working as one, all engrossed with the one work. This you must learn to do, or else you hinder the group. (DNA1–379)

• Another reason for your failure to get all you might out of the present experience is the inordinate pride of the Taurus individual, who is on the first ray where his personality is concerned.
　　...You go bull-headed through life, knocking down and hurting as you go.... You stop not to right or to adjust wrong action, e'en when you recognise it as wrong. (DNA1–471/2)

• The disciple with a first ray personality is apt to be unduly one-pointed in his service or in his particular line of thought and of activity, or else he is entirely engrossed with some individual or group of individuals. This dynamic and intense pre-occupation can often hinder the expansion of consciousness and the unfoldment of that inclusiveness which is essential before any of the major initiations can be taken.... The dual life of the disciple is never an easy one to the man whose personality is basically upon the line of directed power and focused will. ...Oft this directed power is not being adequately diffused, and minor or near objectives being too closely seen, can destroy that which it builds or seeks or loves, through the very intensity of the focused energy. (DNA1–490)

• The first ray personality can always be swept into dynamic usefulness and consequent good health by an act of the will, the spiritual will. Your physical sense of being ill is due purely to spiritual laziness – a thing you can offset at once if you choose. (DNA1–496)

• ...It is the first ray personality, with its quick response to criticism and its dislike of outer control or interference which must be regulated. ...You have to make your own way, then, of learning and of cultivating self-forgetfulness. The man who stands alone, and who has determined that condition of isolation *for himself* has a harder problem, in some ways, and certainly a different problem, than the man who is disciplined by the constant, ceaseless impact of others upon his conscious-ness. You stand very much alone. It has been your own wish, and the right way for you. But you must offset its unavoidable difficulties through a self-imposed discipline. (DNA1–498)

• ...Pride controls so much of your physical plane activity and reactions; note also how your first ray personality and your first ray astral vehicle tend to increase this tendency in you. Here, in the overcoming of pride, lies your major life task and the crux of your life's battle. Sweetness, humility and the willing-ness to recognise values which at present are not quickly recognised by you are for you the way of release.... Your positive and powerful temperament leads you to draw to yourself negative people and you are happier with them than with more positive people. When you can attract the positive kind of people and find your major pleasure in your contacts with the positively polarised disciples of the world, you will have the first indication that the glamour of pride is disappearing. (DNA1–504)

• Your first ray personality does two things to you: It isolates you in your own mind from your associates and you need to learn the necessity for identification with those who are your co-workers....

Your first ray personality, plus your first ray mind, evokes in you a love of power and a desire for that pleasurable sensation which comes from speech which evokes acquiescence. This serves to place you "in the seat of the superior person", as the Chinese call it. You will usually find, my brother, that it is easy to gather around you many little people, of relatively futile accomplishment (from the angle of world service) but that the finer minds have no time for such acquiescence; they proceed upon their way, leaving you to follow after and to catch up with them eventually. (DNA1–587)

• Owing to the dominance of the first ray in your equipment, you have successfully withdrawn yourself from your group brothers; you have considered that they had naught to give you, and you realised that – feeling this way – you had naught for them. Detachment is the path of least resistance for a first ray nature.... Your second ray soul does not sanction detachment, and hence the conflict being waged within your consciousness. (DNA2–523)

• ...Never do you cease fighting and struggling, sometimes under the urge of your soul [second ray] and oft under the influence of a restless and unhappy personality [first ray] emphasis. Can you not begin to cease from strife and struggle, and thus give opportunity for the evolution of that loving spirit which your first ray isolated personality seeks to hide...? (DNA2–698)

The Second Ray as the Personality Ray

• Your *personality ray* is the second Ray of Love-Wisdom and this enables you safely to evoke and use your first ray Will, for it will then be inevitably modified by your personality focus.

You will note, therefore, how this tends to make you fairly well-balanced, when you act as a personality or as a soul. (DNA1–205)

• Only your second ray personality can have the patience to cover the mass of detail needed and to persist in the face of *apparent* nonsuccess. (DNA2–506)

The Third Ray as the Personality Ray

• ...The third Ray of Intelligence...is apt to bring with it the sense of pride of intellect. (DNA1–233)

• ...The third ray faculties and capacities of [the] personality – critical, analytical, separative, prideful and full of self-interest.... (DNA1–233)

The Fourth Ray as the Personality Ray

• Your personality is on the fourth ray, and you have considered this as constituting for you the ray of the artist, of the creative worker. But it is necessary to remember that this is also the Ray of Harmony through Conflict, and it is to this aspect of the ray in relation to your personality that I call your attention. This inner conflict, God-given and of deep spiritual import, is a service. (DNA1–539/40)

The Fifth Ray as the Personality Ray

• The main reason [for your slow progress] lies in your fifth ray personality, wherein the emphasis is laid upon the critical, analytical mind. This leads you to watch and criticise and to argue with yourself and with circumstances. (DNA1–198)

• ...Your rays are such that they constitute a deep pool or well of loving understanding; it is only your fifth ray personality that stands in the way of a full expression of the love which is truly your major and outstanding quality.... It is the task of the fifth ray (when dominating the personality) to dissect, to analyze, and to come to conclusions and this is a glamour, requiring most careful handling or a barrier will be set up.... (DNA1–449)

• Those of you who are in a position to aid unfolding minds, as you are today, and who possess fifth ray personalities as you do, can affect many minds and lay the foundation for lives and activities based upon right thought. It is in your field of activity that the world must eventually find the instruction which will lead to right action, based on right understanding of the Plan, and to a right handling of the younger generation (a thing hitherto totally unknown). In this way, the world may be remodelled by wise planning, placed will (if such a phrase means anything to you. It *involves* conscious focus) and increased activity and momentum. But such right activity will only be possible and the desired ends hastened when people of your generation and opportunity can – in this interlude between the old order and the new – think with clarity, see the issues clearly and in their true relativity, and can inspire the young ones also to see. (DNA1–452)

• Your fifth ray personality makes the reception of illumination easy, for your intellect and your intuition could be put en rapport with facility. (DNA1–556)

The Sixth Ray as the Personality Ray

• ...Your personality ray [sixth] is focused in your astral body [also sixth ray]. The rays – three [physical body], five [mental body] and six [astral body] – are your controlling factors. This gives you devotion and mental control and it should give you real balance but, unfortunately, it does not, because the mind aspect is unduly emphasised and you are afraid of devotion. Yet it is your devotion, my brother, which has brought you to us and not your mental ability. It is your devotion which has led you steadily all these years and produced your service in the world. (DNA1–126)

• Your sixth ray personality produces an intense adherence to your ideals and to the truth, as you see it; it produces also a one-pointedness which has led to a focusing of energy in the head. This has been intensified also, owing to our western civilisation being immersed in the thoughtforms of the Piscean age – the age of the sixth ray which is still with us. (DNA1–236)

• ...It will be your sixth ray vibration which will cause you the most trouble and along which glamour will easily enter. It is, for instance, your personality fanaticism and your personality devotions (both to people and to ideas) which need *tempering* if your first ray [soul] power is to manifest. Your fanatical devotee *will* must be superseded by the *purpose,* ordered and steadfast, of your first ray soul.... The steely, brittle, determined, dynamic will of the devoted aspirant must change into the steadfast, powerful, calm purpose of the soul, working through the disciple. The soul is fluid in adjustment but undeviating in aim. Likewise, the brilliant fanatical devotion to this, that or the other person or ideal must give place to the gentle unchanging love of the soul – the love of your soul for the soul of others. (DNA1–242/3)

• It is particularly wise for sixth ray [personality] people to master the Law of Cycles and of rhythmic growth, for their predisposition to fanatical and violent activity can be offset by wise handling of the life rhythm. (DNA1–256)

• ...The sixth ray quality of your personality...is, as you know, the ray of devotion, of a fanatical idealism, of undue emphasis and this ray, when conditioning the personality, is apt to cause much trouble. The lesser light of that minor ray (in itself, divine) can shut out the full radiance of your soul. (DNA1–322/3)

• Your *personality ray* is the sixth. This gives you power upon the astral plane and, in consequence, it gives you a powerful and sensitive astral body with all the implications of success and failure which go with that situation. (DNA1–646)

• A sixth ray personality is ever sure of his recognition of truth, and is consequently very easily glamoured, and when this is coupled...with a first ray astral body, the difficulty which confronts you as a disciple is very great. (DNA2–674)

The Seventh Ray as the Personality Ray
• The [seventh ray] gives to you, if you can but understand it and choose to use it rightly, the power to take the light which is in you and in the pupil, and apply it to the enlightening of

physical plane living, for the seventh ray is the ray controlling spirit-matter relationships. (DNA1–178)

• The seventh ray in your personality and physical body gives you the desire to use your hands and it determines your life work, because the hands are the agents of the magician.... (DNA1–352)

The Rays of the Mental Body

• ...The mental body of every human being is composed of substance which is governed by the rays, one, four and five. Exceptions to this rule appear, sometimes, on the Path of Discipleship, and are the result of the direct and intelligent action of the Soul, prior to incarnation.... The energies of these three rays, when focused in a personality, provides exactly the right impulse to govern the lower life, both in the case of an undeveloped human being and of a man in the early stages of discipleship and aspiration....

Ray One:

IN UNEVOLVED MAN

1. The will to live or to manifest upon the physical plane.
2. The impulse which works out, therefore, as the instinct to self preservation.
3. The capacity to endure, no matter what the difficulties.
4. Individual isolation. The man is always the "One who stands alone".

IN THE ADVANCED MAN

1. The will to liberation or to manifest consciously upon the plane of the soul.
2. The capacity to react to the plan, or to respond to the recognised will of God.
3. The principle of immortality.
4. Perseverance or endurance upon the *Way*. (EP2–291)

Ray Four

IN UNEVOLVED MAN

1. Aggressiveness and that needed push towards the sensed goal which distinguishes the evolving human being. This goal, in the early stages, will be of a material nature.
2. The fighting spirit or that spirit of conflict which finally brings strength and poise, and which produces eventual integration with

the first ray aspect of deity.

3. That coherent force which makes a man a magnetic centre, whether as the major force in any group unity, such as a parent or a ruler, or a Master in relation to his group.

4. The power to create. In the lower types, this is connected with the impulse, or the instinct, to reproduce, leading consequently to the sex relation; or it may lead to construction of thoughtforms or creative forms of some kind, even if it is only the hut of a savage.

IN THE ADVANCED MAN

1. The Arjuna spirit. This is the urge towards victory, the holding of a position between the pairs of opposites, and the eventual sensing of the middle way.

2. The urge to synthesis (again a first ray impulse) blended with a second ray tendency to love and to include.

3. The attractive quality of the soul as it expresses itself in the relation between the lower and higher selves. This eventuates in the "marriage in the Heavens".

4. The power to create forms, or the artistic impulse.

It will be noted in this connection how accurate was the earlier statement that the artist is found upon all the rays, and that the so-called Ray of Harmony or Beauty is not the only ray upon which the creative worker is found. The mental body of every human being, at some time or another, is found upon the fourth ray and usually when the man is nearing the probationary path. This means that the mental vehicle is governed by an elemental of fourth ray nature or quality and that, therefore, creative, artistic activity is the line of least resistance. We then have a man with an artistic tendency or we have a genius along some line of creative work. When, at the same time, the soul or the personality is also upon the fourth ray, then we will find a Leonardo da Vinci or a Shakespeare. (EP2–291/2)

Ray Five
IN UNEVOLVED MAN

1. The power to develop thought.

2. The spirit of materialistic enterprise, the divine urge, as it evidences itself in the early stages.

3. The tendency to enquire, to ask questions and to find out. This is the instinct to search and to progress, which is, in the last analysis,

the urge to evolve.

4.   The tendency to crystallise, to harden, or to have an "idée fixe". In this connection, it will usually be discovered that the man who succumbs to an "idée fixe" has not only a fifth ray mental body but either a sixth ray personality or a sixth ray emotional body.

IN THE ADVANCED MAN

1.   The true thinker, or mental type – awake and alert.
2.   The one who knows the Plan, the purpose and the will of God.
3.   The one whose intelligence is being transmuted into wisdom.
4.   The scientist, the educator, the writer.   (EP2–293)

The First Ray as the Ray of the Mental Body

• …It is your first ray mind that gives you undoubted mental influence. This is felt most strongly by all who contact you. Being definitely in touch with your soul (which is in its turn under second ray influence) you have a combination of forces which is definitely useful, both to yourself and others. (DNA1–151/2)

• Your *mental body* is a first ray one and this is what makes you a real occult student. Your soul's contact is so definite and real that your mental body builds no barriers between the soul and your personality or between you and your co-disciples. Mentally, you always understand and are inclusive. I do not mean theoretically but in fact.   (DNA1–369/70)

• …The integrated personality force flows through a first ray mental body. This inevitably produces the accompanying characteristics of an intense centralisation (I did not say a selfish one, my brother) and an active assurance, a full fledged ambition (often of an entirely right nature, but occasionally not so right) and a power to analyze and oft to criticise others, their personalities and their tasks.   (DNA1–581)

• Your first ray mind has tended to bring about in you the following conditions:

1.   *A sense (sometimes unrealised) of separativeness….*
2.   *A tendency to criticise….*
3.   *A great facility for over-activity.* You have a mind body

which is in a constant state of fever, with (symbolically speaking, of course) periods of violent activity, amounting almost to delirium.... You are so over-active and your mind ranges so widely here, there and everywhere, that you fail in understanding and in true perception. There has been no time for you to comprehend anything before you are off again in a widely different direction. (DNA1–586)

The Second Ray as the Ray of the Mental Body

• Your *mental body* is on the second ray. This, as you will note, is not usual. It makes illumination the line of least resistance. It facilitates contact with the soul and provides your dominant problem. That problem is the demanding of love and of appreciation where your personality is concerned. Think this out. It means that you can always be depended upon to sacrifice everything in order that the desires, the will and the purpose of the soul – once they are made clear to you – may be truly worked out. Nothing will be permitted by you to arrest your spiritual achievement once the way appears open to you. But it means also, from the lower angle, that you will sacrifice much in order to be loved by people. This matters not at all in the case of the average person for in due time and inevitably a proper sense of proportion will emerge. But it does matter in the case of those who are on the Path of Discipleship and who face at some not so distant time preparation for initiation. Watch this with care and discover for yourself the situation. One clue to understanding would be that you study whether or not, in moments of personality emergency, you sacrifice your sense of truth or your friends. (DNA1–336)

• You have a second ray *mental body* and, therefore, are not adhering to the rule which usually governs the choice of the forces isolated in any particular mental body. Those upon the Path do not always adhere to the rules. This type of governing mental energy enables you to do three things:

1. Respond with facility – if you choose – to the impulses of your second ray soul.

2. Hold the mind steady in the light and thereby discern the basic principles which your first ray personality can so easily recognise.
3. Work with order, skill and precision in your chosen field of service.

You must, at the same time, guard against too much attention to detail which is always the line of least resistance and of satisfactory experience to those who possess your combination of ray forces. (DNA1–500/1)

The Third Ray as the Ray of the Mental Body

• …Your *mental body* is on the third Ray of Active Intelligence which is also your personality ray. This does two things for you: It definitely facilitates the integration of your personality, and is also enables you to contact your soul with relative ease, if you so choose. Nevertheless, it also emphasises all the third ray faculties and capacities of your personality – critical, analytical, separative, prideful and full of self-interest – and, as you are definitely going through a process of rapid integration, this produces situations which require most careful handling and watching. (DNA1–233)

The Fourth Ray as the Ray of the Mental Body

• Your *mental body* is on the fourth Ray of Harmony through Conflict and hence your pliability, your sense of relationship and your rapid grasp of mental truth. Illusion will ever be a more ready snare to you than glamour. (DNA1–133)

• Your *mental body*…is upon the fourth Ray of Harmony through Conflict. Hence your power to harmonise, to unify and to comprehend. (DNA1–168)

• Your *mental ray* is that of the fourth, the Ray of Harmony through Conflict, of beauty through order, and of unity through understanding. This, being on the line of your soul ray [second ray], will tend to bring about rapid contact with the soul, via the mind, if you apply yourself with diligence to the task involved. Your whole life problem is, therefore, that of relationships, both within yourself and in your chosen field of service. This is naturally true of all, but your particular battlefield in this connection lies in the reconciling of the forces warring within your own nature and in your particular environment.... It is the battlefield of higher relations – those between the soul and the personality, and between what you are in this life and the environment in which you find your chosen field of service. Your personal release lies in the production of harmony through conflict, and your best technique is to produce this harmonising influence within your environment *as the result* of your inner conflict, silently waged in the shrine of the mind. (DNA1–178/9)

• The ray of the mind, the fourth ray, is the controlling ray of your personality, and that means that the power to react to soul illumination is yours. The goal of your meditation should be *light*. (DNA1–196)

• ...The ray of your *mental body* is that of the fourth, which facilitates your task of responding to the light of the soul, for it gives you a mind nature which can react easily to your second ray soul, for it is on the same line of force. (DNA1–197)

• Your *mental body* is on the fourth Ray of Harmony through Conflict and this, at times, upsets your balance and your equilibrium. Your desire for harmony sometimes produces short-sighted vision and you tend to act precipitately. When this occurs, you later discover that you initiated conflict instead of having instituted harmony, as had been your original intention. But you can learn much thereby, because, in the last analysis, the fourth ray governs humanity itself as well as this planet, the earth; your fourth ray mind can always, therefore, put you in touch with the world of men, and do it with greater safety than can your emotional nature [sixth ray]. This fact, coupled with the wisdom and love of your personality, should aid you greatly in the task of working with people which is your chosen field of endeavour and expression. (DNA1–205)

• What, my brother, are the characteristics of a fourth ray

mental body? Let me list a few of them for you, leaving you to make your own application, in truthfulness and understanding.

Destructive	*Constructive*
An inner mental battle	The resolution of the pairs of opposites.
Many antagonisms	Non-partisanship. The Middle Way.
Prejudice	Tolerant understanding.
Personality unity and synthesis . . .	Group unity and synthesis.
Discord, interior and exterior	Harmony within and without.
Environal problems	Environal peace.
Imposition of the personal will . . .	Expression of the will-to-love.

There are, of course, many other qualities and tendencies but I have enumerated those of the greatest usefulness to you. I would remind you that the fourth ray is, when a part of the personality force equipment, the expression of the will-to-love (either in the material sense or in the spiritual). It is, therefore, allied to the first ray, through its will emphasis. (DNA1–257/8)

• Your *mental body* is on the fourth ray; hence your power to harmonise and to avert conflict, thus acting as a calm centre in the whirlpool of activity with which you are surrounded. (DNA1–275)

• Your *mental body* has been outstandingly a fourth-ray one, giving you a love of harmony which has aided you in organisation rule, a love of beauty which enabled you to see the real, and a discrimination which has enabled you to gather around yourself that which unfolded beauty to you – books and beautiful things. But it also gave you, as it ever does, a spirit of conflict, urging you forward to fresh victories in the cause of harmony. (DNA1–402)

• Your *mental body* is on the fourth ray. Hence the conflict and hence, at the same time, the deep-seated love of harmony. These have warred together in your life.... It is possible to love harmony so much that you will fight to get it and struggle to achieve it; in this way you enter into a world of glamour from which it is oft difficult to emerge. (DNA1–485)

• Your *mental body*...is on the fourth Ray of Harmony through Conflict and hence the intensity of your mystical interior life.... It is the factor in your life which makes you magnetic and loved. (DNA1–632)

• Your *mental body* is upon the fourth ray, which gives you your love of the arts and sciences; it is, however, for you basically the ray which brings – and which should bring – conflict into your life and your relationships. This idea has much value and usefulness to you, for it has been the conflict in your life...which can make you a strong hand in the dark to others. Forget this not, but battle on, remembering that you travel not alone. (DNA1–640)

• Your *mental body* is definitely on the fourth ray and it is through this fourth Ray of Harmony through Conflict that you can establish a rapid rapport with your brothers. It makes for understanding, intelligently applied, and for the emergence of beauty through that established rapport. It is the quality in you which gives you an ordered sense of colour, proportion and of harmony in your planned environment. It also evokes in you at times a violent reaction to that which seems incorrect, inharmonious and out of tune or line. (DNA1–646/7)

• Your *mental body*...is of the fourth ray type. This means that harmony appeals to you and the bringing together of opposites into an intelligent unity. But it is a harmony interpreted in terms of emotion.... You must ponder on harmony as the mind understands it, and remember that only those succeed in resolving discord into harmony who themselves work from a stable centre of adjustment. (DNA1–658/9)

• Your *mental body* is governed by the fourth ray, producing that love of art and literature which distinguishes you, and providing also that field of conflict which characterises your entire life. (DNA1–665)

• [A number] of the group members have the fourth Ray of Harmony through Conflict controlling the mental body, hence consequent conflict and proffered opportunity, plus an expressed ambition for the achievement of psychic harmony between the soul of form and the soul itself. It is through the conflict between these two that harmony becomes possible. This is the ray of testing, the energy which brings about trial. People struggle with ideas, with attaining the goal of their current idealism and are driven by longing to find peace, joy and divine assurance. After the cycle of lives in which the mental ray varies from life to life, there arrives an incarnation wherein the ray of harmony through conflict dominates; then the disciple is specifically put to the proof and is tested and tried in order to demonstrate to him the gain or the non-gain of the past cycle of living experience. Such a proposition [today] faces…humanity, one of whose controlling rays is the fourth. (DNA2–735)

The Fifth Ray as the Ray of the Mental Body

• *The mental body* in your case is governed by fifth ray energy. This is a pronounced condition and constitutes much of your life difficulty. It is, in the case of all aspirants thus conditioned mentally, the paramount cause of their *non*-magnetic behaviour, using that word in its psychological implications. I would remind you that being non-magnetic at your stage of development means that (even though you may have some measure of soul contact) you cannot radiate that soul life to others as you would like to do, for your dominant fifth ray mental body (the Ray of Concrete Science…) is insulated, isolated and has a natural tendency to that discrimination which leads to separativeness. The reverse effect is also true. The radiation of others can be also shut off and hence your inability to register telepathic impressions. The value of a fifth ray mind is however very great, for it means a keen and useful mind and (ponder on this) an open door to inspiration. (DNA1–120)

• The ray of your *mental body* is the fifth, and because it is the same ray as that of your personality, you will have to guard with care against mental crystallisation, and the undue influence of the critical mind. This ray gives you ability in the field of knowledge, but it must be balanced by the unfoldment of the intuition; it gives you the power to master your chosen field of knowledge, but that power must be balanced by the simultaneous mastering of the world wherein love and wisdom control. (DNA1–315)

• …Your fifth ray quality of mind can serve a useful group purpose. You are in a position to build a protecting wall (but not a separating barrier) around the group as a whole; it is to this activity I call you at this time. (DNA1–316)

• …Your fifth ray quality…is that of knowledge, and which, when present, can produce illumination. It is that quality which permits the man who has it, to *stand steady in the light,* to *rest in pure being,* and to *become the true Observer.* These qualities of steadiness with the intent to reflect light, of centralisation of the self, and of right observation are essential to this group. (DNA1–316/7)

• This fifth ray mind gives you the enquiring, questioning nature which is one of your outstanding characteristics– a great asset when rightly used; a major problem and real deterrent to the inflow of soul light when over-emphasised. (DNA1–350)

• …The one-pointedness of your fifth ray mind has determined the nature of your mental approach to problems and to people. (DNA1–352)

• Your *mental body* is on the fifth Ray of Concrete Knowledge or Science. Hence your interest and usefulness in the science of astrology which is in many ways the science of sciences. Hence also your keen mind, your untiring search for truth and your power to achieve light on many matters. The one point you should remember is that the fifth ray is a crystallising factor and (in conjunction with the will and power developed by you in your last life) could tend to make you dogmatic and consequently separative. This must be offset by your second ray soul. (DNA1–437)

• Your *mental body* is on the fifth ray and, therefore, you have an intensely analytical mind. I would, however, remind you that you are analytical but not discriminating. Ponder on this distinction. (DNA1–520)

• Your *mental body* is on the fifth ray, giving you your grip of facts and your grasp of the contours of the occult sciences. But this mental body must be guided into being an instrument of illumination and not simply a recorder of facts; this only becomes possible when head and heart vibrate in unison. (DNA1–540)

• ...Your fifth ray mentality...renders you non-magnetic and gives you a vertical and not a horizontal attitude to life. (DNA1–541)

• The fifth Ray of Concrete Knowledge is, in reality, that on which a man learns to use all acquired knowledge of the "form divine" in such a way that the inner life is served and the outer form becomes the magnetic expression of the divine life. It is the ray of *intelligent love* above all else, just as the second ray is the ray of *intuitive love* – a fact which is seldom remembered or known. (DNA1–542)

The Rays of the Astral Body

The First Ray as the Ray of the Astral Body

• ...Your *astral body* [as well as your mental body] is...upon the first ray which is an unique occurrence and rarely to be found. It is here that the sense of separateness enters in, for that first ray tendency does to you two things:

    a. It feeds your sense of separativeness and thus tends to isolate you.
    b. It fosters your fear of attachment.

Thus you are oft emotionally and astrally detached and isolated from those who love you and from your fellow-men. Hence there is a continuing conflict between your loving soul and your isolated, lonely, astral vehicle. (DNA1–370)

• Your *astral body* is also governed by the first ray. This is an exception to the general rule that the second and sixth rays govern the astral bodies of all humanity. This rule varies occasionally in the case of disciples. (DNA1–427)

• …You have a first ray *astral body*. This is again an exception to the usual rule. In the case of the disciple who is occupied with some particular rounding-out process this exception does occur, and the first ray personality of your last incarnation left you the legacy of a first ray astral body in this. (DNA1–466)

• Your *astral body* is on the first Ray of Will or Power and hence much of your difficulty in the past. A first ray astral body is a powerful asset but requires most careful watching and skilful harnessing. When not rightly handled, it is easily stirred up into storms and tempers or into the condition wherein the dramatic "I" is centralised in the life. (DNA1–501)

The Second Ray as the Ray of the Astral Body

• Your *astral body* is on the second ray…giving you those difficulties and those opportunities which lead eventually to expansions of consciousness and that sensitivity to the psyche in others which has been the basis of much of your most successful work. (DNA1–133)

• Your *astral body* is…a second ray aggregation of energies and hence the influence of love which you carry everywhere with you. I would remind you, however, that when the soul and the astral body are both on the same ray, there is presented always an engrossing problem of balance. (DNA1–152)

• Your second ray *astral body* greatly facilitates your work, giving you understanding and harmlessness; your emotions thus do not interfere with your judgment and your decisions. (DNA1–168)

• Your *astral body* has been governed by the second ray, and from certain points of view, this has been the most powerful influence in your personality equipment; it has been the balancing factor to the first-ray line energy, expressed by your soul and personality rays. (DNA1–402)

• Your *astral body* is on the second ray, and this fact much facilitates the task of your soul, and will account for the ability which you will discover in yourself to be a transmitter of light and love to others. It is this alignment between your soul and your astral body which gives you the intuitive insight you can use, if you remain humble and continue loving. (DNA1–640)

The Sixth Ray as the Ray of the Astral Body

• *The astral or emotional body* is conditioned by the sixth ray of devotion or of idealism, but this can be most easily transferred and transformed under the influence of the second Ray of Love-Wisdom. Your task this life is to make this possible so that, in your next life, you can have an astral body conditioned by the second ray. Your ability to go forward in the face of obstacles in order to attain your ideal is your outstanding asset, and one that will land you eventually at your goal. (DNA1–120)

• ...You have oriented the astral body to the higher values and impressions and have done it so successfully that your emotional sensitivity to others is now definitely a working asset. (DNA1–122)

• Your *astral or emotional body* is on the sixth ray.... In your case, this sixth ray energy shows itself predominantly as devotion to duty as realised, and to responsibility as recognised, and not so much in devotion to persons or even ideals. This has constituted a paramount balancing factor in your life. (DNA1–179)

• Your *astral body* is on the sixth ray. This gives you a one-pointed attitude to life and primarily, in your case, to the things of the spiritual world.... This ray also enables you to make a fairly facile soul contact, should you so desire. (DNA1–197)

• Your *astral body* is...upon the sixth Ray of Devotion. This gives you idealism, devotion to causes, your power to sacrifice and your determination always to produce good out of seeming evil. (DNA1–205)

• It should be remembered that the rays themselves have their secondary attributes and just as the sixth ray – expressed in your personality – can lead to the fanatical following of the ideal (whatever that may connote to you) so the same ray in the astral body produces the expression of devotion.... This devotion where you are concerned is not devotion to your own selfish interests but it is for you a great extroverting factor. It leads you along the way of service. (DNA1–255)

• Your *astral body* is on the sixth ray but...its major quality is devotion and devoted persistence, and not fanaticism. This energy is of immense value to you because it is, curiously enough, your only link with the great second ray of love in this particular incarnation. But it is a strong and powerful link. (DNA1–315)

• Another source of your trouble is to be found in your sixth ray astral body (the ray of idealistic, fanatical devotion) for it produces a real lack of balance, an undue attention to details of process, and of devotion to those details from the emotional satisfaction which comes from this attention; this brings about a failure to understand the larger issues and an inability to move gently on the Way. (DNA1–415)

• This [sixth] ray force gives you devotion, idealism, a dynamic will to pierce through all glamours and misconceptions and thus achieve truth and freedom, both for yourself and for your group and those you serve. (DNA1–438)

• Your *astral body* is on the sixth ray.... This gives you intensity in aspiration and the dynamic will to push forward which has sufficed hitherto to carry you over all obstacles. You have succeeded in avoiding the usual difficulties of...fanatical adherences to people or schools of thought. (DNA1–447)

• Your *astral body* is on the sixth ray and this intensifies your Taurian tendencies for, as the Bull rushes straight forward seeing only that which lies directly ahead, so does the sixth ray fanatic. When, however, this aptitude is applied to the path of service, much progress can be made. (DNA1–486)

• Your *astral body* is upon the sixth ray. This gives you the one-pointedness which is such an asset to any disciple, but it also gives a measure of narrowness which at times handicaps you. (DNA1–540)

• ...A sixth ray astral body (where a disciple is concerned) predicates intense adherence to a line of thought, to an idea, a group, a person or an attitude or to a preconceived notion. These may be right or wrong but the tendency to adherence is powerfully present and can be a great asset or a major hindrance. In any case – again for a disciple – any *idée fixe* (beyond that of a right spiritual orientation) can be a deterrent to progress, if fanatically motivated. (DNA1–582/3)

• ...Your sixth ray astral body intensifies your problem for it leads you to be devoted to the superficial phenomena which you regard as realities. (DNA1–637)

• Your *astral body* is definitely sixth ray and hence predisposes you to Piscean attitudes, emotional *idées fixes,* violent astral storms, great devotions which call your emotional reactions into play on matters and subjects which, in this day of world suffering and crisis, do not warrant attention and constitute an easy tuning-in on glamour and illusion. (DNA1–659)

• Because of that fixed devotion, they can walk undeviatingly upon the Way. But they are apt to forget that – equally because of that devotion – they ray forth a quality which stimulates its correspondence in others. That is why sixth ray people can easily form a group around themselves. But they seldom succeed in holding those thus attracted for very long, because they do not understand the reason for this facility and ascribe it ever to wrong causes.... In your case [your sixth ray astral body] produces [a] sense of inferiority.... I would ask you to change your point of view and to regard your sixth ray astral body as a powerful piece of equipment to be used in service. (DNA2–477)

The Rays of the Physical Body

• ...The brain is ever composed of atoms and cell units which vibrate to the energy of the ray which controls the physical body. This is a basic occult fact given out in a definite statement for the first time but ever deducible and implied when the student studies intelligently and has a real grasp of basic esoteric implications. (DNA2–494)

The First Ray as the Ray of the Physical Body

• Your *physical body* is of a dominant first ray type. This again is not usually so except in the case of disciples, who are liable to build vehicles of any type of force to meet the emergency, the need or the service of a particular life. This first ray body enables you to handle spiritual energy upon the physical plane. It enables you also to act as a force transmitter and distributor. (DNA1–336/7)

The Third Ray as the Ray of the Physical Body

• You have a third ray (the Ray of Intelligent Activity) *physical body.* This is largely controlled, interiorly, by your fifth ray mind. (DNA1–121)

• [Your difficulty] also lies in your third ray *physical body* which, again upon the mental line, increases the activity of your critical personality. It is yourself, however, whom you mainly criticise, but this can be as wrong and as unnecessary as criticising others. (DNA1–198)

• You have a third ray *physical body*. This gives you contact and brings you down to earth, a thing that a sixth ray person predominantly needs, particularly when highly developed. It aids you in expression upon the physical plane; it makes a focal point for the manifestation of the soul, for it is peculiarly the ray through which the third aspect of divinity sweeps into expression; it can produce the potency of personality expression but it can also prove a definite hindrance. (DNA1–255)

• Your *physical body* is on the third Ray of Active Intelligence. This was the factor which brought you originally into the business field and has, therefore, inclined you to field work, and organisation work. (DNA1–379)

• Your *physical body* is on the third Ray of Active Intelligence. This has given you your capacity to work upon the physical plane, to handle money (though not in your own interests) and has tied you in closely with the material life of your environment, in a curiously symbolic manner. (DNA1–402)

• Your third ray physical body inclines you to great physical activity (such as rapid movement and rapid speech); it keeps you working at something all the time and often at something quite unproductive of good results, and not proportionate to the labour expended. (DNA1–415)

• Your *physical body* is on the third ray. This gives you an active, intelligent grip upon life and a coordinated physical vehicle. (DNA1–540)

• ...Your third ray physical body...demands change and requires variety; it dislikes quietness and stability. (DNA1–541)

The Sixth Ray as the Ray of the Physical Body

• As your *physical body* is also upon the sixth ray, your brain is consequently most responsive to your astral impulses. (DNA1–233)

• Your *physical body* is also on the sixth ray which makes it – and, therefore, your brain – predominantly the servant of your astral body but it also makes you intuitive or astral-buddhic. Therefore, I would have you note that, in your case, there is an exception to the usual rule controlling the physical body, for very few physical bodies are on the sixth ray, as is yours. (DNA1–520)

The Seventh Ray as the Ray of the Physical Body

• Your *physical body* is on the seventh ray, which gives you a sense of the relationship between spirit and matter, between soul and body and enables you, if so you will, to be a constructive agent in magical work. (DNA1–133)

• ...Your *physical body* is on the seventh ray. Hence your Masonic opportunity and your ability to organise and to rule. I would remind you all that when the statement is made that the physical body is upon the seventh ray, it means that the atoms of the brain, in particular, are coloured and motivated by seventh ray energy. So it is with all the rays upon which a physical vehicle may be found. This provides a definite opportunity to those so constituted at this time in connection with the seventh ray, as it is coming into influence so rapidly. At the same time it provides a problem – that unending problem of the balancing of forces which is the major task of the initiate or of those in training for initiation. (DNA1–168)

• Your *physical body* is on the seventh Ray of Ceremonial Order or Magic; here is to be found the source of much of your ill-health. The seventh plane is the plane upon which spirit must express itself. It is the receptacle of spiritual energy. Your physical vehicle and medium of expression is of such a sensitive and refined nature and so frail a receptacle that your life problem is to handle wisely the spiritual energy which seeks to pour through. (DNA1–438)

• Your *physical body* is on the seventh Ray of Ceremonial Order or Magic, and hence your interest in spiritualism.... (DNA1–549)

• Your *physical body* is upon the seventh ray and this makes for integration and for efficiency. (DNA1–583)

• Your *physical body* is upon the seventh ray...accounting, as it does, for your interest in music, ritual, psycho-analysis. The goal of all these three methods of expression is to bring together and relate harmoniously the soul and the form, which is the major task of the seventh ray upon the seventh or physical plane. (DNA1–640)

Initiation
and the Rays

• Each initiation gives more control on the rays, if one may so express it, although this does not adequately convey the idea. Words so often mislead. At the fifth initiation, when the adept stands Master in the three worlds, He controls more or less (according to His line of development) the five rays that are specially manifesting at the time He takes the initiation. At the sixth initiation, if He takes the higher degree, He gains power on another ray, and at the seventh initiation He wields power on all the rays. The sixth initiation marks the point of attainment of the Christ, and brings the synthetic ray of the system under His control. We need to remember that initiation gives the initiate *power on the rays,* and not *power over the rays,* for this marks a very definite difference. Every initiate has, of course, for his primary or spiritual ray one of the three major rays, and the ray of his Monad is the one on which he at length gains power. The love ray, or the synthetic ray of the system, is the final one achieved. (IHS–17)

• 1. The magical force of the seventh Logos is felt at the first Initiation.

   2. The aggressive fire of the sixth Logos is felt at the second Initiation.

   3. The illuminating light of the fifth Logos is felt at the third Initiation.

   4. The harmonising life of the fourth Logos is felt at the fourth Initiation.

   5. The blending power of the third Logos is felt at the fifth Initiation.

6. The unifying heat of the second Logos is felt at the sixth Initiation.

7. The dynamic electricity of the first Logos is felt at the seventh Initiation. (TCF–433)

• All who are in these groups have taken the first initiation, as have so many thousands of people in the world today. Many have taken the second initiation, particularly those who are working in fifth ray Ashrams and in third ray Ashrams, for such disciples are distinguished by a lack of emotional emphasis.

Group initiation has been forced upon the Hierarchy by the rapid unfoldment of the spiritual consciousness in humanity, an unfoldment which demonstrates – no matter what the ray – as goodwill. This goodwill is not to be interpreted as the sentimental sixth or second ray untrained aspirant is prone to interpret it. It can take many forms: it can show itself as sacrifice on the part of science and a dedication of the fruits of scientific research to human welfare; it may take shape in the third ray aptitude to dedicate great wealth to philanthropic or educational enterprises. In neither of these cases is the disciple apparently distinguished by a so-called loving nature. Yet the results of their application to science or their accumulation of the crystallised prana of the financial world are turned to the helping of mankind. This will be a hard saying for some of you who rate an irritable remark by a co-disciple as something disgraceful and belittle the efforts of the money-maker, and do both with a sense of self-righteous congratulation. (DNA2–336/7)

• The second initiation is a profoundly difficult one to take. For those upon the first or second rays of aspect it is probably the most difficult of them all. The astral nature is deeply self-centred, and this the inflow of soul energy in the initiatory period intensifies; it is endowed with acute emotionalism and swift response to glamour. Where there is so much first ray energy to be found...there will be a strong conviction of destiny, a pronounced sense of power, and the feeling that you can see through people – from a superior position – so that their faults and failures and their little human failings loom large in your consciousness. (DNA2–525/6)

• As the three rays which govern the lower triplicity blend and synthesise and produce the vital personality, and as they in their turn dominate the ray of the dense physical body, the lower man enters into a prolonged condition of conflict. Gradually and increasingly, the soul ray, "the ray of persistent and magnetic grasp", as it is occultly called, begins to become more active; in the brain of the man who is a developed personality, an increased awareness of vibration is set up. There are many degrees and stages in this experience, and they cover many lives. The personality ray and the egoic ray at first seem to clash, and then later a steady warfare is set up with the disciple as the onlooker – and dramatic participator. Arjuna emerges into the arena of the battlefield. Midway between the two forces he stands, a conscious tiny point of sentient awareness and of light. Around him and in him and through him the energies of the two rays pour and conflict. Gradually, as the battle continues to rage, he becomes a more active factor, and drops the attitude of the detached and uninterested onlooker. When he is definitely aware of the issues involved, and definitely throws the weight of his influence, desires, and mind on to the side of the soul, he can take the first initiation. When the ray of the soul focuses itself fully through him, and all his centres are controlled by that focused soul ray, then he becomes the transfigured Initiate, and takes the third initiation. The ray of the personality is occultly "extinguished" or absorbed by the ray of the soul, and all the potencies and attributes of the lower rays become subsidiary to and coloured by the soul ray. The disciple becomes a "man of God", – a person whose powers are controlled by the dominant vibration of the soul ray and whose inner, sensitive mechanism is vibrating to the measure of that soul ray which – in its turn – is being itself reoriented to, and controlled by, the monadic ray. The process then repeats itself:–

1. The many rays which constitute the lower separative man are fused and blended into the three personality rays.
2. These are, in their turn, fused and blended into a synthetic expression of the dominant self-assertive man, the personal self.
3. The personality rays then become one ray and in their turn become subservient to the dual ray of the soul. Again, therefore, three rays are blended and fused.
4. The soul rays dominate the personality and the three become again the one, as the dual ray of the soul and the blended ray of the personality vibrate to the measure of the highest of the soul rays – the ray of the soul's group, which is ever regarded as the true egoic ray.
5. Then, in time, the soul ray begins (at the third initiation) to blend with the ray of the Monad, the life ray. The higher initiate is therefore a dual and not a triple expression.
6. In time, however, this realised duality gives place to the mysterious, indescribable process called *identification* which is the final stage of soul unfoldment. It is useless to say more for what might be said could only be comprehended by those preparing for the fourth initiation, and this treatise is written for disciples and initiates of the first degree. (EP2–17/18)

• ...Disciples upon the different rays will all have the same goal, make the same experiments, go through the same experience and arrive equally at divine expression. However, their qualities and their modes of approach, their reactions and their distinctive natures will differ according to their ray type; this constitutes a most interesting and little known phase of our study of initiation. Initiation has been a blanket happening, and no note has been made of the ray implications. This I propose to remedy.

Each of the seven initiations, for instance, is an exemplification or a revealer of one of the seven ray qualities or tendencies; it is governed and conditioned always by a certain ray, and this is one of the factors which disciples have to learn and grasp whilst preparing for an initiation, because it involves success in handling and manipulating certain types of divine energy.

Each of the initiations brings one or other of the seven centres into full functioning activity, not from the angle of awakening or of stimulation, but from the angle of a "wheel turning upon itself". (RI–338)

• ...There comes a life cycle wherein the disciple reverses himself upon the Wheel of Life (the zodiacal wheel) and from going clockwise around the zodiac, he now begins to go anti-clockwise; he learns that the substance aspect of his nature may still be conditioned by the forces flowing through them sequentially and serially, and according to his horoscope and according to the exoteric mode of the zodiacal revolution; at the same time, the disciple is receiving energy currents from the reversed wheel whereon he, as a soul, finds himself. He is consequently the recipient of two currents of energy, going in reverse directions; hence the increased conflict in his life and circumstances; these constitute the reason for the tests of initiation....

You have, therefore:

Initiation 1. Birth
Sacral centre	7th ray		Physical plane
Beginnings	Relationship	Sex Magic	

Initiation 2. Baptism
Solar plexus centre	6th ray		Astral plane
Dedication	Glamour	Devotion	

Initiation 3. Transfiguration
Ajna centre	5th ray		Mental plane
Integration	Direction	Science	

Initiation 4. Renunciation
Heart centre	4th ray		Buddhic plane
Crucifixion	Sacrifice	Harmony	

Initiation 5. Revelation
Base of spine	1st ray		Atmic Plane
Emergence	Will	Purpose	(RI–339/40)

Group Initiation

• ...One of the prime prerequisites for initiation is a clear and concise recognition of one's own group, not through a process of wishful thinking, but through factual co-operation and work upon the physical plane. I said *group,* my brother, and not organisation, for they are two very different things.

Have carefully in mind, therefore, the fact of group initiation, and forego the process of considered thought anent *your* preparation for initiation. Some groups are being prepared for initiation in which the following factors control – as far as the individual is concerned:

1. A group of men and women whose souls are on some one ray are gathered together subjectively by a Master on the same ray, for group training.
2. Opportunity is given to such people to contact on the physical plane some of those who are thus subjectively linked, and thus mutually convey a sense of group solidarity. The subjective relationship is assured by an objective contact. Recognition is therefore a preliminary test of initiation, and this should be remembered.
3. Such people thus being trained and related are, from the angle of the initiation to be taken, at the same point in evolution. They are taking the same initiation and are being subjected to the same tests and difficulties. These tests and difficulties are due to the fact of the personality ray which may be (and usually is) quite different to the soul ray. It is the personality ray which works to prevent contact, to mislead in recognition, to retard progress and to misinterpret information. As long as a disciple in training is focused in his personality, group initiation will not be possible for him, his recognition of co-aspirants will be fleeting and rapidly disturbed by the critical lower mind, and a wall of thoughtforms, created by the personality, anent the group members, will be thrown up and prevent a united moving forward through the Door of Initiation.

4. Group initiation cannot be achieved by a group in training until the members, as a group, have developed their particular "spiritual enterprise". It is the law of the spirit that the disciple must appear before the Initiator empty-handed, but that in group formation the group members unitedly contribute something to the enrichment of the Ashram. This may take the form of some considered project in line with the Plan, whereby they testify to their comprehension of that Plan and demonstrate to the initiate-company in which they find themselves, and those senior disciples to whose contact they are to be admitted, that they have already proven their fitness for acceptance and have proven it along the line of service. It has to be a group enterprise, a group service and a group contribution. The specific contribution of the individual does not appear.

This thought of group initiation must be remembered, for it will colour all that I shall seek to convey to your minds and will hasten the day of your own acceptance.

No one is admitted (through the processes of initiation) into the Ashram of the Christ (the Hierarchy) until such time as he is beginning to think and live in terms of group relationships and group activities. Some well-meaning aspirants interpret the group idea as the instruction to them that they should make an effort to form groups – their own group or groups. This is not the idea as it is presented in the Aquarian Age, so close today; it *was* the mode of approach during the Piscean Age, now passed. Today, the entire approach is totally different. No man today is expected to stand at the centre of his little world and work to become a focal point for a group. His task now is to discover the group of aspirants with which he should affiliate himself and with whom he must travel upon the Path of Initiation – a very different matter and a far more difficult one. (RI–342/4)

Initiation I. The Birth at Bethlehem. Ray VII.
The Energy of Order or Ceremonial Magic.

• [The] incoming of a ray always produces an intensified period of initiatory activity, and this is the case today. The major effect, as far as humanity is concerned, is to make possible the presentation of thousands of aspirants and applicants for the first initiation; men on a large scale and in mass formation can today pass through the experience of the Birth Initiation. Thousands of human beings can experience the birth of the Christ within themselves and can realise that the Christ life, the Christ nature and the Christ consciousness are theirs.... These great initiations, implemented by the ray energies, must be registered in the physical brain and recorded by the waking consciousness of the initiate, and this must be the case in this amazing period wherein – for the first time since humanity appeared on Earth – there can take place a mass initiation. The experience need not be expressed in occult terms, and in the majority of cases will not be; the individual initiate who takes this initiation is aware of great changes in his attitude to himself, to his fellowmen, to circumstances and to his interpretation of life events. These are peculiarly the reactions which attend the first initiation; a new orientation to life and a new world of thought are registered by the initiate. This will be equally true on a large scale where modern man, the world initiate of the first degree, is concerned. Men will recognise the evidences in many lives of the emergence of the Christ-consciousness, and the standard of living will increasingly be adjusted to the truth as it exists in the teachings of the Christ....

In connection with the individual and the first initiation, the seventh ray is always active and the man is enabled consciously to register the fact of initiation because either the brain or the mind (and frequently both) are controlled by the seventh ray. It is this fact which is of importance today in connection with humanity, for it will enable mankind to pass through the door admitting them to the first initiatory process....

The seventh ray is, par excellence, the medium of relationship. It brings together the two fundamental aspects of spirit and matter. It relates soul and form and, where humanity is concerned, it relates soul and personality. In the first initiation, it makes the initiate aware of that relation; it enables him to take advantage of this "approaching duality" and – by the perfecting of the contact – to produce upon the physical plane the emergence into manifestation of the "new man". At the first initiation, through the stimulation brought about by seventh ray energy, the personality of the initiate and the hovering over-shadowing soul are consciously brought together; the initiate then knows that he is – for the first time – a soul-infused personality. His task is now to grow into the likeness of what he essentially is. This development is demonstrated at the third initiation, that of the Transfiguration.

The major function of this seventh ray is to bring together the negative and positive aspects of the natural processes. It consequently governs the sex relationship of all forms; it is the potency underlying the marriage relation, and hence as this ray comes into manifestation in this world cycle, we have the appearance of fundamental sex problems – license, disturbance in the marriage relation, divorce and the setting in motion of those forces which will eventually produce a new attitude to sex and the establishing of those practices, attitudes and moral perceptions which will govern the relation between the sexes during the coming New Age.

The first initiation is therefore closely related to this problem. The seventh ray governs the sacral centre and the sublimation of its energy into the throat or into the higher creative centre; this ray is therefore setting in motion a period of tremendous creative activity, both on the material plane through the stimulation of the sex life of all peoples and in the three worlds through the stimulation brought about when soul and form are consciously related. The first major proof that humanity (through the medium of the majority of its advanced people) has undergone the first initiation will be the appearance of a cycle of entirely new creative art. This creative urge will take forms which will express the new incoming energies. Just as the period governed by the sixth ray has culminated in a world wherein men work in great workshops and factories to produce the plethora of objects men deem needful for their happiness and well-being, so in the seventh ray cycle we shall see men engaged on an even larger scale in the field of creative art. Devotion to objects will eventually be superseded by the creation of that which will more truly express the Real; ugliness and materiality will give place to beauty and reality. On a large scale, humanity has already been "led from darkness to light" and the light of knowledge fills the land. In the period which lies ahead and under the influencing radiation of the seventh ray, humanity will be "led from the unreal to the Real". This the first initiation makes possible for the individual and will make possible for the mass of men.

Seventh ray energy is the energy needed to bring order out of chaos and rhythm to replace disorder. It is this energy which will bring in the new world order for which all men wait; it will restore the ancient landmarks, indicate the new institutions and forms of civilisation and culture which human progress demands, and nurture the new life and the new states of consciousness which advanced humanity will increasingly register. Nothing can arrest this activity; all that is happening today as men search for the new ways, for organised unity and peaceful security, is being implemented through the incoming Ray of Order or Ceremonial Magic. The white magic of right human relations cannot be stopped; it must inevitably demonstrate effectively, because the energy of this seventh ray is present, and the Lord of the Ray is co-operating with the Lord of the World to bring about the needed "re-forming". Soul-infused personalities, acting under this ray influence, will create the new world, express the new qualities and institute those new regimes and organised modes of creative activity which will demonstrate the new livingness and the new techniques of living. It is the distortion of these seventh ray ideals and the prostitution of this incoming energy to serve the unenlightened and selfish ambitions of greedy men which has produced those totalitarian systems which today so terribly imprison the free spirit of men.

To sum up what I have said:

1. The energy of the seventh ray is the potent agent of initiation when taken on the physical plane, that is, during the process of the first initiation.

2. Its effect upon humanity will be:
    a. To bring about the birth of the Christ-consciousness among the masses of intelligently aspiring human beings.
    b. To set in motion certain relatively new evolutionary processes which will transform humanity (the world disciple) into humanity (the world initiate).
    c. To establish in a new and intelligible manner the ever-existent sense of relationship and thus bring about upon the physical plane right human relations. The agent of this is goodwill, a reflection of the will-to-good of the first divine aspect. Of this first Ray of Will or Purpose, goodwill is the reflection.
    d. To readjust negative and positive relationships, and – today – this will be carried forward primarily in connection with the sex relation and marriage.
    e. To intensify human creativity and thus bring in the new art as a basis for the new culture and as a conditioning factor in the new civilisation.
    f. To reorganise world affairs and so initiate the new world order. This is definitely in the realm of ceremonial magic.

3. The stimulation of this seventh ray will, in relation to the individual initiate,
    a. Bring into being upon the mental plane a widespread and recognised relation between the soul and the mind.
    b. Produce a measure of order in the emotional processes of the initiate, thus aiding the preparatory work of the second initiation.
    c. Enable the initiate – upon the physical plane – to estab-

lish certain service relationships, to learn the practice of elementary white magic, and to demonstrate the first stage of a truly creative life.

As far as the individual initiate is concerned, the effect of seventh ray energy in his life is potent in the extreme; this is easily realised, owing to the fact that his mind and his brain are conditioned by the seventh ray at the time that the initiatory process is consciously taking place. The effect of this upon the mental plane is similar to that seen – on a much larger scale – in the planet, for it was this ray energy which the planetary Logos utilised when He brought together the major dualities of spirit and matter at the commencement of His creative work. The two aspects of the mind (the lower concrete mind and the soul, the Son of Mind) become more closely related and enter eventually into a conscious, recognised association *on the astral plane;* it is the seventh ray which restores order within the astral consciousness, and (on the mental plane) it is this influence which produces creativity, the organising of the life, and the bringing together "within the head" of the lower and higher energies in such a manner that "the Christ is born"....

Finally, it is seventh ray energy which – in the initiatory process between the first and the second initiations – enables the initiate (in his physical plane life) to demonstrate a developing sense of order and of organisation, to express consciously and increasingly a desire to help his fellowmen, and thereby establish relationship with them, and to make his life creative in many ways.

All these factors are embryonic in his nature, but he now begins to *consciously* lay the foundation for the future initiatory work; the physical disciplines are at this time of great importance, though their value is frequently over-emphasised and their effect is not always good; the relationships established and fostered are sometimes of small value, owing to the disciple being usually self-centred and thus lacking – from ignorance and lack of discrimination – complete purity of motive. Nevertheless, the changes brought about by the influence of this ray become increasingly effective from life to life; the disciple's relation to the Hierarchy, the reorganising of his life on the physical plane, and his growing effort to demonstrate the esoteric sense of white magic will become more and more vital, until he is ready for the second initiation. (RI–567/75)

Initiation II. The Baptism in Jordan. Ray VI.
The Energy of Idealism and Devotion.

• In the initiatory process between the first initiation of the Birth of the Christ and the beginning of the conscious unfoldment of the Christ life and awareness, the life of the initiate has undergone a pronounced reorientation. He is now capable of an equally pronounced and often fanatical adherence to the programme of aspiration and of devotion to the good (as he sees it at this stage).... The disciple is learning to discipline his lower nature and to achieve a measure of mastery over his physical inclinations; he thus releases physical energy and brings order into his life. This takes a very long time and may cover a cycle of many incarnations. He is constantly fighting against his lower nature, and the requirements of his soul (as he somewhat ignorantly interprets them) are in constant session against the animal nature, and increasingly in relation to the emotional nature.

...He discovers that he lives in a chaos of emotional reactions and of conditioning glamours. He slowly begins to realise that in order to take the second initiation he *must* demonstrate emotional control; he realises also that he must have some knowledge of those spiritual energies which will dissipate glamour, plus an understanding of the technique whereby illumination from the mind – as the transmitting agent of the light of the soul – can dispel these glamours and thus "clarify the atmosphere", in the technical sense.

I might emphasise that as yet no initiate demonstrates complete control during the intermediate period between any initiation and the next higher initiation; the intermediate period is regarded as "a cycle of perfecting"....

The initiatory process between the first and the second initiations is for many the worst time of distress, difficulty, realisation of problems and the constant effort to "clear himself" (as it is occultly called), to which the disciple is at any time subjected....

As regards humanity as a whole, polarised as it is in the emotional nature, the effect of this sixth ray is potent in the extreme. Its energy has been playing upon men ever since it came into incarnation, and the last one hundred fifty years have seen that potency become extremely effective. Two factors have enhanced this effect:

1. The sixth Ray of Idealism or of Devotion is the ray which normally governs the astral plane, controlling its phenomena and colouring its glamour.
2. The stream of energy, coming into our planetary life from the constellation Pisces, has for two thousand years conditioned human experience and is peculiarly fitted to blend with and complement this sixth ray energy and to produce exactly the situation which is today governing world affairs.

The united activity of these two great streams of cosmic energy, playing upon and through the third planetary centre, Humanity, has created the unique condition in which "the race of men" can stand before the planetary Initiator, the Christ, and under the focused stimulation of the Hierarchy, pass through the appropriate initiation.

It should here be remembered that the masses of men can and will take the first initiation, but that a very large group of aspirants (far larger than is realised) will pass through the experience of the second initiation, that of the purifying Baptism. These are the people who express the essential qualities of ideological recognition, devoted adherence to truth as sensed, profound reaction to the physical disciplines (imposed since they participated in the first initiation many lives earlier) and a growing responsiveness to the aspirational aspect of the astral body; this aspiration is occupied with reaching out towards contact with and expression of the mental principle. This particular group in the human family are "kamamanasic" initiates, just as those taking the first initiation are "physico-etheric" initiates.

It is the activity of this sixth ray which has brought out into the light of day the growing ideological tendencies of mankind....

The work of sixth ray energy, the result of the long cycle of Piscean energy, and the impact of the incoming Aquarian energy will bring a potent transformation in the "watery realm" of the astral plane.... The sixth ray will bring together all these energies in time and space: ray energy, Piscean energy, Aquarian energy and the energy of the astral plane itself; this again produces a vortex of force which is invocative of mental energy; it is a controlling factor, which has plunged humanity into a tumultuous awareness of clashing ideologies, which has precipitated a reflected vortex in the world war, and which is responsible for the present crisis and point of tension [published 1948]....

As regards the individual initiate who is to undergo the initiation of the Baptism, the effect of sixth ray energy upon his nature is easily apparent, owing to the extreme potency of the second aspect of the personality in the three worlds, his astral body or nature. In the early stages of the impact of sixth ray energy upon his emotional nature a perfect vortex of force is generated, his emotional reactions are violent and compelling, his glamours are intensified and controlling, and his aspiration steadily mounts, but is at the same time limited and hindered by the strength of his devotion to some sensed ideology. Later, under the influence of an increasing soul contact (itself the second aspect of his essential divinity), his emotional, kamic and aspirational nature becomes quieter and is more controlled through the agency of the mind; his alignment becomes astral-mental-soul. When this state of consciousness has been achieved and the "waters" of the astral body are quiet and can reflect the beautiful and the true, and when his emotions have been purified by intense self-effort, then the disciple can step into the baptismal waters; he is then subjected to an intense purificatory experience which, occultly speaking, enables him "for ever to step out of the waters and be no longer in danger of drowning or of submergence"; he can now "walk on the surface of the sea and with safety proceed onward towards his goal".

The effect of sixth ray activity upon the mental nature is, as you may imagine, a tendency – first of all – to the crystallising of thought, a reaction to imprisoning ideologies, and a fanatical mental adherence to mass ideals, with no understanding of their relationship to the need of the time or to their intended creative aspects. Later, as the disciple prepares for the second initiation, these tendencies are transformed into spiritual devotion to human welfare and to a one-pointed adherence to the Plan of the Hierarchy; all *emotional* reaction to the Hierarchy of Masters fades out, and the disciple can now work without being hindered by constant astral disturbances.

The effect of sixth ray energy upon the integrated personality of the disciple can only be described as producing a condition wherein he is definitely astral-buddhic in his nature; gradually his one-pointed emotional effort towards orientation to the soul makes him "an aspiring point of tension, oblivious of crisis and firmly anchored in the love which streams forth from the soul".

Let me sum up what I have said anent the effect of sixth ray energy:

1. The energy of the sixth ray produces two major results:
   a. An embryonic realisation of the will nature which determines the life of the initiate.
   b. A pronounced conflict between the lower and the higher self. This reveals to the initiate the ancient conflict between the emotional nature and true realisation.

This brings about a basic reorientation of the life of the initiate and of humanity as a whole.

2. In connection with humanity, the effects of the sixth ray are as follows:
   a. The development of a tendency to clarify the world atmosphere, thus releasing the energy of goodwill.

    b.   The production of a condition wherein "the race of men" can take either the first or the second initiation.

    c.   The sudden and powerful emergence· of the world ideologies.

    d.   A basic transformation within the astral plane itself which is producing points of crisis and a point of tension.

3.   In relation to the individual initiate, the sixth ray produces:

    a.   An acute situation wherein a vortex of force is generated.

    b.   In this vortex all the emotional and ideological reactions of the aspirant are intensified.

    c.   Later, when this subsides, the initiate's alignment becomes astral-mental-soul.

    d.   There takes place, in connection with his mental vehicle, a crystallisation of all thought and a fanatical adherence to mass idealism.

    e.   These tendencies are later transformed into spiritual devotion to human welfare.

    f.   The personality becomes definitely astral-buddhic in nature and expression.

...It is the activity of the seventh Ray of Order and of the sixth Ray of Idealism which has generated the tendency in humanity towards the white magic of right human relations. They have fostered the trend to ideological control of the human consciousness. It is the passing out of the Piscean Age with its type of energy, and the coming into power of the Aquarian Age (with its potent purificatory energies and its quality of synthesis and universality) which will make the new world order possible. It is therefore apparent that the opportunity confronting humanity has never been so promising and that the corporate relation and fusion of all these energies makes the manifestation of the Sons of God and the appearance of the Kingdom of God an inevitable happening in our planetary life. (RI–575/584)

Initiation III. The Transfiguration. RAY V.
The Energy of Concrete Knowledge.

• As all disciples have to be focused on the mental plane and must operate from that level of consciousness, the understanding of this type of consciousness is one of major importance. It is glibly and most easily said that disciples and (necessarily so) initiates must use the mind, and that their polarisation must be mental. But what does this mean? Let me give you some concise definitions of this ray energy, leaving you to make your own individual application, and from your study of these concepts anent the mind, learn to gauge your own mental condition.

1. The energy of what is so peculiarly called "concrete science" is the quality or the conditioning nature of the fifth ray.

2. It is pre-eminently *the substance* of the mental plane. This plane corresponds to the third subplane of the physical plane, and is therefore gaseous in nature – if you care to use its correspondence as a symbol of its nature. It is volatile, easily dispersed, is the receptive agent of illumination, and can be poisonous in its effect, for there are undoubtedly conditions in which "the mind is the slayer of the Real".

3. This energy is characterised by three qualities:
   a. The quality which is the result of relationship with the Spiritual Triad. We call this "abstract mind" and the impact which affects it comes from the atmic level of the Spiritual Triad, that of spiritual will.
   b. The quality which in this solar system is easily responsive to the major ray of the planet, that of love-wisdom. So responsive is it that – in conjunction with emanations from the three worlds – it has produced the one existent form upon the mental plane. This form (in the planetary sense) is that of the Kingdom of God and, in the individual sense, is that of the ego or soul.
   c. The quality which is basically related to the emanations

or vibrations arising from the three worlds; these creatively result in the myriads of thoughtforms which are found upon the lower levels of the mental plane. It might therefore be said that these qualities or aspects of the fifth ray of spiritual energy produce:

> Pure thought
> The thinker or the Son of Mind
> Thoughtforms

4. This energy (as far as mankind is concerned) is the thoughtform making energy, and all impressions from the physical, etheric and astral planes force it into activity on the level of concrete knowledge, with a resultant kaleidoscopic presentation of thoughtforms.

5. It is fundamentally the most potent energy at this time in the planet, because it was brought to maturity in the first solar system, that of active intelligence.

6. It is the energy which admits humanity (and particularly the trained disciple or initiate) into the mysteries of the Mind of God Himself. It is the "substantial" key to the Universal Mind.

7. It is profoundly susceptible to the energy of Love-Wisdom, and its fusion with the love aspect is given the name of "wisdom" by us, because all wisdom is knowledge gained by experience and implemented by love.

8. This energy, in its three aspects, is related in a peculiar sense to the three Buddhas of Activity. These great Lives reached Their present state of development in the previous solar system.

9. This energy, in so far as it is considered as the mental energy of a human being – and this is one of its minor limitations though a major one for a human being – is the higher correspondence of the physical brain. It might be said that the brain exists because the mind exists and needs a brain as its focal point upon the physical plane.

10. The quality of this energy of concrete knowledge or science is twofold:

     a. It is extraordinarily responsive to impressions coming from some source or other.

     b. It is rapidly thrown into forms in response to impression.

11. The impressions received come from three sources and are sequentially revealed to man. These three are:

     a. Impressions from the three worlds; these come, first of all, from the individual and then, secondly, from the levels of planetary consciousness.

     b. Impressions from the soul, the Son of Mind, upon the level of mentality itself.

     c. Impressions from the Spiritual Triad, via the antahkarana; these come when the antahkarana is constructed or in process of construction.

12. This energy is essentially a light-bearer. It responds – again sequentially in time and space – to the light of the Logos. It is for this reason that the mind is regarded both as illumined when higher contacts are present and as an illuminator where the lower planes are concerned.

13. This energy is (from the human standpoint) awakened and brought into activity through the action of the five senses which are the conveyors of information from the three worlds to the mental plane. It might be said that:

     a. Five streams of informative energy, therefore, make their impact upon the concrete mind and emanate from the physico-astral plane.

     b. Three streams of energy, coming from the soul, also make an impression upon the concrete mind.

     c. One stream of energy – during the initiatory process – contacts the mind. This comes from the Spiritual Triad and utilises the antahkarana.

14. The energy of this fifth ray might he regarded as the *commonsense,* because it receives all these impacts of varying energies, synthesises them, produces order out of the many ceaseless impacts and interprets them, thus creating the multiplicity of forms to which we give the name of "world thought".

15. This energy transforms the divine ideas into human ideals, relating the knowledges and sciences of humanity to these ideals, thus making them workable factors in human evolution, its cultures and civilisations.

There is much more that I could add, but the above gives you a series of simple definitions of value as you study the mental unfoldment of the disciple, as he undergoes the initiatory process which is our theme at this time. It also throws light upon the ray effects upon humanity *as a whole.* This ray energy is indeed sadly concrete in its expression in our Aryan race – a race, however, which will see more people take initiation than ever before in human history, and which will, in a peculiar sense, see *the descent* of the Kingdom of God to Earth as a result of *the ascent* of so many upon the ladder of evolution....

Today in our Aryan age and race, we see the vital expression of this fifth ray energy. When I use the word "race" I deal not with man-made or pseudo-scientific differentiations of nations and races or types. I deal with a state of consciousness which is the Aryan or mental consciousness or state of thinking; this finds its exponents and its "race members" in every nation, without any distinction or omissions. This I would have you carefully remember, for there is no new race in process of appearing, from the territorial angle; there is only a general distribution of those persons who have what have been called the sixth root race characteristics. This state of consciousness will find its expression in people as far apart racially as the Japanese and the American or the Negro and the Russian. It posits an ability to function with clarity upon the mental plane, to collate information, rightly to interpret and relate that information, and to create the needed thoughtforms or concepts for those interpretations....

Today we find this ray energy expressing itself mainly through science – a science sadly debased and corrupted by materialism and human greed, but a science which (when animated entirely by goodwill) will lift humanity on to higher levels of consciousness, thus laying the foundation for that time when humanity on a large scale can pass through the Transfiguration Initiation. Steps in this direction are already being laid and the existence of the press, the radio and the rapid means of transportation have done much to further the revelation of that unity and that Oneness which is the major characteristic of the Universal Mind....

The existence of a closed mind on a national scale is dangerous in the extreme, just as the individual is in a dangerous "state of mind" when he closes it to world contact, world news and world understanding, and when he refuses to admit new ideas and new modes of behaviour. Fortunately, the influence of this fifth ray energy – which is always present, whether the ray is in incarnation or not – is steadily leading humanity towards illumination.

This ray energy operates always in connection with the Law of Cleavages. Today, tremendous cleavages between the past and the present are in order. The importance of this statement is to be found in the fact that – for the first time in human history – humanity is aware of cleavage *at the time* it is being brought about. Hitherto cleavages have been noted during an historical retrospect. Today, all men everywhere are conscious of the fact that the old order, the old cultures and civilisations are rapidly passing away, and they are universally clamouring for the new. Everywhere men are laying the foundation for the new order, the coming of which is threatened only by one country, Russia, owing to its separativeness (and not because of its ideology), and by one world group in every country, those guilty of financial greed and consequent aggressiveness....

The outstanding expression of this fifth ray energy can be seen in the rapid formulating of the many ideologies which have taken place since the year 1900. Such words as Fascism, Communism, National Socialism, Socialism as the British accept it, and the names of many schools of psychology and philosophy, were unknown one hundred years ago; today they are the common talk and phrases of the man in the street. The inflow of this mental energy into the world of men, the attainment in consciousness of mental ability by many thousands, and the achievement of mental polarisation by aspirants all the world over, are all due to the activity of this fifth ray energy; this may be regarded as preparatory work for the first and the second initiations. Some of this success is due also to a little-realised function of this fifth ray energy – that of telepathic interplay. Few people realise in the slightest degree how naturally telepathic every human being is or how impressionable are their minds; this again is an effect of fifth ray influence.

The creation (and, I should add, the over-creation) of the millions of material things which men everywhere regard as essential to their well-being is also the result of the creative activity of the fifth ray consciousness. This is, of course, as it demonstrates upon the physical plane. When it demonstrates upon the mental plane, we then talk of ideas, concepts, philosophies and ideologies. When it demonstrates upon the astral plane, we are aware of the religious impulse, of mysticism and of the emotional and conditioning desires. All these aspects are present in the consciousness of men everywhere today. Everything is crystallising in human consciousness, and this takes place in order to make man aware of where he stands upon the ladder of evolution, and of what is wrong and what is right. All this again is due to the influence of fifth ray energy. This will begin to transform human living and human desires and also human affairs and attitudes, and will lead eventually (in the middle of the sixth root race) to the great Transfiguration Initiation in which the reality that lies behind all human phenomena will stand revealed....

Let me now summarise the effects of this fifth ray energy in relation to humanity and to the individual initiate:

1. I gave, first of all, fifteen items of information anent this fifth ray energy, or fifteen definitions of its activity. These will warrant careful study.
2. The effect of this fifth ray energy upon humanity in this fifth root race was considered; it was noted that this Aryan effect was dominant and dynamic in the extreme and that

it has greatly hastened human evolution.

3. I pointed out the close relation between love and mind, as follows:

   a. Ray II and Ray V
   b. Plane II and plane V
   c. Solar system II and root race V

   In all these relationships, the fifth in order is the prime agent and the revealer of the second type of spiritual energy.

4. The fifth ray energy produces three major areas of thought, or three prime conditions wherein the thoughtform-making energy expresses itself:

   a. Science . . . . education . . . . . . medicine
   b. Philosophy . . . . ideas . . . . ideals
   c. Psychology . . . . in process of modern development

5. This fifth ray energy operates in connection with the Law of Cleavages.

6. It is also responsible for the rapid formation of great conditioning ideologies.

7. This fifth ray energy is the important factor in making possible the first major initiation, the Transfiguration Initiation.

8. Fifth ray energy works in three ways in connection with the three aspects of the personality:

   a. As the transmuting agent . . . . the physical body
   b. As the transforming agent . . . . the astral body
   c. As the transfiguring agent . . . . the mental body

This gives you much food for thought; it indicates the personality goal and the mode whereby it is attained. After the third initiation, we reach out in consciousness to higher expansions of consciousness and will then enter a realm of ideas which are not yet easy for the disciple to appreciate or to understand. (RI–589/602)

Initiation IV. The Renunciation. RAY IV.
The Energy of Harmony through Conflict.

• This fourth ray...is out of incarnation, as far as the reincarnating egos or souls of men are concerned. From another angle, however, it is always active and ever present, because it is the ray which governs the fourth kingdom in nature, the human kingdom in the three worlds of strictly human evolution. (RI–603)

• The whole of human history has been conditioned by the fourth Ray of Harmony through Conflict, and it is this ray which has determined the ring-pass-not within which humanity must work.

At this time, the effect of this ray is predominantly of a group nature, and there are – except in the ranks of disciples of the Great White Lodge – no fourth ray souls in incarnation. Once humanity has decided upon the goal and the method of reconstruction and of reorganisation which is to take place within the periphery of the fourth ray ring-pass-not, then (if humanity's decision is correct and is not postponed) many fourth ray souls will resume incarnation, and so implement human decision. This will mark a great turning point in human history and will enable seventh ray energy to be turned to the best advantage. (RI–605)

• Fundamentally, this fourth ray is that which is responsible for the strains and the stresses, and for the initial conflict between the major pair of opposites to which we give the name of spirit-matter. It is this fourth ray energy which makes apparent the distinction (so often misunderstood by man) between good and evil. In Atlantean days, the leaders of men, under the influence of this paramount fourth ray energy, made a decision which laid the emphasis upon the matter aspect, according to their desire and their emotional reaction, which is present in the essential duality of manifestation, and thus inaugurated the Age of Materialism. This age has wrought itself out through its accompanying greeds, hate, separativeness and aggression. During the present century, this materialism led to the world

war which was in reality the expression of a shifting orientation, and therefore to a certain extent, of a coming triumph of
Good.

The balance is slowly, very slowly, swinging over to the side
of the spirit aspect of the duality; it has not yet swung, even in
intention, completely over, but the issues are becoming increasingly clearer in men's minds and the indications are that man
will eventually decide correctly, will attain a point of balance
or equilibrium, and will finally throw the weight of public
opinion on the side of spiritual values, thus leading to a
collective renunciation of materialism, particularly in its grosser
and physical forms. The time is not yet, but a great awakening
is in process; men, however, will only see correctly when this
Principle of Conflict is properly evaluated as a spiritual necessity and is used by humanity as an instrument to bring about
emergence from the wrong controls and principles. Just as the
individual disciple uses it to emerge out of the control of
matter in the three worlds, beginning with the emergence from
the control of the physical body, passing out of the control of
the emotional nature, and formulating for himself a spiritual
ideology which enables him to pass out of the control of the
three worlds of forms, and so begin to function as a soul-
infused personality, so mankind also has to do the same in
mass formation.

This whole process culminates when the fourth initiation, the
Great Renunciation, is taken by man today, and by humanity
in some distant future; this "point of emergence" is reached by
right decision and as a result of a right use of the Principle of
Conflict.

It will be obvious to you that this Principle of Conflict is
closely related to death. By death, I mean extraction from form
conditions – physical, emotional or mental; I mean cessation of
contact (temporarily or permanently) with physical form, with
astral glamour and with mental illusion; I mean the rejection of
Maya, the name of that all-inclusive effect which overwhelms
a man who is immersed in materialism of any kind, and is
therefore overcome (from the soul angle) by life in the three

worlds. It is the Principle of Conflict, latent in every atom of substance, which produces, first of all, conflict, then renunciation, and finally emancipation; which produces war in some form or another, then rejection, and finally liberation.... There is deep occult significance to the thought, often voiced, that death is the great Liberator; it means that the Principle of Conflict has succeeded in bringing about conditions wherein the spirit aspect is released (temporarily or permanently) from imprisonment in some kind of form life, either individual or group.

You will all, as disciples or aspirants, be able to interpret the working of this principle as you watch the effect, in your own lives, of the action of the strains and stresses, the points of crisis or of tension which the conflict between soul and personality produces. Conflict is always present prior to renunciation, and it is only at this fourth great spiritual crisis that conflict, as we understand it, ends. (RI–605/7)

• This Principle of Conflict is a familiar one to every struggling aspirant and conditions his whole life, producing crises and tensions, sometimes almost past endurance; they indicate nevertheless rapid development and steady progress.... It is a conflict which has engulfed the masses in every land, which is still producing physical conflict, emotional strain and tremendous mental issues, and which will greatly lessen when the masses of people everywhere are convinced that right human relations are of far greater importance than greed, human pride, territorial grabbing, and material possessions. (RI–610/11)

• It will be obvious that this ray energy [of Harmony], embodying the Principle of Conflict, has a unique and curious effect upon *relationships*. This is due to the interrelation of this Ray of Harmony through Conflict and the second Ray of Love-Wisdom; this second ray is primarily the ray of right human relations – as far as the fourth kingdom in nature is concerned. The energy of love governs all relations between souls and controls the Hierarchy, the Kingdom of Souls; the energy of wisdom should govern all relations within the fourth kingdom, the human; some day it will inevitably do so, hence the emphasis laid upon the need for soul-infused personalities in the world today, as promulgated by all true esoteric schools.

It might be said that the effect of the Principle of Conflict, operating under Ray IV and controlled by Ray II, will be – as far as humanity is concerned – to bring about right human relations and the growth of the universal spirit of goodwill among men. Only the most benighted and uncouth of thinkers would fail to see that these two results of the conflict, engendered at this time, are the two most desirable factors for which all men of goodwill should work. The inflow of energy into humanity at this time is all in favour of such efforts, and the Principle of Conflict has worked so effectively that all men are desiring *harmony,* peace, equilibrium, right adjustment to life and circumstances, and right and balanced human relations.

...The masses of the people in all lands have been convinced by the evidence made available by the Principle of Conflict that basic changes in man's attitude and goals must be brought about if humanity is to survive; they are, in their own ways (wisely or unwisely), seeking a solution.

The war has produced much good – in spite of the destruction of forms. The causes of war are better understood; the issues involved are slowly being clarified; information about all nations – even when incorrectly presented – has awakened mankind to the fact of the One World; the community of pain, sorrow, anxiety, starvation and despair have brought all men closer together, and this relation is a far greater breeder of harmony than man realises; the world of men today is more closely knit *subjectively* (in spite of all outer cleavages and conflicts) than ever before in human history; there is a firmer determination to establish right human relations and a clearer perception of the factors involved; the new *Principle of Sharing,* inherent in the second Ray of Love-Wisdom which is concerned so fundamentally with relationships, is gaining ground, and its potency is being released by the activity of the fourth Ray of Harmony through Conflict. This Principle of Sharing, though still divorced from any *official* sanctions, *is* under consideration and will some day be the governing factor in the economic life of the world, regulated and controlled by those men who are alert to human need upon the physical plane. (RI–611/13)

• Everywhere the fourth Ray of Harmony through Conflict is active in the human family and is dominating human affairs; everywhere in the life of the individual, in the lives of groups, organisations and churches, in the life of nations and in the life of mankind as a whole, the issues are being clarified, and humanity is being led from one renunciation to another, until some day the human kingdom will unitedly take the fourth initiation and the Great Renunciation will be accepted; this step, lying far ahead as yet in the future, will affiliate humanity with the Hierarchy and release millions of men from the thralldom of materialism. This moment in human history will inevitably come. The first indication that the distant vision has been glimpsed might perhaps be noted in the prevalent instinct to *share,* motivated at present by the instinct to self-preservation, but definitely developing as a possible mode of action upon the far horizon of man's thinking. True sharing definitely involves many little renunciations, and it is upon these small renunciations that *the capacity* for freedom is slowly being generated and *the habit* of renunciation can eventually be stabilised; this capacity and these habits, these unselfish activities and these spiritual habitual attitudes are the preparatory stages for the Initiation of Renunciation, just as the effort to serve one's fellowmen is preparatory to the taking of the third Initiation, of the Transfiguration. (RI–614)

• *The overshadowing* of all disciples and initiates, and the consequent stimulation of their natures and of their environment, must inevitably produce conflict; the outpouring of the stimulating love of God into the hearts of men must equally and inevitably produce conflict; the line of cleavage between men of goodwill and the unresponsive natures of those uninfluenced by this quality will be made abundantly, usefully and constructively clear. It will be obvious also that when Christ establishes the "centre or focal point of the divine Purpose" in some definite place on Earth, its radiation and implementary potency will also produce the needed conflict which precedes the clarification and the renunciation of obstructions.

But there will come a point in all these three spheres of Christ's proposed activity when conflict will be superseded by harmony; this is due to the fact that the energy of harmony through conflict is under the control or influence of the energy of the second Ray of Love-Wisdom. As far as humanity as a sum total is concerned, the conflict of ideas and of emotional desire is today so acute that it will finally exhaust itself, and men will turn, with relief and with a longing to escape from further turmoil, towards right human relations; this will consti-tute the first major human decision leading to the longed-for harmony. The attitude of the masses will then be soundly tending towards harmony, owing to the work of the men and women of goodwill as they implement the "streaming forth of the love of God into the hearts of men". (RI–617/18)

• In the world at this time the two aspects of this fourth ray – the aspect or Principle of Conflict and the aspect or Principle of Harmony – are struggling to bring about the liberation into equilibrium of mankind. Until quite lately, the Principle of Conflict has grown increasingly in power, yet as a result of this conflict a definite trend towards harmony can be seen emerging in human thinking; *the concept* of harmony through the estab-lishing of right human relations is slowly coming into recog-nition. The activities of mankind, and particularly of govern-ments, have been ignobly selfish and controlled by the concepts of fighting, aggression and competition for untold millenia; the territories of the planet have changed hands many times and the earth has been the playground of a long succession of con-querors; the heroes of the race – perpetuated in history, stone and human thinking – have been the warriors, and conquest has been an ideal. The world war (1914-1945) marked a culminat-ing point in the work of the Principle of Conflict and, as I have shown, the results of this work are today inaugurating a new era of harmony and co-operation because the trend of human thinking is towards the cessation of conflict. This is an event of major importance and should be regarded as indicating a turning point in human affairs. This trend is impulsed by a weariness of fighting, by a changing rating as to the values in human accomplishment, and by a recognition that true greatness is not expressed through such activities as those of Alexander the Great, Julius Caesar, Napoleon or Hitler, but by those who see life, humanity and the world as one united whole, interrelated, co-operative and harmonised. Those who struggle for this world unity, and who educate the race in the Principles of Harmony and of right human relations, will some day be recognised as the true heroes.

The factor that must and will relate the Principle of Conflict to the expression of harmony and bring about the new world order, the new civilisation and culture, is the trend and the voice of public opinion, and the opportunity offered to people everywhere to bring about social security and right human relations. It is not the government of any nation which will bring this about, but *the innate rightness* of the people themselves when they have been educated to see the issues clearly, the relationships which should be established, and the immense subjective unity of mankind. This will not come about without an intensive period of planned education, of a truly free press and radio – both free to speak the exact truth and to present the facts as they occur, without being controlled or influenced by governmental interference, pressure groups, religious organisations, or by any dictating parties or dictators. (RI–621/2)

• The disciples of the world today are submerged in an ocean of warring energies; the Principle of Conflict touches every life, is potent in the consciousness of each individual aspirant, and is conditioning the mass consciousness of mankind. Emotionally and physically, the masses in every land are roused by this conflict; the disciples on earth and the thinking people everywhere are aroused mentally, as well as emotionally and physically, and hence the intensity of their problem. The *points of crisis* in the lives of disciples have – during the past few decades – been many; a *point of tension* has now been reached of an extreme nature; how rapidly can this tension bring about the needed *point of emergence?*

...The disciple knows, however, that – as a result of conflict – the complete harmonising of his entire nature will be brought about; the fusion of soul and personality will be consummated, and for this he works. The same principle can also be applied by him in his consideration of general human affairs; he needs to see in all world conflict the needed steps towards an eventual harmony – a harmony based upon a true mental perception and a sound idealism. It is this process of developing mental understanding and a sound rational yet spiritual attitude which is now going on; the emergence of the many ideologies are the guarantee that the true idealism will eventually appear and control – the ideal of right human relations; it is the struggle between emotional control and a steadily developing mind control which is conditioning mankind at this time. When a mental, an emotional and a physical conflict are raging simultaneously, the results must necessarily be difficult, but they are surmountable.

Today, the conflicts are numerous, vital and unavoidable; they are present in the individual consciousness and in the mass consciousness; they present constant points of crises and are today bringing about a point of world tension which seems well-nigh unbearable. But ahead of the individual disciple and of humanity lies a point of emergence.

What must the disciple do whilst the point of tension is dominating him and his fellowmen? The answer is a simple one. Let each disciple and all groups of disciples develop the ability to think sanely, with right orientation and a broad point of view; let them think truly, evading no issues, but preserving always a calm, dispassionate and loving understanding; let them demonstrate in their environment the qualities which will establish right human relations and show on a small scale the behaviour which will some day characterise enlightened humanity; let them not be discouraged, but let them hold firmly to the conviction of the inevitable spiritual destiny of humanity; let them realise *practically* that "the souls of men are one" and learn to look beyond the immediate outer seeming to the inner (and sometimes remote) spiritual consciousness; let them *know* that the present world conflict will be terminated.

The perfect outcome of the conflict will necessarily be lacking, for perfection is not yet possible to man; nevertheless, a situation can be brought about which will permit the return of the Christ into objective relation with mankind, and which will enable Him to set about His task of resurrecting the human spirit, out of the tomb of materialism into the clear light of spiritual perception. For this, all men must work. (RI–637/8)

Initiation V. Revelation. RAY I.
The Energy of the Will-to-Good. Power.

• This initiation has always been called in the Christian church by the name of the Resurrection, whereas it is the seventh initiation which is the true resurrection. The correct name for the fifth initiation is the Initiation of Revelation; this signifies the power to wield light as the carrier of life to all in the three worlds, and to know likewise the next step to be taken upon the Way of the Higher Evolution. This Way is revealed to the initiate in a new light and with an entirely different significance when the fifth initiation is taken. It is the true time of emergence from the tomb of darkness and constitutes an entrance into a light of an entirely different nature to any hitherto experienced.

...The Master, as He emerges at the fifth initiation into the light of day, realises in that light:

1. The true and hitherto unknown significance of the three worlds which he has viewed almost entirely from the angle of *meaning*. Now its *significance* is apparent, and the revelation is so tremendous that "he withdraws into the world of light and joins his brothers. He gathers all his forces and *seeks new light upon the Plan*. That light shines forth and with the force of its revealing power, new loyalties arise, new goals are seen, and that which shall be and the thing which is, both become lost in the radiant light of revelation."

2. That the first vibration or influencing energy of the cosmic ray of prevailing energy in its highest aspect is the Ray of Love-Wisdom, and this is now contacted; this is made possible by the Master's response to the first Ray of Power or of the Will-to-Good, experienced in its second aspect at the fifth initiation. Forget not that all rays have three aspects, and that all three can be contacted by the human consciousness of the spiritual man, thus placing at his disposal the energies of the seven rays and of the twenty-one forces. It is this synthesis which is revealed at the fifth initiation....

3. From that height also, the mystery of the human soul is revealed and a great triangular pattern will be seen, relating the human spirit to the world of forms, to the united Hierarchy and to the Council Chamber of the Lord....

The first Ray of Will or Power is distinguished by the highest *known* divine quality (there are others still higher). In the word, GOODWILL, the secret purpose of the planetary Logos is hidden. It is being slowly brought to the attention of humanity by means of the three phases: God is Love. Good-will. The Will-to-Good. These three phases, in reality concern the three aspects of the first ray.

When a Master takes the fifth initiation, He already knows the significance of the fist two aspects, and must become consciously aware of the highest aspect: the Will-to-Good....

As this first ray is not in incarnation at this time, and therefore souls who can fully express it are absent, the entire theme anent this type of energy, and its influence and quality when related to the energies and the forces is most difficult to express. Each great ray, as it comes into incarnation, transforms the speech of the cycle, enriches the existent vocabulary, and brings new knowledge to humanity; the many civilisations – past and present – are the result of this.

I would ask you to consider the relation of the fifth initiation, the fifth Ray of Science and the first Ray of Will, for there lies the key to the revelation accorded to the initiate-Master.

As you can see, we are venturing into realms far beyond your comprehension; but the effort to grasp the unattainable and to exercise the mind along the line of abstract thought is ever of value.

It must be remembered therefore (and I reiterate) that the revelation accorded to the disciple-initiate is along the line of the first Ray of Will or Power, and that is a ray which is as yet a long way from full manifestation. From one angle, it is of course always in manifestation for it is the ray which holds the planet and all that is upon it in one coherent manifesting whole; the reason for this coherent synthesis is the evolutionary effort to work out divine purpose. The first ray ever implements that purpose. From another angle, it is cyclic in its manifestation; here I mean from the angle of *recognised* manifestation – and such is the case at this time. (RI–643/6)

To Serve

Ray Methods of Activity

• We might...take the seven Rays and give the names for the three ways in which the groups on any particular ray interact with each other, remembering that as we consider them, we are really studying the twenty-one vibrations of the Law of Attraction or motion....

I. Ray of Power.
 1. Destruction of forms through group interplay.
 2. Stimulation of the Self, or egoic principle.
 3. Spiritual impulse, or energy.

II. Ray of Love-Wisdom.
 4. Construction of forms through group intercourse.
 5. Stimulation of desire, the love principle.
 6. Soul impulse, or energy.

III. Ray of Activity or Adaptability.
 7. Vitalising of forms through group work.
 8. Stimulation of forms, the etheric or pranic principle.
 9. Material impulse, or energy.

IV. Ray of Harmony, Union.
 10. Perfecting of forms through group interplay.
 11. Stimulation of the solar Angels, or the manasic principle.
 12. Buddhic energy.

V. Ray of Concrete Knowledge.
 13. Correspondence of forms to type, through group influence.

    14. Stimulation of logoic dense physical body, the three worlds.

    15. Manasic energy or impulse.

VI. Ray of Abstract Idealism or Devotion.

    16. Reflection of reality through group work.

    17. Stimulation of the Man through desire.

    18. Desire energy, instinct and aspiration.

VII. Ray of Ceremonial Order.

    19. Union of energy and substance through group activity.

    20. Stimulation of all etheric forms.

    21. Vital energy. (TCF–1222/3)

• It would be well to remember that disciples on the first ray understand discipleship largely in terms of energy, or force, or activity, whilst disciples on the second ray understand it more in terms of consciousness or initiation. Hence the divergence of expressions in ordinary use, and the lack of comprehension among thinkers. It might prove useful to express the idea of discipleship in terms of the different rays – meaning by this, discipleship as it manifests on the physical plane in service:

1st Ray . . Force	Energy	Action	The Occultist.
2nd Ray . Consciousness .	Expansion . . .	Initiation	The true Psychic.
3rd Ray . Adaptation . . .	Development .	Evolution	The Magician.
4th Ray . Vibration	Response	Expression . . .	The Artist.
5th Ray . Mentation	Knowledge . .	Science	The Scientist.
6th Ray . Devotion	Abstraction . .	Idealism	The Devotee.
7th Ray . Incantation . . .	Magic	Ritual	The Ritualist.

Remember carefully that we are here dealing with disciples. Later on as they progress, the various lines approximate and merge. All have been at one time magicians, for all have passed upon the third ray. The problem now is concerned with the mystic and the occultist, and their eventual synthesis. A careful study of the foregoing will lead to the realisation that the difficulties between thinkers, and between disciples of all groups, consist in their identifying themselves with some form, and in their inability to understand the different points of view of others. As time elapses, and they are brought into closer relationship with the two Masters with whom they are concerned (their own inner God and their personal Master), the inability to co-operate and to merge their interests in the good of the group will pass away, and community of endeavour, similarity of object, and mutual co-operation will take the place of what is now so much seen, divergence. We might well ponder on this, for it holds the key to much that is puzzling and, to many, distressing. (IHS–80/81)

• …Each ray worker and server will be found to render his service along peculiar and specific lines. These indicate for him the line of least resistance and, consequently, of the greatest efficiency. These methods and techniques will constitute the inner structure of the coming Science of Service, and they will be discovered through the admission of the Ray hypothesis and an observation of the methods employed by these clearly isolated Ray types and groups. These differing ways of service, all of them, work in conformity with the Plan, and together produce a synthetic whole. The ray or rays in manifestation at any one time will determine the general trend of the world service, and those servers whose egoic ray is in incarnation, and who are endeavouring to work with right activity, will find their work facilitated if they understand that the trend of affairs is with them and that they are following the line of least resistance at that period. They will work with greater facility than will the disciples and aspirants whose egoic ray is out of manifestation. This recognition will lead to a careful study of times and seasons, thus there will be no waste effort, and real advantage can be taken of the qualifications and aptitudes of the servers available. All will be in conformity with the Plan. A consideration of the rays in or out of manifestation, and a recognition of the disciples and servers available on the physical plane at any one time, is part of the work of the Masters in the Hierarchy. (EP2–138/9)

• The seven ray types will work in the following ways, which

I am stating very briefly for to do more than that might limit the expression of those who do not know enough to be discriminating as to their characteristics, and might unduly qualify and colour the experience of those servers who recognise (as some already do) their ray. They might, with entirely good intention, seek to force the ray qualities of their souls into dominance before the personality ray is adequately known or controlled. Other servers frequently confuse the two rays and deem their soul ray to be of a particular type, whereas it is only their personality ray to which they predominantly conform, and by which they are pre-eminently governed. Is it not possible for us to observe here the care with which the Teachers of these truths and the custodians of the coming revelation, must proceed? They have to guard the aspirants from premature knowledge, which they might theoretically grasp but which they are not yet ready practically to apply.

Ray I. Servers on this ray, if they are trained disciples, work through what might be called the imposition of the Will of God upon the minds of men. This they do through the powerful impact of ideas upon the minds of men, and the emphasis of the governing principles which must be assimilated by humanity. These ideas, when grasped by the aspirant bring about two developments. First, they initiate a period of destruction and of a breaking up of that which is old and hindering, and this is later followed by the clear shining forth of the new idea and its subsequent grasping by the minds of intelligent humanity. These ideas embody great principles, and constitute the New Age ideas. These servers, therefore, work as God's destroying angels, destroying the old forms, but nevertheless, behind it all lies the impetus of love.

With the average aspirant, however, who is on the first ray, the activity is not so intelligent. He grasps the idea that is needed by the race, but he will seek to impose it primarily as his idea, something which he has seen and grasped and which impatiently he seeks to impose upon his fellow men for their good, as he sees it. He inevitably destroys as fast as he builds, and finally destroys himself. Many worthy aspirants and disciples in training for service at this time work in this sad way.

Some of the Masters of the Wisdom and Their groups of disciples are actively engaged at this time in an endeavour to impose certain basic and needed ideas upon the races of men, and much of Their work is being prepared for by a group of Destroying Disciples, and also by a group of Enunciating Disciples, for these two types of work carry forward their task as a unit. The idea to be dominant in the future is proclaimed in writing and by the voice, by one Group. The Group of Destroyers takes it up, and proceed to break up the old forms of truth so as to make room and way for the new emerging idea.

Ray II. Servers on this ray ponder, meditate upon and assimilate the new ideas associated with the Plan, and by the power of their attractive love, they gather together those who are at that point in their evolution where they can respond to the measure and rhythm of that Plan. They can select, and train those who can "carry" the idea deeper into the mass of humanity. We should not forget that the work of the Hierarchy at this time, and the task of the New Group of World Servers is primarily associated with ideas. The disciples and servers on the second ray are "busy building habitations for those dynamic entities whose function it has ever been to charge the thoughts of men and so to usher in that new and better age which will permit the fostering of the souls of men". So runs the *Old Commentary,* if I thus modernise its ancient wording. By magnetic, attractive, sympathetic understanding, and the wise use of slow action, based on love, do the servers on this ray work. Today their power is becoming dominant.

Ray III. The servers on this ray have a special function at this time in stimulating the intellect of humanity, sharpening it and inspiring it. They work, manipulating ideas so as to make them more easy of comprehension by the mass of intelligent men and women who are to be found in the world at this time and whose intuition is not yet awakened. It is to be noted how the work of the true servers is largely with the new ideas and not with the business of organisation and of criticism (for these two go hand in hand). Ideas are taken by the third ray aspirant, as they emerge from the elevated consciousness of Those for whom the first ray works and are rendered attractive by the second ray worker (attractive in the esoteric sense) and adapted to the immediate need and rendered vocal by the force of the intellectual third ray types. In this lies a hint for many of the third ray personalities to be found working in various fields of service at this time.

Ray IV. This ray is not in incarnation at the time and therefore few fourth ray egos are available in world service. There are, however, many fourth ray personalities and they can learn much by the study of the work of the New Group of World Servers. The major task of the fourth ray aspirant is to harmonise the new ideas with the old, so that there can be no dangerous gap or break. They are those who bring about a "righteous compromise", and adapt the new and the old so that the true pattern is preserved. They are engaged with the bridging process, for they are the true intuitives and have a capacity for the art of synthesis so that their work most definitely can help in bringing forward a true presentation of the divine picture.

Ray V. The servers on this ray are coming rapidly into prominence. They are those who investigate the form in order to find its hidden idea, its motivating power, and to this end they work with ideas, proving them either true or false. They gather into their ranks those whose personalities are on this ray and train them in the art of scientific investigation. From the sensed spiritual ideas, lying behind the form side of manifestation, from the many discoveries in the ways of God with man and nature, from the inventions (which are but materialised ideas) and from the witness to the Plan which law portrays, they are preparing that new world in which men will work and live a more deeply conscious, spiritual life. Disciples working along these lines in every country today are more active than at any other time in human history. They are, knowingly and unknowingly, leading men into the world of meaning, and their discoveries will eventually end the present era of unemployment, and their inventions and improvements, added to the steadily growing idea of group interdependence (which is the major message of the New Group of World Servers) will eventually ameliorate human conditions so that an era of peace and leisure can supervene. You will note that I do not say "will supervene", for not even the Christ Himself can predict exactly the time limit within which changes can eventuate, nor the reaction of humanity to any given point of revelation.

Ray VI. The effect of the activity of this ray, during the past two thousand years, has been to train humanity in the art of recognising ideals, which are the blue prints of ideas. The main work of the disciples on this ray is to capitalise on the developed tendency of humanity to recognise ideas, and – avoiding the rocks of fanaticism, and the dangerous shoals of superficial desire – train the world thinkers so ardently to desire the good, the true and the beautiful, that the idea which should materialise in some form on earth can shift from the plane of the mind and clothe itself in some form on earth. These disciples and servers work consciously with the desire element in man; they work scientifically with its correct evocation. Their technique is scientific because it is based upon a right understanding of the human material with which they have to work.

Some people have to be galvanised into activity by an idea. With these the first ray disciple can be effective. Others can be reached more easily by an ideal, and will then subordinate their personal lives and wishes to that ideal. With these the sixth ray disciple works with facility, and this he should endeavour to do, teaching men to recognise the truth, holding steadily before them the ideal, restraining them from a too energetic and fanatical display of interest, in the need for the long pull. The sixth ray, it should be remembered, when it constitutes the personality ray of a man or a group, can be far more destructive than the first ray, for there is not so much wisdom to be found, and, as it works through desire of some kind, it is following the line of least resistance for the masses, and can therefore the more easily produce physical plane effects. Sixth ray people need handling with care, for they are too one-pointed and too full of personal desire, and the tide of evol-

ution has been with this type for a very long time. But the sixth
ray method of evoking desire for the materialising of an ideal
is indispensable, and, fortunately, there are many aspirants and
disciples on this ray available today.

Ray VII. This ray provides at this time an active and
necessary grouping of disciples who are eager to aid the Plan.
Their work lies naturally on the physical plane. They can
organise the evoked ideal which will embody as much of the
idea of God as the period and humanity can evidence and
produce in form upon the earth. Their work is potent and
necessary and calls for much skill in action. This is the ray that
is coming into power. None of these ray participants in the
hierarchical crusade today can really work without each other,
and no group can carry on alone. The difference between the
methods of the old age and that of the new can be seen
expressed in the idea of leadership by one and leadership by a
group. It is the difference between the imposition of an individual's response to an idea upon his fellow men and the reaction
of a group to an idea, producing group idealism and focalising
it into definite form, carrying forward the emergence of the
idea without the dominance of any one individual. This is the
major task today of the seventh ray disciple, and to this end he
must bend every energy. He must speak those Words of Power
which are a group word, and embody the group aspiration in
an organised *movement*, which, it will be noted is quite distinct
from an organisation. A striking instance of the use of such a
Word of Power being enunciated by a group has lately been
given in the Great Invocation which has been used with marked
effect. It should continue to be used, for it is the inaugurating
mantram of the incoming seventh ray. This is the first time
such a mantram has been brought to the attention of humanity.

All these rays work today for the carrying out of a specific
group idea of seven Masters Who, through Their picked and
chosen servers, are actively participating in the work which is
the initiatory work of the seventh ray. It is also linked up with
the incoming Aquarian influence. The Masters, with their large
group of disciples, functioning on all the five planes of human

unfoldment, have studied minutely Their accepted disciples, the disciples under supervision and not yet accepted, and the aspirants of the world. They have selected a number of them to weld together into a group upon the outer physical plane. The basis of this selection is:–

a. Sensitivity to the Aquarian influence.
b. Willingness to work in a group as an integral part of the group, and having no idea of personal ambition or any wish to be a leader. Where the desire to be a leader exists, that disciple is automatically (though only temporarily) disqualified for this particular endeavour. He can still do good work, but it will be secondary work, and more closely affiliated with the old age than with the work of the New Group of World Servers.
c. A dedication that holds nothing back that can *rightly* be given.
d. A harmlessness which, though not yet perfected, exists as an ideal towards which the aspirant is constantly striving.

In this work many can have a part. The Law of Service has been thus outlined in an endeavour to make one of the most esoteric influences in the solar system somewhat clearer in our minds. I call you to service, but would remind you that the service discussed here will only be possible when we have a clearer vision of the goal of meditation, and learn to preserve, during the day, the attitude of inner spiritual orientation. As we learn to obliterate and efface out of our consciousness ourselves as the central figure in our life drama, then and then only can we measure up to our real potentialities as servers of the Plan. (EP2–140/46)

The New Group of World Servers

• The emergence of the New Group of World Servers today is an indication that there are enough egoic ray types in physical manifestation, and that a sufficient number of personalities are responding to soul contact, so that a group can be formed that can be definitely *impressed as a group.* This is the first time that such a situation has been possible. Up till this century, individuals could be impressed, here and there, in different parts of the world, and at widely separated times and periods. But today *a group can respond* and their numbers are relatively so great that there can be formed upon the planet a group composed of a number of persons of such radiatory activity that their auras can meet and contact each other. Thus one group – subjective and objective – can be functioning.

There are today enough centres of light, scattered all over the world, and enough disciples and aspirants, that the little beams or threads of light (speaking symbolically) which radiate from each of them, can meet and interlace, and form a network of light in the world. This constitutes the magnetic aura of the New Group of World Servers. Each individual in the group is sensitive to the Plan, either through his own personal know-ledge through contact with his soul, or because his intuition tells him that what the Group, which attracts him, accepts as its immediate work is for him true and right, and with it all that is highest and best in him can co-operate. Each individual in that Group will work in his own particular surroundings according to his ray and type. That again will be coloured by his race and nation. But the work is the better carried forward as the units in the Group meet the need in their own peculiar environment, in the manner that is, for them, the simplest and best way, belonging as they do by habit and training in that particular setting. This should be remembered. (EP2–139/40)

• As the members of this…[New Group of World Servers] meditate and serve, they will gradually find that they are becoming aware of an inner group – the Ashram of the Master on Whose ray the individual server is to be found. This will necessarily vary according to the ray; the ray – it must be remembered – determines the quality and the nature of the service to be rendered. Gradually the neophyte swings into the rhythm of the Ashram, and gradually his meditation changes and falls into line with the instinctual and constant ashramic meditation. (DNA2–205)

• ...The invocative appeal of the united Hierarchy and of the New Group of World Servers will be so potent that it will evoke a response from humanity and a cycle of organisation, of planning and of effective expression will follow. Reflection, meditation and visualisation will give place to scientific *thinking* (which is essentially meditation) and to the needed physical plane activity.

This will take place, esoterically speaking, under the impression of the Masters upon the three major rays. The first Ray of Will or Power (the Ray of the divine Destroyer) is already actively working, destroying the old and outworn conditions and bringing about the wreckage of the old civilisation so that the new order can be effectively brought into expression. As the Christ said, when He instituted the Christian civilisation of the past two thousand years (which has gone so sadly far from His original intention), you "cannot put new wine in old bottles". The war (1914-1945) started the needed process of destruction, and the post-war period is carrying forward the planned undertaking. It is nearing its desired finish, if men work towards the freedom for which all their souls long.

The second Ray of Love-Wisdom, through the many extant educational processes and through the modern *conflict of ideas* (producing thus a borderland between the areas of influence of the first and second rays) is opening the minds of thousands of people. The pronounced contrast in ideas – as, for instance, the contrast between totalitarianism and the democratic freedom of thought (does such democratic freedom really exist, my brother?) – is forcing men to think, to reflect, to question and to meditate. The world is thereby greatly enriched, and the whole human family is transiting out of a pronounced cycle of karma yoga into the required cycle of raja yoga, from unthinking activity into a period of illumined mind control. It is a mental illumination which is brought about by the meditative and the reflective activity of humanity as a whole, and this is carried forward under the guidance of the New Group of World Servers, working under hierarchical impression.

Members of all the ray types are to be found in the New

Group of World Servers, either through the activity of the personality ray or of the soul ray; therefore, the energies of all the rays are being brought to bear upon this creative period in modern human history. It is interesting to have in mind the fact that through the medium of all the fighting forces of the world (naval, military and air) much needed hierarchical work is being accomplished; the energy of the fourth Ray of Harmony through Conflict is making itself phenomenally felt – this time in conjunction with the unusual activity of the first ray. Therefore, through the Forces of Light, liberation into freedom will come and it will mean the freedom of all mankind. I make here no defence of war or of fighting, brother of mine. I simply deal with world conditions as they exist today, and with the processes and the methods which are characteristic of the civilisations which have already disappeared and of the civilisation out of which we are today emerging. As man leaves the animal, the strictly physical and the highly emotional and inflammable stages behind him and *learns to think,* then (and only then) will war cease. Fortunately for humanity, this is happening most rapidly.

For the first time in human history, the lines of demarcation between that which is right from the angle of the spiritual values (the essential freedom of the human spirit) and that which is wrong (the imprisonment of the human spirit by materialistic conditions) are clearly perceived by the majority of the nations of the planet. Within the United Nations is the germ and the seed of a great international and meditating, reflective group – a group of thinking and informed men and women in whose hands lies the destiny of humanity. This is largely under the control of many fourth ray disciples, if you could but realise it, and their point of meditative focus is the intuitional or buddhic plane – the plane upon which all hierarchical activity is today to be found.

The fifth Ray of Concrete Knowledge is also expressing itself powerfully in the meditation and the reflection of the world scientists in all fields of human interest; in their hands the form of the new civilisation is being constructed. I would remind you that when I use the word "scientist", I refer to all who are working in the social sciences and the economic sciences as well as the large group of chemists, biologists, physicists, etc., who are usually covered by that term. The organising, defining power of the mental plane is being brought to bear upon all phases of human life by the scientists of all the many schools of thought; out of this meditative and creative thought which they all so admirably demonstrate will come the structure of the new civilisation.

The sixth ray disciple is active also in organising the mystical aspiration of the masses of men everywhere which is in itself a most potent energy; these aspirational men (no matter what may be their immediate aspiration) are necessarily polarised upon the astral plane but are not yet capable of the clear mental perception of the massed intelligentsia or susceptible to the influence of the accurate, esoteric approach. Their guided, mystical orientation will be one of the most powerful factors in the destruction of the old values and in the massed recognition of the spiritual truth which underlies all life; it is with this reorientation that sixth ray disciples, wielding sixth ray energy, are occupied at this time. You need to remember that the one-pointed attitude of the mystic, functioning in group formation, will be a powerful factor in the creative work being done by the Hierarchy and by the New Group of World Servers, because theirs will be a massed effect, and usually wielded unconsciously.

Under the influence of disciples on the seventh Ray of Organisation or of Ceremonial Order, that powerful physical concretisation of energy which we call "money" is proving a topic of the most definite concentration; it is being most carefully considered, and the minds of thinking financiers and of wealthy humanitarian persons and philanthropists will be gradually led forward from a strictly philanthropic activity to an activity which is impulsed and brought into expression by spiritual insight, and by *a recognition of the claims of Christ* (no matter by what name He may be called in the East or in the West) upon the financial reservoir of the world. This is a hard thing to bring about, for the subtle energies of the inner worlds take much time in producing their effects upon the objective, tangible plane of divine manifestation. Money is not yet used divinely, but it will be. Nevertheless, the task is well in hand and is engaging the attention of disciples upon all the rays, under the guidance and the impression of the powerful seventh ray Ashram – now already in process of externalisation.   (DNA2–218/222)

• There are many first ray workers finding their way into the ranks of the workers among the New Group of World Servers. Unless these workers are swept by love, their first ray energy will wreck the work of the group. Yet they are needed at this time, for they have the strength to stand unmoved at the centre. It is the conjunction of the first and second ray workers which can carry the world through the coming crisis of Reconstruction....   (EXH–335)

Right Human Relations

• [The work of the first ray] disciples and initiates who are working under the direction of the Master M...lies in the field of right human relations and in the production of that synthesis of effort which will create a new intuitional consciousness and – consequently – a changing political consciousness and situation in which the family of nations will stand together for certain basic values. These are fundamentally three in number:

1. The freedom of the individual. These freedoms have been voiced for us in the words of that great first ray disciple, Franklin D. Roosevelt. They are the four essential freedoms.
2. Right international interplay, necessitating finally the abolition of war.
3. Clean political regimes, free from graft, selfish ambition and dirty political manoeuvring.

In the achievement of these ends...the disciples of synthesis and the instigators of right political relationships will work in close co-operation with disciples upon the second ray whose task it is to educate the general public in the truer values. A trained and enlightened public, shouldering right responsibility, will elect only those men whose vision is in line with the new ethics, the new science of right human relations, and who recognise as a basic political tenet the equality of all men – an equality founded on a universal and basic divinity. (EXH–578/9)

Rays Conditioning Group Service

• ...Divine creativity will express itself when all of you in the group begin to study your rays from the angle of group service, and not so much from the angle of your own individual conditioning. Which of you investigates his ray equipment of energy from this standpoint? Do not the majority of you regard the subject much along the following lines: This ray in my equipment enables me to be and do thus, and so this ray complicates my life; this ray needs stronger emphasis in my life; such and such a ray gives me this or that quality or capacity. Disciples must learn to study the group equipment as a whole, and discover where a potency of which they may be the custodian can enrich the group life, enhance its effort and round out its presentation as a serving unit in the world of men. The responsibility of wielding force is a fact to be emphasised in the consciousness of all disciples; it will lead to a more deeply conscious and intelligent use of ray energy. (DNA2–583)

• ...Each ray works or pours its energy through one or other of the centres in the etheric body of that Entity Who informs an entire kingdom in nature, and then through that particular centre galvanises the individualising unit into the needed activity. Later, when the ray effects, psychologically speaking, are better understood, and the centres, with their seven ray vibrations, have been more deeply studied, it will be found that through a particular centre and along a particular ray vibration, forms of life and centres of consciousness can be contacted and known. This applies to all forms in all kingdoms, subhuman or superhuman. One of the first ways in which man is learning this truth is through the discovery of that vibration – emanating from a particular Master – which produces a reaction in himself, and which calls forth a response. Thus he is enabled to find out upon which ray his soul is found and to which ray group he should be attracted. This is of importance to the aspirant, and should be considered more carefully than has hitherto been the case, for by it the aspirant determines the nature and the quality of his soul type, and of the centre through which he (occultly speaking) goes out upon the Path. He discovers likewise the group of forms and of lives with which he is linked, to which he must render service, and by which he can be served. (EP1–260/1)

• Within the group life, the individual will not be dealt with as such by those who seek to train, teach and weld the group into an instrument for service. Each person will be regarded as a transmitter of the type of energy which is the predominant energy in any ray type, – either egoic or personality rays. Each can in time learn to transmit the quality of his soul ray to the group, stimulating his brothers to greater courage, clearer vision, finer purity of motive, and deeper love, and yet avoid the danger of vitalising his personality characteristics. This is the major difficulty. To do this effectively and correctly, we must all learn to think of each other as souls, and not as human beings. (EP2–181)

The Dissipation of Glamour

• Speaking symbolically, I would say that the planetary astral body (viewing it from soul levels) is lost in the depths of a surrounding fog. When at night you look out at some clear sky, you see the stars and suns and planets shining with a clear cold brilliancy and with a twinkling blazing light which penetrates for many millions of miles (or light years as they are called) until the human eye registers them…. Looking, however, at the astral body of the planet, could you but do so, you would see no such clear shining but simply a murky ball of seeming steam and mist and fog. This fog is of a density and thickness which would indicate not only impenetrability but also those conditions which are unfavourable to life. …And in that fog –

seeing all things misshapen and distorted – labour the sons of men. Some are so habituated to the fog and the density that they remain oblivious of its existence, regarding it as right and good and the unchangeable place of their daily life. Others have caught faint glimpses of a clearer world wherein more perfect forms and shapes can be seen and where the fog hides not a dimly sensed reality – though what that reality may be they know not. Still others, such as yourselves, see before you an open path leading to the clear light of day. (GWP–69/70)

• ...Groups working consciously at the service of dissipating glamour will have the following characteristics:
1. They will be composed of sixth ray aspirants and disciples, aided by second ray spiritual workers.
2. They will be formed of those who:
    a. Are learning or have learnt to dissipate their own individual glamours and can bring understanding to the task.
    b. Are focussed upon the mental plane and have, therefore, some measure of mental illumination. They are mastering the Technique of Light.
    c. Are aware of the nature of the glamours which they are attempting to dissipate and can use the illumined mind as a searchlight.
3. They will count among their numbers those who (occultly speaking) have the following powers in process of rapid development:
    a. The power not only to recognise glamour for what it is, but to discriminate between the various and many types of glamour.
    b. The power to appropriate the light, absorbing it into themselves and then consciously and scientifically project it into the world of glamour....
    c. The power to use the light not only through absorption and projection but also by a conscious use of the will, carrying energy upon the beam of projected light. (GWP–201/2)

• The factor which leads to the dissipation of glamour is devotion – devotion to an individual, to a Master...or to some idealistic project. It is finally an unlimited devotion to the Way, to the treading of the Path at any cost, and to the unswerving attachment to service – as constituting the major technique of the Path. (RI–682/3)

• The individual glamours of which the disciple becomes aware are...of five types of force.... They are:

1. The forces of his dense physical nature and of the vital body which latter, functioning through the dense physical nature, produce a condition of maya or of uncontrolled energy.

2. The forces of the astral nature, based upon desire and upon sentiency. These, at this stage, fall into two groups which we call pairs of opposites. Their potency is accentuating at this period of individual history, for the disciple is polarised in the majority of cases in his astral body and is, therefore, subject to the glamours produced by the interplay of the opposites, plus the condition of maya, referred to above.

3. The forces of the lower mental nature, of the chitta or mind-stuff of which the mental body is composed. This is coloured by past activity, as is the substance composing all the vehicles. This adds to maya and glamour, the state of illusion.

4. The personality ray then emerges and intensifies all these three aspects of force expression, producing eventually their synthetic work. Then we have the emerging of what has been called "the threefold glamorous condition", into one major glamour.

5. The soul ray or energy is all this time steadily increasing its rhythmic potency, and seeking to impose its purpose and will upon the personality. It is the united relation and the interplay between these two which – when a point of balance has been achieved – sweeps the man on to the Probationary Path, on to the Path of Discipleship, and right

up to the gate of initiation. There, standing before the Gate, he recognises the final duality which awaits resolution. The Dweller on the Threshold and the Angel of the PRESENCE.

The nature of these glamours differs with different people, for the ray quality determines the type of glamour or illusion to which a man will easily succumb, and that kind of glamour which he will most easily create....

I can indicate the major glamours (and under this term I include the various maya and illusions) to which the ray types predispose the man.... Yet remember this, my brother:

The issue is certain and determined for, in this solar system, the triumph of the soul and its final dominance and control is a foregone conclusion, no matter how great the glamour or how fierce the strife....

RAY I.

The glamour of physical strength.

The glamour of personal magnetism.

The glamour of self-centredness and personal potency.

The glamour of "the one at the centre".

The glamour of selfish personal ambition.

The glamour of rulership, of dictatorship and of wide control.

The glamour of the Messiah complex in the field of politics.

The glamour of selfish destiny, of the divine right of kings personally exacted.

The glamour of destruction.

The glamour of isolation, of aloneness, of aloofness.

The glamour of the superimposed will – upon others and upon groups.

RAY II.

The glamour of the love of being loved.

The glamour of popularity.

The glamour of personal wisdom.

The glamour of selfish responsibility.

The glamour of too complete an understanding, which negates right action.

The glamour of self-pity, a basic glamour of this ray.

The glamour of the Messiah complex, in the world of religion and world need.

The glamour of fear, based on undue sensitivity.

The glamour of self-sacrifice.

The glamour of selfish unselfishness.

The glamour of self-satisfaction.

The glamour of selfish service.

RAY III.

The glamour of being busy.

The glamour of co-operation with the Plan in an individual and not a group way.

The glamour of active scheming.

The glamour of creative work – without true motive.

The glamour of good intentions, which are basically selfish.

The glamour of "the spider at the centre".

The glamour of "God in the machine".

The glamour of devious and continuous manipulation.

The glamour of self-importance, from the standpoint of knowing, of efficiency.

RAY IV.

The glamour of harmony, aiming at personal comfort and satisfaction.

The glamour of war.

The glamour of conflict, with the objective of imposing righteousness and peace.

The glamour of vague artistic perception.

The glamour of psychic perception instead of intuition.

The glamour of musical perception.

The glamour of the pairs of opposites, in the higher sense.

RAY V.

The glamour of materiality, or over-emphasis of form.

The glamour of the intellect.

The glamour of knowledge and of definition.

The glamour of assurance, based on a narrow point of view.

The glamour of the form which hides reality.

The glamour of organisation.

The glamour of the outer, which hides the inner.

RAY VI.

The glamour of devotion.

The glamour of adherence to forms and persons.

The glamour of idealism.

The glamour of loyalties, of creeds.

The glamour of emotional response.

The glamour of sentimentality.

The glamour of interference.

The glamour of the lower pairs of opposites.

The glamour of World Saviours and Teachers.

The glamour of the narrow vision.

The glamour of fanaticism.

RAY VII.

The glamour of magical work.

The glamour of the relation of the opposites.

The glamour of the subterranean powers.

The glamour of that which brings together.

The glamour of the physical body.

The glamour of the mysterious and the secret.

The glamour of sex magic.

The glamour of the emerging manifested forces.

I have here enumerated many glamours. But their names are legion, and I have by no means covered the possibilities or the field of glamour. (GWP–116/23)

• ...Ambition and love of power, backed by frantic desire and unscrupulousness form the "Dweller" for the first ray types. (TWM–239)

• First ray people can overcome glamour with relative ease once they become aware of it as a personality limitation. (GWP–222)

• Second ray aspirants are usually fully aware of any glamour which may be seeking to hold them because they have an innate faculty of clear perception. Their problem is to kill out in themselves their rapid response to the magnetic pull of the astral plane and its many and widespread glamours. They are not so frequently responsive to *a* glamour as to all glamours in a relatively temporary manner but one which is nevertheless exceedingly delaying to their progress. Because of their clear-sightedness, they add to this sensitivity to glamour an ability to suffer about it and to register their responsiveness as a sin and failure and thus delay their liberation from it by a negative attitude of inferiority and distress. (GWP–222/3)

• …The power of fear is enormously aggravated by the thoughtform we ourselves have built of our own individual fears and phobias. This thoughtform grows in power as we pay attention to it, for "energy follows thought", till we become dominated by it. Second ray people are peculiarly a prey to this. For the majority of them it constitutes the "dweller on the threshold".… (TWM–238/9)

• Third ray people are as susceptible to [glamour] as are those of the sixth ray and their devious, twisting, planning minds and the rapidity with which they can deceive themselves (and seek often to deceive others) greatly hinders their work of clearing away glamour. Their pronounced tendency to be the victims of glamour is evidenced by the inability of the third ray aspirant and disciple to convey his meaning clearly by speech. He has guarded himself for many lives by devious formulations of thought and of ideas and can seldom convey his meaning clearly. This is why sixth ray people and third ray people almost inevitably prove themselves unable to teach. Both these groups…would greatly hasten the process of dissipation if they would force themselves to speak or write their thoughts clearly, if they would never be ambiguous or deal in half thoughts, innuendo or suggestion. They should clearly enunciate the ideas with which they may be dealing. (GWP–222)

• Fourth ray people are peculiarly prone to fall into glamour and thus to produce a condition which is one of extreme difficulty. I might define their problem by saying that they tend to bring their illusions down to the astral plane and there clothe them with glamour and have consequently a double problem upon their hands; they are faced with a unification of glamour and illusion. They are, however, the group of souls which will eventually reveal the true nature of the intuition and this will be the result of their illusory glamorous fight in the world of appearances. (GWP–223/4)

• Fifth ray people suffer the least from glamour but are primarily the victims of illusion, and for them the Technique of the Presence is all-important because it brings in a factor which the true fifth ray person is apt to negate and refuse to admit, the fact of the Higher Self. He feels self-sufficient. They respond so easily and with such satisfaction to the power of thought; pride in their mental competence is their besetting sin and they are, therefore, set in their purposes and preoccupied with the world of the concrete and the intellectual. The moment that the Angel of the Presence is a reality to them, their response to illusion weakens and disappears. Their major problem is not so much the negation of the astral body, for they are apt to despise its hold, but they have a major difficulty in recognising that which the mind is intended to reveal – the divine spiritual Self. Their lower concrete mind interposes itself between them and the vision. (GWP–223)

• The majority of those [working at the dissipation of glamour in their own lives] are sixth ray aspirants – those who have sixth ray personalities or whose soul ray is the sixth, plus those on all rays who have powerful sixth ray astral vehicles. These make the most effective workers in the group but are subject to one major difficulty. In spite of aspiration and good intention, they are seldom aware of the glamours which control them. It is exceedingly hard to induce the sixth ray aspirant to admit that he is held by a glamour, particularly when it is glamour of spiritual connotation and of a very high order. In their case, the glamour is enhanced by the energy of devotion which stiffens it and brings in a quality which makes it most difficult to penetrate. Their complete assurance proves a serious obstacle to clear-sighted work because that has all to go before the work of dissipation can be carried forward successfully. (GWP–221/2)

• *The glamour of devotion* causes many probationary disciples to wander circuitously around in the world of desire. This is primarily a glamour which affects sixth ray persons and is particularly potent at this time owing to the age-long activity of the sixth Ray of Devotion during the rapidly passing Piscean Age. It is today one of the potent glamours of the really devoted aspirant. They are devoted to a cause, to a teacher, to a creed, to a person, to a duty, or to a responsibility. Ponder on this. This harmless desire along some line of idealism which confronts them becomes definitely harmful both to themselves and to others, because through this glamour of devotion they swing into the rhythm of the world glamour which is essentially the fog of desire. Potent desire along any line, when it obliterates the wider vision and shuts a man within a tiny circle of his own desire to satisfy his sentiment of devotion, is just as hampering as any of the other glamours, and is even more dangerous because of the beautiful colouring which the resultant fog takes on. A man gets lost in a rapturous mist of his own making, which emanates from his astral body and which is composed of the sentimentalising of his own nature about his own desire and devotion to the object of his attracted attention.

With all true aspirants, owing to the increased potency of their vibrations, this devotional sentiment can be particularly difficult and bring about a lengthy imprisonment. One illustration of this is the sentiment of devotion poured out in a glamorous ecstasy by probationary disciples upon the Masters of the Wisdom. Around the names of the Members of the Hierarchy and around Their work, and the work of the initiates and the disciplined disciples (mark that phrase) a rich glamour is created which prevents Them ever reaching the disciple or his reaching Them. It is not possible to penetrate the dense glamour of devotion, vibrating with dynamic ecstatic life, which emanates from the concentrated energy of the disciple, working still through the solar plexus centre.

For this glamour there are some age-old rules: Contact the greater Self through the medium of the higher Self and thus lose sight of the little self, its reactions, its desires, and intentions. Or: The pure love of the soul which is not personalised in any way and which seeks no recognition can then pour into the world of glamour which surrounds the devotee, and the mists of his devotion (upon which he prides himself) will melt away. (GWP–77/9)

• What I have now to say will not be followed with ease or with due appreciation by the sixth ray disciple, because the methods employed by Those Who are handling and directing the new [seventh ray] energies are not comprehensible by him, grounded as he is in the methods of the past; hence the appearance of the fundamentalist schools, found in every field of thought – religious, political and even scientific. Again, when the sixth ray disciple attempts to use the new incoming energies, they express themselves for him upon the astral plane and the result is astral magic, deepened glamour and pronounced deception. To this fact must be ascribed today the appearance of teachers, claiming to teach magic, to bring about certain magical results, to work with rays of differing colours and to utilise Words of Power, to pronounce decrees and to be repositories of the hitherto unrevealed wishes and secrets of the Masters of the Wisdom. It is all a form of astral glamour, and the contacting upon the astral plane of that which will later precipitate upon earth. But the time is not yet and the hour for such usages has not arrived. The sense of time and the understanding of the correct hour for the carrying out of the Plan in its future detail has not been learnt by these sincere, but deluded, people and – focused as they are upon the astral plane and undeveloped as they are mentally – they misinterpret to themselves and for others that which they there psychically sense. They know far too little and yet believe that they know much. They speak with authority, but it is the authority of the unexpanded mind. The expression of old magical patterns, the digging up of hints and indications of crystallised and worn-out methods from the ancient past is all too prevalent at this time and is responsible for much deception of the masses and consequent mass delusion. (DN–121/2)

• The seventh ray person is faced with the difficulty of being able to create exceedingly clear-cut thoughtforms and the glamours, therefore, which control him are precise and definite and, to him, all compelling. They rapidly crystallise, however, and die their own death. (GWP–222)

Healing and the Rays

• *There is naught but energy, for God is life. Two energies meet in man, but other five are present. For each is to be found a central point of contact. The conflict of these energies with forces and of the forces twixt themselves produce the bodily ills of man. The conflict of the first and second persists for ages until the mountain top is reached – the first great mountain top. The fight between the forces produces all disease, all ills and bodily pain, which seek release in death. The two, the five, and thus the seven, plus that which they produce, possess the secret. This is the fifth Law of Healing within the world of form.*

This Law [Law V] can be resolved into certain basic statements which can be tabulated as follows:

1. We live in a world of energies and are a constituent part of them ourselves.
2. The physical vehicle is a fusion of two energies and seven forces.
3. The first energy is that of the soul, the ray energy. It is the producer of conflict as the soul energy seeks to control the forces.
4. The second energy is that of the threefold personality – the personality ray....
5. The forces are the other energies or ray potencies which control the seven centres and are dominated either by the energy of the personality or by that of the soul.
6. Two conflicts, therefore, proceed between the two major energies and between the other energies, focused through the seven centres.

7.   It is the interplay of these energies which produces good health or bad. (EH–136/7)

The Rays of Healer and of Patient
(From Fifteen Statements on Healing and the Seven Rays)

3.   No matter upon which ray the healer may be found, he must always work through the second subray of that ray – the ray of love-wisdom in each ray. By means of this, he becomes connected with or related to the governing soul and personality rays. The second ray has the capacity of all-inclusiveness.

4.   The second ray and the second subray on all rays are themselves dual in expression. The healer must learn to work through the love aspect and not through the wisdom aspect. This takes much training in the practice of spiritual differentiation.

5.   Those vehicles in the form nature which are on the line of [rays] 2-4-6 must be used by the healer when practising the healing art. If he has no vehicles or bodies on this line of basic energy, he will not be able to heal. This is seldom realised. It is rare, however, to find an equipment lacking all second ray energy outlets.

6.   Those healers who are on the second ray, or who are equipped with a powerful second ray vehicle, are usually great healers. The Christ, being the truest exponent of the second ray ever known on earth, was greatest of all the healing sons of God.

7.   The ray of the soul conditions and determines the technique to be employed. The ray in the personality vehicles most closely related to the second ray (for which all the subrays act as channels) is the one through which the healing energy must flow.

8.   The second subray of the soul ray determines the approach to the healing problem immediately confronting the healer; this energy is transmuted into healing force when passing through the appropriate personality vehicle. To be appropriate it must be on the line of 2-4-6. (EH–696)

• It will be apparent to the most superficial reader that the variation or the identity between the rays of the healer and his patient constitutes a factor of importance: many conditioning factors will be presented; there will also be present a contrast between the soul rays and the personality rays of both parties concerned. You may have, therefore, conditions in which:

1. The soul rays are identical and the personality rays are different.
2. The personality rays are the same but the soul rays are not.
3. The rays are similar in both cases.
4. The rays of neither soul nor personality are the same.
5. The soul ray is not known but the personality ray is apparent. The ray of the personality is easily ascertained, but there is often no indication as to the soul ray. This can apply to both healer and patient.
6. Nothing is known anent the rays of either party.

I am not bringing in to this discussion any reference to the rays of the mental, astral or physical vehicles, though they have a definite and sometimes decisive effect and the knowledge is most useful when known....

In *Discipleship in the New Age* the rays are given of a large number of disciples. You might, as an experimental exercise, take these various rays, as assigned, and place each of these disciples in the part of either healer or patient, and see what centres would be employed in the case of some disease (each based in a different location in the human body), and then attempt to decide what method, mode or procedure the healer would be wise to follow. At the same time you should remember two things: first, that all these people are members of a second ray Ashram; also that they are disciples, and consequently their rays are apparent and obvious to the healer, which greatly helps. You could determine also what ray energy should be employed in the healing process, through what centre in yourself, as the healer, and the disciple as a patient, you should work.... Then, having through the use of the imagination worked at an imaginary healing, look around among your friends and acquaintances for those whom you believe possess similar ray conditions and – if they are ailing or ill – seek to help them in the same way as you attempted to aid an imaginary patient; note then what happens....

The...subject can perhaps be clarified by certain statements....

1. The healer should ascertain his rays, and then proceed with his work on the basis of that information. When that knowledge is not available, he should refrain from the attempt to heal.

2. When unable – from lack of this knowledge – to carry forward the healing work, let him confine himself to the task of acting as a channel for the energy of love to the patient.

3. The healer will find it easier in most cases to ascertain his rays, or one of them at least, than to know the rays of the patient....

4. The healer, having to his satisfaction determined upon the rays or ray conditioning him, should then prepare himself...[by familiarising] himself with...the rays of the patient, if feasible; these, if known, will condition his approach.

5. Thus prepared, the healer focuses his attention in his own ray. When he only possesses general and not specific knowledge of his own ray or rays and those of the patient, the healer may proceed upon the surmise that one or both are along the line of [rays] 1-3-5-7 or 2-4-6 and act upon that general assumption.... The problem then is whether the relation between the healer and patient will be from personality to personality, from soul to soul, or from personality to soul and vice versa.

6. When the relation is that of personality to personality (and this will be the most usual), the energy with which the healer will work is simply that of planetary prana....

7. Where the relation is that of the soul of the healer to the personality of the patient, the healer will work with ray energy, pouring his own ray energy through the centre

which is controlling the diseased area. When both the soul of the healer and that of the patient are working in co-operation there can be the blending of two energies or (where similar rays are present) the strengthening of one energy and a greatly hastened work of healing or of dissolution. (EH–698/703)

The Seven Healing Techniques

• It will be obvious to you that even if the techniques or the seven modes of healing – relating as they do to the energies of the seven rays – were exactly imparted to you, it would be rare indeed to find a healer who was competent to use them in this interim period in world affairs. ...The soul ray of the average aspirant is seldom in control to such an extent that it can bring adequate illumination and ray potency; until it is in control, these ray methods and techniques, determining the use and direction of the ray energies, are useless. This should not bring to you disappointment, but simply an attitude of expectancy, particularly where the younger students and readers are concerned. All things considered, this hiatus between expectancy and possibility is exceedingly good. (EH–693)

• Some disciple in the early part of [the 21st] century will take [the following] techniques or magical statements, relating to the healing work, and interpret them and elucidate them. They are susceptible of three significances, the lowest of which the modern student may succeed in interpreting for himself if he reflects adequately and lives spiritually. Here are the seven statements.

1. *The first ray technique.*
    Let the dynamic force which rules the hearts of all within Shamballa come to my aid, for I am worthy of that aid. Let it descend unto the third, pass to the fifth and focus on the seventh. These words mean not what doth at sight appear. The third, the fifth, the seventh lie within the first and come from out the Central Sun of spiritual livingness. The highest then awakens within the one who knows and within the one who must be healed and thus the two are one. This is mystery deep. The blending of the healing force effects

the work desired; it may bring death, that great release, and re-establish thus the fifth, the third, the first, but not the seventh.

This dynamic first ray energy is usually employed by the trained spiritual healer when it is apparent to him that the patient's hour has come and release approaches. In cases where the first ray is the soul ray of either healer or patient, this application of first ray energy must move from head centre to head centre, and from thence to the area of distress and to the centre allied with the location. This may cause (when healing is possible and karmically correct) a temporary increase of the trouble; this is owing to the fact that the incoming energy "expels dynamically" the very seed or roots of the disease. There may be a rise in temperature, or a collapse of some kind or another, and for this the healer, the patient and the attendant physician must be prepared and should take the needed physical steps for amelioration – steps as ordained by the orthodox medical profession, which will offset the purely physical reaction. Where the soul ray of the patient is not on the first ray, but the first ray is the ray of the personality, the healer must use great caution in applying first ray energy, and should proceed very slowly and gradually through the centre on the line of 1-3-5-7 which is nearest to the seat of trouble, passing the energy through that centre and thence to the centre (which-ever that may be) found in the locality of the disease. If that particular centre happens to be on the line of 3-5-7, the healer will have to exercise special care, or else the dynamic first ray energy will destroy and not heal.

2. *The second ray technique.*

Let the healing energy descend, carrying its dual lines of life and its magnetic force. Let that magnetic living force withdraw and supplement that which is present in the seventh, opposing four and six to three and seven, but dealing not with five. The circular, inclusive vortex – descending to the point – disturbs, removes and then supplies and thus the work is done.

The heart revolves; two hearts revolve as one; the twelve within the vehicle, the twelve within the head and the twelve upon the plane of soul endeavour, co-operate as one and thus the work is done. Two energies achieve this consummation and the three whose number is

a twelve respond to the greater twelve. The life is known and the
years prolonged.

If this ancient statement is read in the light of any knowledge
you may have (and you probably have more than you realise),
particularly knowledge anent the centres, the primary or easiest
interpretation will appear.

3.   *The third ray technique.*
    The healer stands and weaves. He gathers from the three, the five,
    the seven that which is needed for the heart of life. He brings the
    energies together and makes them serve the third; he thus creates a
    vortex into which the one distressed must descend and with him goes
    the healer. And yet they both remain in peace and calm. Thus must
    the angel of the Lord descend into the pool and bring the healing life.

The "pool of waters" figures here and may cause much questioning as to its significance. Its elementary interpretation relates
in reality to the central and major cause of much disease…, the
emotional nature, which it is the task of the third aspect of
divinity to control. Ponder on this, for much enlightenment
may come.

The next healing technique is longer and far more abstruse.
There is little of it that you will understand; it is entirely
related, as far as our theme is concerned, to man himself and
to the aphorism: "Man, *know* thyself."

4.   *The fourth ray technique.*
    The healer knows the place where dissonance is found. He also
    knows the power of sound and the sound which must be heard.
    Knowing the note to which the fourth great group reacts and linking
    it to the great Creative Nine, he sounds the note which brings release,
    the note which will bring absorption into one. He educates the
    listening ear of him who must be healed; he likewise trains the
    listening ear of him who must go forth. He knows the manner of the
    sound which brings the healing touch; and also that which says:
    Depart. And thus the work is done.

This fourth technique is one that – in default of true ray
knowledge – can be of general usefulness, because this fourth
ray governs the fourth kingdom in nature, the human. The

healer along this line of work (and such healers are practically nonexistent at this time because the fourth ray is not in incarnation) heals primarily through the use of the appropriate sound or sounds. In the early stages when this technique comes into demonstration, music will be largely used by the healer to bring about a cure or to facilitate the process of death or departure. It will, however, be music with one constantly recurring chord, which will embody the note of the fourth ray and of the human kingdom. Healing by the means of sound will be one of the first healing unfoldments to be noted at the close of the [21st] century. More teaching along this line would be useless until the fourth ray again cycles into manifestation.

5. *The fifth ray technique*

That which has been given must be used; that which emerges from within the given mode will find its place within the healer's plan. That which is hidden must be seen and from the three, great knowledge will emerge. For these the healer seeks. To these the healer adds the two which are as one, and so the fifth must play its part and the five must play its part and the five must function as if one. The energies descend, pass through and disappear, leaving the one who could respond with karma yet to dissipate and taking with them him who may not thus respond and so must likewise disappear.

The obvious and simplest meaning of the fifth ray mode of healing is that the healer, working scientifically and largely on concrete levels, employs all aids to bring about a cure, starting with appropriate physical care and passing on to subtler modes of healing. Again I would point out that physical aid can be as divinely used as the more mysterious methods which the metaphysical healer of the present time believes to be so profoundly more effective. Just as all modern knowledge, developed on the physical plane, through the personalities of men and women of insight and genius everywhere, is useful to the disciple and initiate, in time and space, so it is with the medical sciences. Just as right application of these varying sciences has to be made by the disciple or the initiate in order to bring about spiritual results, so must it be when the healer is at work.

All work becomes spiritual when rightly motivated, when wise discrimination is employed and soul power is added to the knowledge gained in the three worlds. The dynamic use of energy in one of its seven streams, added to the sane understanding and work of the modern physician, aided by the healer (who works as does a catalyst), can produce miracles when destiny so ordains. The metaphysical healer who works solely on the subtler levels is like the spiritual worker who fails so constantly to precipitate the needed financial assets on the physical plane. This is caused frequently by a subtle – though usually unrecognised – sense of superiority with which the average healer and the esotericist views his problem of materialisation of either physical health or money. Ponder on this and realise that fifth ray methods carry through to the physical plane; there they engender conflict and eventually produce a physical precipitation of the desired nature. In what I have said anent the fifth ray techniques, I have given more hints and information than in any of the others.

6. *The sixth ray technique.*

Cleaving the waters, let the power descend, the healer cries. He minds not how the waters may respond; they oft bring stormy waves and dire and dreadful happenings. The end is good. The trouble will be ended when the storm subsides and energy has fulfilled its charted destiny. Straight to the heart the power is forced to penetrate, and into every channel, nadi, nerve and spleen the power must seek a passage and a way and thus confront the enemy who has effected entrance and settled down to live. Ejection – ruthless, sudden and complete – is undertaken by the one who sees naught else but perfect functioning and brooks no interference. This perfect functioning opens thus the door to life eternal or to life on earth for yet a little while.

This technique is curiously potent and sudden when the healer is on the sixth ray; the results are drastic and full of pain, but the results are sure – healing or death, and oft the latter. The sixth ray healer is seldom disciplined or wise at this time, owing to this being the end of the sixth ray cycle. When again the sixth ray comes into manifestation, humanity will have progressed far along the Path and the present aggressive, too sure, fanatical sixth ray healer will not reappear. Today they are the majority, and their work is not good; it is well-intentioned, but the technique is ignorantly applied and the end justifies not the assurance of the healer, leading to frequent deception of the patient.

7. *The seventh ray technique.*

Energy and force must meet each other and thus the work is done. Colour and sound in ordered sequence must meet and blend and thus the work of magic can proceed. Substance and spirit must evoke each other and, passing through the centre of the one who seeks to aid, produce the new and good. The healer energises thus with life the failing life, driving it forth or anchoring it yet more deeply in the place of destiny. All seven must be used and through the seven there must pass the energies the need requires, creating the new man who has for ever been and will for ever be, and either here or there.

In this technique you have the clue to them all, for the work of the seventh ray healer is to bring together the life and the substance which will take the place of the substance which is diseased and bring new life to aid the recovery. The glory of life lies in consummation and in emergence. This is the prime task and the prime reward of all true healers. It is this technique of attraction and substitution which will be brought to a fine point of scientific expression in the coming new age wherein the seventh ray will dominate our planet, producing that which is new and needed and determining the coming culture, civilisation and science. (EH–706/13)

Disease and the Rays

• All disease and ill health are the result of the activity or the inactivity of one or other of the seven types of energy as they play upon the human body. All physical ills emerge out of the impact of these imperfect energies as they make their impact upon, enter into and pass through the centres in the body. All depends upon the condition of the seven centres in the human body; through these the impersonal energies play, carrying life, disease or death, stimulating the imperfections in the body or bringing healing to the body. All depends, as far as the human being is concerned, upon the condition of the physical body, the age of the soul and the karmic possibilities. (EH–304/5)

• According to the temperament so will be the types of disease, and the temperament is dependent upon the ray quality. People on the different rays are predisposed to certain disorders.

...The more advanced the aspirant, the greater probability there is that the diseases from which he suffers will be pronounced and powerfully demonstrating, on account of the inflow to a greater or less degree of the stimulating force of the soul. (EH–66/67)

• Exemption from the effects of human ills is no indication of spiritual superiority. It might simply indicate what one of the Masters has called "the depths of spiritual selfishness and self-satisfaction". The initiate of the third degree can hold himself exempt, but this is only because he has completely freed himself from glamour and no aspect of the personality life has any further power over him. All the ray types are equally subjected to these particular problems. The seventh ray, however, is more susceptible to the problems, difficulties and diseases incident to the blood stream than are any of the other ray types. The reason is that this is the ray which has to do with the expression and manifestation of life upon the physical plane and with the organisation of the relationship between spirit and matter into form. It is concerned therefore today, as it seeks to create the new order, with free circulation and with a consequently intended freedom of humanity from the ills and problems of the past. (EH–128/9)

• The effects of this [seventh] ray force are most peculiar and will be a great deal more prevalent than heretofore, as this ray is now coming into power. It is this energy which is largely responsible for infections and contagious diseases. The keynote of the work of the seventh ray is to bring together life and matter upon the physical plane. This, however, when viewed from the angle of imperfection, is a bringing together (if you can understand the implications) of Life, the lives and the general livingness of the creative process. This is symbolised by the promiscuity and the endless moving interplay of all life within all lives. The result is therefore the activity of all germs and bacteria within the medium which will best nurture them. (EH–304)

• On the astral plane there will...be found in every astral body seven...focal points through which energy can enter, raying forth then into the vital centres in the etheric physical body as seven differentiated types of force. These types of force produce both bad and good effects, according to the quality of the negative dense physical body. These differ according to the type of ray or force, and it may be interesting if I here indicate to you the good and the bad effects and the corresponding diseases.

Astral Force	Centre	Bad Aspect	Disease	Good Aspect
First ray. Will or Power.	Head	Self-pity. The dramatic I.	Cancer.	Sacrifice. Dedication of the I.
Second ray. Love-Wisdom.	Heart	Self-love. Personality.	Heart trouble. Stomach trouble.	Soul love. Group love.
Third ray. Activity.	Sacral	Sexuality. Over-activity.	Social diseases.	Parental love. Group life.
Fourth ray. Harmony.	Ajna	Selfishness. Dogmatism.	Insanities.	Mysticism.
Fifth ray. Knowledge.	Throat	Lower psychism.	Wrong metabolism. Certain cancers.	Creativity. Sensitivity. Inspiration.
Sixth ray. Devotion.	Solar Plexus	Emotionalism.	Nervous diseases. Gastritis. Liver trouble.	Aspiration. Right direction.
Seventh ray. Organisation.	Base of the spine.	Self-interest. Pure selfishness. Black Magic.	Heart diseases. Tumours.	White magic.

(EH–50/1)

• Where there is no free play between the etheric body and the astral body, you will have trouble. Where there is no free play between the etheric body and the physical body, involving also the nerve ganglia and the endocrine system, you will also have trouble. The close relation between the seven major centres and the seven major glands of the physical system must never be forgotten. The two systems form one close interlocking direct-orate, with the glands and their functions determined by the condition of the etheric centres. These, in their turn, are con-ditioned by the point in evolution and gained experience of the incarnate soul, by the specific polarisation of the soul in incarnation, and by the rays (personality and soul) of the man. Forget not, that the five aspects of man (as he functions in the three worlds) are determined by certain ray forces; you have the ray of the soul, the ray of the personality, and the rays of the mental, the astral and the physical bodies. All these will, in the coming New Age, be definitely considered and discovered, and this knowledge will reveal to the healer the *probable* con-dition of the centres, the order of their awakening, and their individual and basic note or notes. The new medical science will be outstandingly built upon the science of the centres, and upon this knowledge all diagnosis and possible cure will be based. (EH–77)

Medical Practice in the New Age

• Medical men in the New Age will eventually know enough to relate these various ray forces to their appropriate centres; hence they will know which type of force is responsible for conditions – good or bad – in any particular area of the body. Some day, when more research and investigation have been carried forward, the science of medicine will be built upon the fact of the vital body and its constituent energies. It will then be discovered that this science will be far simpler and less complicated than present medical science. Today, medicine has reached such a point of complexity that specialists have perforce been needed who can deal with one area of the body and with its effect upon the entire physical vehicle. The average general practitioner cannot cope with the mass of detailed knowledge now gathered re the physical body, its various systems, their interrelation and their effect upon the many organisms which constitute the whole man. Surgery will remain occupied with the anatomical necessities of the human frame; medicine will shift its focus of attention, before long, to the etheric body and its incident circulatory systems of energy, its interlocking relationships and the flow between the seven centres, between the centres themselves and the areas which they control. This will mark a tremendous advance in wise and useful approach; it will produce a basic simplification; it will lead to more correct methods of healing, particularly as clair-voyant vision is developed and becomes recognised by science, and known to be an extension of a normal sense. (EH–276/7)

Conclusion

• Be not discouraged, my brother. If you and all your group brothers will work on these ray ideas and deal with yourselves as unified *wholes* and not with yourselves as composites, you will soon be ready for group work.... (DNA1–198)

• And so they stand – Humanity and the Hierarchy. And so you stand, my brother, personality and soul, with freedom to go forward into the light if you so determine or to remain static and unprogressive, learning nothing and getting nowhere; you are equally free to return to identification with the Dweller, negating thus the influence of the Angel, refusing imminent opportunity and postponing – until a much later cycle – your determining choice. This is true of you and of Humanity as a whole. Will humanity's third ray materialistic personality dominate the present situation or will its soul of love prove the most powerful factor, taking hold of the personality and its little issues, leading it to discriminate rightly and to recognise the true values and thus bring in the age of soul or hierarchical control? Time alone will show. (GWP–160)

• I wonder sometimes if any of you realise the epoch-making importance of the teaching which I have given out anent the seven rays as manifesting energies. Speculations as to the nature of the divine Trinity have ever been present in the discussions and thinking of advanced men – and that since time began and the Hierarchy started its agelong task of influencing and stimulating the human consciousness – but information anent the seven Spirits before the Throne of the Trinity has not been so usual and only a few writers, ancient or modern, have touched upon the nature of these Beings. Now, with all that I have given you concerning the seven rays and the seven Ray

348

Lords, much more can be discovered; these seven great Lives can be seen and known as the informing essences and the active energies in all that is manifested and tangible upon the physical plane as well as on all the planes of divine expression; in saying this, I include not only the cosmic physical plane (composed of our seven systemic planes) but the cosmic astral and the cosmic mental planes also. (EH–583)

• As meditation is practised, as the lower bodies are pains-takingly dominated…it will become increasingly possible to bring into the lower personality on the physical plane that spiritual illumination and that divine energy which is the soul's heritage. Little by little the light will shine forth, year by year the strength of the higher contact will grow, gradually the downpour of divine love and wisdom into the head centres will be increased until eventually the entire lower man will be transformed, his sheaths will be refined, controlled and used, and he will demonstrate upon earth the powers of Director, Teacher or Manipulator according to the major ray upon which his Monad may be found. (RI–7)

• My prayer and wish is that your goal may be clear to your vision and that the "strength of your heart" may be adequate to the undertaking. (RI–703)

Training for new age discipleship is provided by the *Arcane School*. The principles of the Ageless Wisdom are presented through esoteric meditation, study and service as a *way of life*.

Write to the publishers for information.

Index